What American Needs to Know About the Qur'an

A History
of
Islam & the United States

William J. Federer

What Every American Needs to Know About the Qur'an -*A History of Islam & the United States* By William J. Federer

Library of Congress HISTORY / EDUCATION

paperback book
ISBN 0-9778085-5-6
ISBN13 978-0-9778085-5-7
EAN 9780977808557
ebook
ISBN 0-9778085-6-4
ISBN13 978-0-9778085-6-4
EAN 9780977808564

FREE EBOOK

As owner of this book, you can receive as a limited-time offer a free ebook of this title, which contains additional chapters.

Email: **wjfederer@gmail.com**
with subject line **Q2011**
and the ebook will be sent to you via reply email.

Amerisearch, Inc., P.O. Box 20163, St. Louis, MO 63123,
1-888-USA-WORD, 314-487-4395 voice/fax
www.Amerisearch.net, wjfederer@gmail.com

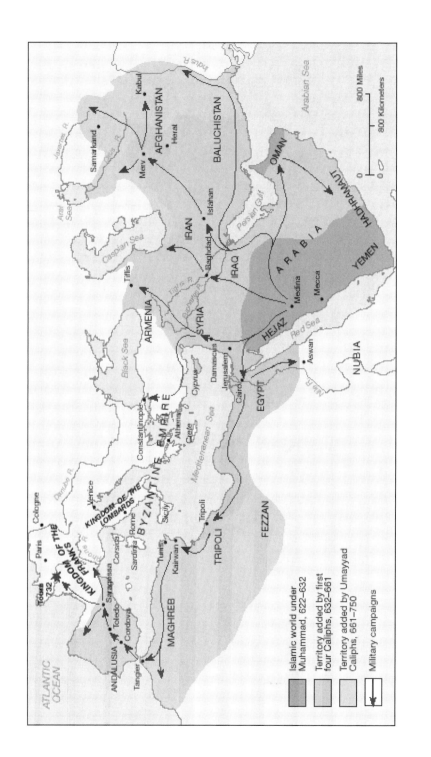

ATLANTIC OCEAN

KINGDOM OF THE FRANKS

Cologne
Paris
Tours 732

Venice
KINGDOM OF THE LOMBARDS
Corsica
Rome
Sardinia
Sicily

Saragossa
Toledo
Cordova
ANDALUSIA
Tangier

MAGHREB

Tunis
Kairwan
TRIPOLI
Tripoli

FEZZAN

BYZANTINE EMPIRE
Athens
Constantinople
Crete
Cyprus

Black Sea

Danube R.

Mediterranean Sea

Rhine R.

ARMENIA
Tiflis

Caspian Sea

Aral Sea

Jaxartes R.

Oxus R.
Samarkand
Merv
Kabul
AFGHANISTAN
Herat
BALUCHISTAN
Indus R.

IRAN
Isfahan
Baghdad
IRAQ
Tigris R.
Euphrates R.
SYRIA
Damascus
Jerusalem
Cairo

EGYPT
Nile R.
Aswan
NUBIA

Red Sea

HEJAZ
Medina
Mecca
ARABIA

Persian Gulf
OMAN
HADHRAMAUT
YEMEN

Arabian Sea

0   800 Miles
0   800 Kilometers

Islamic world under Muhammad, 622–632

Territory added by first four Caliphs, 632–661

Territory added by Umayyad Caliphs, 661–750

Military campaigns

CONTENTS

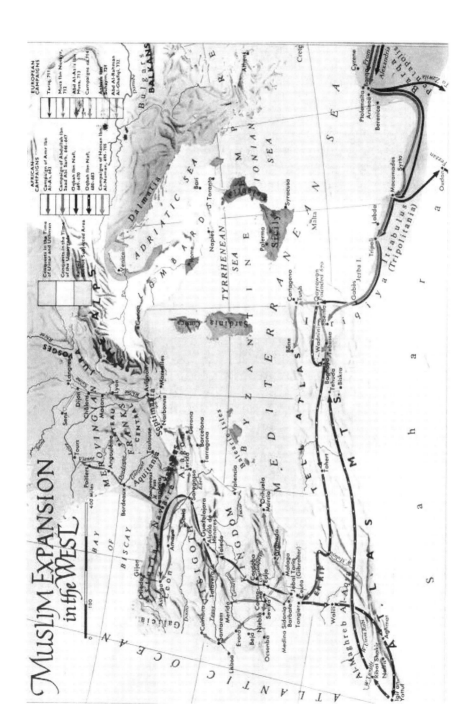

PREFACE

Thousands of books, documents and articles have been researched over several years in preparation for this book.

You will be fascinated by this fast-paced history of the world from a perspective you have never imagined.

Current events will come into focus in the back drop of 1,400 years of inconceivable yet true events and conflicts.

Every effort has been made to present this information objectively. It is hoped this work is received that way.

You will not be the same after you have read what every American needs to know about the *Qur'an*.

"Islam has always been a part of America's story."

> Barack Hussein Obama
> June 4, 2009
> Cairo, Egypt

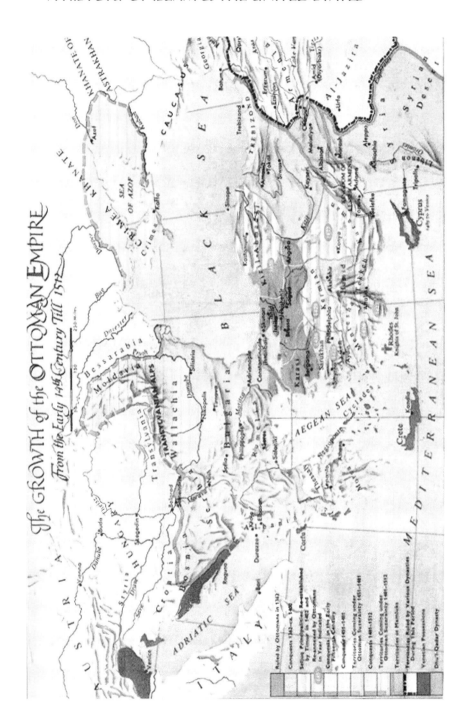

INTRODUCTION

In 2006, Keith Ellison of Minnesota became the first Muslim elected to the U.S. Congress. As reported by Niraj Warikoo in the *Detroit Free Press*, Dec. 25-26, 2006, Keith Ellison told his supporters:

> You can't back down. You can't chicken out. You can't be afraid. You got to have faith in Allah, and you've got to stand up and be a real Muslim.

Ellison, who said little of being a Muslim while campaigning, went on to tell his Islamic audience:

> We're going to continue to face them. They're not going to stop right away. But if you, and me too, stick together, if we believe in Allah, subhanahu wa ta'ala, if we turn to the *Qur'an* for guidance, we'll find an answer to the questions we have.

If one turns for guidance to the *Qur'an*, which Keith Ellison swore into office upon, one finds many disconcerting verses within its chapters, called suras:

> Believers, take neither the Jews nor the Christians for your friends. (Sura 5:51)

> Infidels are those who declare: "God is the Christ, the son of Mary." (Sura 5:17)

> Infidels are those that say 'God is one of three in a Trinity." (Sura 5:73)

> Make war on the infidels who dwell around you. (Sura 9:123)

> The infidels are your sworn enemies. (Sura 4:101)

> When you meet the infidel in the battlefield, strike off their heads. (Sura 47:4)

Mohammed is Allah's apostle. Those who follow him are ruthless to the infidels. (Sura 48:29)

Prophet, make war on the infidels. (Sura 66:9)

Kill the disbelievers wherever we find them. (Sura 2:191)

The only reward of those who make war upon Allah and His messenger... will be that they will be killed or crucified, or have their hands and feet on alternate sides cut off, or will be expelled out of the land. (Sura 5:33)

Fight those who believe not in Allah nor the Last Day, nor hold that forbidden which hath been forbidden by Allah and His Messenger, nor acknowledge the religion of Truth, (even if they are) of the People of the Book, until they pay the jizya with willing submission, and feel themselves subdued. (Sura 9:29)

Therefore, when ye meet the Unbelievers (in fight), smite at their necks; At length, when ye have thoroughly subdued them, bind a bond firmly (on them): thereafter (is the time for) either generosity or ransom. (Sura 47:4)

Believers, do not make friends with those who have incurred the wrath of Allah. (Sura 60:13)

Never be a helper to the disbelievers. (Sura 28:86)

꙳

QUESTIONS?

Are these verses from the *Qur'an* taken out of context? Does it matter if a politician swears on a *Qur'an*? Is it Islamophobic to be concerned? Is Islam a peaceful religion?

A stock investment may sound good, but the investor must do diligence and examine the track record of its past performance. Similarly, one must examine the track record of Islam's past performance to see how the *Qur'an* has been interpreted throughout history.

As the axiom goes, "past performance is the best indicator of future behavior."

⸎

CONSTITUTION & *QUR'AN*

"When the first Muslim American was recently elected to Congress, he took the oath to defend our Constitution using the Holy Qur'an."
-President Obama, Cairo, Egypt, June 4, 2009

The dilemma is, how can one swear to defend something upon a book that espouses the opposite?

The **First Amendment** to the U.S. Constitution states that Congress shall make no law prohibiting the free exercise of religion, yet Mohammed said "Whoever changes his Islamic religion, kill him." (*Hadith Sahih al-Bukhari*, Vol. 9, Book 84, No. 57). Islamic law relegates non-Muslims to "dhimmi" status, where they are not to propagate their customs amongst Muslims and cannot display a Cross or Star of David.

The **First Amendment** states Congress shall not abridge "the freedom of speech," yet Islamic law enforces dhimmi status on non-Muslims, prohibiting them from observing their religious practices publicly, raising their voices during prayer , ringing church bells or say anything considered 'insulting to Islam.'

The **First Amendment** states Congress cannot take away "the right of the people to peaceably assemble," yet Islamic law states non-Muslims cannot repair places of worship or build new ones, they must allow Muslims to participate in their private meetings, they cannot bring their dead near the graveyards of Muslims or mourn their dead loudly.

The **First Amendment** states Congress cannot take away the right of the people "to petition the Government for a redress of grievances," yet Islamic law states non-Muslims are not to harbor any hostility towards the Islamic state or give comfort to those who disagree with Islamic government

The **2nd Amendment** states "the right of the people to keep and bear arms shall not be infringed," yet Islamic law states non-Muslims cannot possess arms, swords or weapons of any kind.

The **3rd Amendment** states one cannot be forced to "quarter" someone in their house, yet Islamic law states non-Muslims must entertain and feed for three days any Muslim who wants to stay in their home, and for a longer period if the Muslim falls ill, and they cannot prevent Muslim travelers from staying in their places of worship.

The **4th Amendment** guarantees "the right of the people to be secure in their persons, houses, papers, and effects against unreasonable searches and seizures," yet Islamic law states if a non-Muslim rides on a horse with a saddle and bridle, the horse can be taken away.

The **5th Amendment** states that "no person shall be held to answer for a capital or otherwise infamous crime...without due process of law," yet Mohammed said "No Muslim should be killed for killing a Kafir (infidel)." (*Hadith Sahih al-Bukhari,* Vol. 9, No. 50).

The **6th Amendment** guarantees a "public trial by an impartial jury" and the **7th Amendment** states "the right of trial by jury shall be preserved," yet Islamic law does not give non-Muslims equal legal standing with Muslims, even prohibiting a non-Muslim from testifying in court against a Muslim.

The **8th Amendment** states there shall be no "cruel and unusual punishments inflicted," yet the *Qur'an* states:

Cut off the hands of thieves, whether they are male or female, as punishment for what they have done — a deterrent from Allah. (Sura 5:38)

A woman who has been raped is also punished "with a hundred stripes." (Sura 24:2)

The **13th Amendment** states there shall be no "slavery or involuntary servitude," yet the *Qur'an* accommodates slavery as Mohammed owned slaves.

The **14th Amendment** guarantees citizens "equal protection of the laws," yet the *Qur'an* does not consider non-Muslims equal to Muslims.

The **15th Amendment** guarantees "the right of the citizens...to vote shall not be denied...on account of race, color, or previous condition of servitude," yet strict interpretation of Islamic law does not allow voting, as democracy is considered people setting themselves in the place of Allah by making the laws.

The **16th Amendment** has some similarities with Islamic law, as "Congress shall have the power to lay and collect taxes on incomes from whatever source derived." Mohammed said "Fight those who believe not in Allah...until they pay the jizya [tax] with willing submission, and feel themselves subdued." (Sura 9:29)

The **19th Amendment** allows women to vote, yet in strict Islamic countries women cannot vote.

The **21st Amendment** allows for the sale of liquor, yet Islamic law states non-Muslims are not to sell or drink wine and liquor openly.

&

THE *HADITH*

In addition to the *Qur'an*, Muslims respect the "Hadith" - sayings of Mohammed recounted by his wives, relatives and warriors. *Hadith Sahih al-Bukhari* states:

No Muslim should be killed for killing a kafir
(a disbeliever). (Volume 1, Book 3, No. 111)

BIOGRAPHY OF MOHAMMED

The *Qur'an* and the *Hadith* are complemented by
the ***Sirat Rasul Allah,*** *(Life of the Prophet of Allah),* the
first biography of Mohammed, written by Ibn Ishaq (d.
768) about a hundred years after Mohammed's death. Ibn
Ishaq was "the first to collect the accounts of the
expeditions of the Messenger of Allah and record them."
The *Sirat Rasul Allah,* edited by Ibn Hisham (d. 834), has
the story of Mohammed's cousin and son-in-law, Ali:

Ali Ibn Abi Talib encountered a man called
Umru and told him, "I indeed invite you to Islam."
Umru said, "I do not need that." Ali said,
"Then I call you to fight."
Umru answered him, "What for my
nephew? By God, I do not like to kill you."
Ali said, "But, by God, I love to kill you."
(*The Biography of the Prophet,* part 3, p. 113; see
also *al-Road al-Ánf* part 3, p. 263.)

AMERICA'S KNOWLEDGE OF ISLAM

America's lack of knowledge of Islam is
understandable, as *Newsweek Magazine* (Sept. 2005)
reported Americans identify themselves as:

85 percent Christian, consisting of:
58 percent Protestant
22 percent Catholic
5 percent other Christian
2 percent Jewish
1 percent Atheist
0.5 percent Buddhist
0.5 percent Hindu
10 percent other/non-reporting
and only 1 percent Muslim

Most Americans know of Islam from news stories of:

Suicide bombings &terrorist attacks
Women wearing burkas
Men's faces covered with scarves
Militants with machine guns
Shouting in Arabic, burning cars in Paris
Death penalty for leaving Islam
Videos of hostages beheaded
Riots over Dutch cartoons
Threats on the Pope
Wanting to destroy Israel
Cheering when Twin Towers fell on 911.

Americans are in disbelief that some Muslim sects practice honor-killing of daughters who "dishonor" their family by dating non-Muslims, men having four wives, stoning of adulteresses, court-ordered gang rapes, cutting off hands of thieves, female circumcision and impalements.

RELIGION OF PEACE

Islam is the opposite of freedom. It means surrender, submission or subjugation. A Muslim is someone who has submitted. A "dhimmi" is a non-Muslim forced to submit.

Mohammed divided the world into two parts: those who have submitted to the will of Allah and those yet to submit. He called these the House of Islam (dar al-Islam) and the House of War (dar al-harb).

Whereas "world peace" to a Westerner means peaceful coexistence, "world peace" to a Muslim means "world Islam," the world submitting to the will of Allah.

MUSLIMS: MODERATE VS VIOLENT

Moderate Muslims think the world will submit to Allah figuratively or in the distant future, maybe at the Hour of Judgment. Therefore, since it is so far off, it is acceptable to get along with non-Muslims in the present.

Fundamental violent Muslims think the world is submitting to Allah now and feel they are fulfilling Islam's "manifest destiny" by making it happen. They are willing to fight moderate Muslims, considering them backslidden from obeying the commands of Mohammed.

Moderate Muslims hesitate to speak out against fundamental violent Muslims, as occasionally one does and they are threatened, intimidated, change their names for protection, have fatwas put on them and even killed.

So there could, in a sense, be three groups of Muslims: a minority of fundamental violent ones, a majority of moderate ones who are afraid of the fundamental violent ones, and the courageous dead ones who were not afraid of the fundamental violent ones.

Stanely Kurtz, a senior fellow at the Ethics and Public Policy Center, wrote in his article "Tribes of Terror" (Claremont Review of Books, Winter 2007/2008, p. 41):

> A given theologian's "true" Islam is one thing; "actual existing" Islam on the ground is another.

COURAGEOUS MODERATE MUSLIMS

Moderate Muslims receive death threats from fundamental violent Muslims and are criticized by CAIR, Council on American-Islamic Relations, a front group whose leaders are connected with supporting terrorism (Randall Todd "Ismail" Royer indicted for training terrorists on American soil, June 27, 2003; Bassem K. Khafagi arrested for funneling money to terrorists, January, 2003; Siraj Wahhaj alleged co-conspirator to blow up New York City monuments in the 1990s).

Moderate Muslims attended the Secular Islam Summit in St. Petersburg, Florida, and released "The St. Petersburg Declaration, " March 5, 2007:

> We are secular Muslims, and secular persons of Muslim societies. We are believers, doubters, and unbelievers, brought together

by a great struggle, not between the West and Islam, but between the free and the unfree. We affirm the inviolable freedom of the individual conscience. We believe in the equality of all human persons. We insist upon the separation of religion from state and the observance of universal human rights. We find traditions of liberty, rationality, and tolerance in the rich histories of pre-Islamic and Islamic societies. These values do not belong to the West or the East; they are the common moral heritage of humankind.

We see no colonialism, racism, or so-called "Islamophobia" in submitting Islamic practices to criticism or condemnation when they violate human reason or rights.

We call on the governments of the world to reject Sharia law, fatwa courts, clerical rule, and state-sanctioned religion in all their forms; oppose all penalties for blasphemy and apostasy, in accordance with Article 18 of the Universal Declaration of Human rights; eliminate practices, such as female circumcision, honor killing, forced veiling, and forced marriage, that further the oppression of women; protect sexual and gender minorities from persecution and violence; reform sectarian education that teaches intolerance and bigotry towards non-Muslims; and foster an open public sphere in which all matters may be discussed without coercion or intimidation.

We demand the release of Islam from its captivity to the totalitarian ambitions of power-hungry men and the rigid strictures of orthodoxy. We enjoin academics and thinkers everywhere to embark on a fearless examination of the origins and sources of Islam, and to promulgate the ideals of free scientific and spiritual inquiry through cross-cultural translation, publishing, and the mass media.

We say to Muslim believers: there is a noble future for Islam as a personal faith, not a political doctrine; to Christians, Jews, Buddhists, Hindus, Baha'is, and all members of non-Muslim faith communities: we stand with you as free and equal citizens; and to nonbelievers: we defend your unqualified liberty to question and dissent.

Before any of us is a member of the Umma, the Body of Christ, or the Chosen People, we are all members of the community of conscience, the people who must choose for themselves.

⤙

MOHAMMED'S CHILDHOOD

Mohammed was born around 570 AD into the Quraysh tribe, being a descendant of Adnan, who is said to have descended from Ishmael.

Mohammed's father, Abd Allah, died six months before he was born. Mohammed's mother, Amina, died when he was 6 years old. At the age of 8, his grandfather and guardian, Abd al-Muttalib, died. Mohammed was then given to his uncle, Abu Talib.

Mohammed's first biography, *Sirat Rasoul Allah*, written by Ibn Ishaq and edited by Ibn Hisham, recorded how for a time, Mohammed's mother, Amina, gave him to a Bedouin nursing mother named Halimai and her husband to raise, but he was returned to him with the account:

> It was not longer than a month after our return that his milk-brother came running to me and his father, saying, "Two men dressed in white garments have taken hold of my brother, and have thrown him on the ground. They ripped open his belly, and are squeezing him."

I and his fosterfather hastened out and found him standing apparently unharmed but with his countenance quite altered.

We questioned him, and he said, "Two men dressed in white garments came to me, who threw me down, opened my abdomen and searched in it for I know not what."

We returned with him to our tent, and his fosterfather said to me, "O Halima! I fear something has happened to the boy. Carry him to his family ere the injury becomes apparent!"

Accordingly, we took him back to his mother, who asked, "What has brought you here, when you were so anxious that he should remain with you?"

I replied, "Allah has caused my son to grow and I have done my duty, but I feared that something might befall him and therefore I have brought him back to you as you desired."

She said, "Such is not the case! Tell me the truth about it." And she would not let me alone until I had told her everything.

Then she asked, "Are you afraid that he is possessed by Satan?" and I replied, "Yes." She said "No, by Allah!" ("Siratu'l Rasul of Ibn Hisham" vss. 105-106, Mizanu'l Haqq, page 347, and Anas Ibn Malik, Mishkat IV, page 367)

෯

MOHAMMED TRAVELS WITH UNCLE

At age 13, with his mother and grandfather dead, Mohammed was raised by his uncle, Abu Talib, a textile merchant who went on camel caravans to foreign lands.

Mohammed could not read, so what he learned about Judaism, Christianity, Zoroastrianism, Manichaeism and Arabian pagan religions, such as Sabeans, came mostly from stories and oral traditions he heard on these travels.

෯

QUR'AN: MANICHAEISM INFLUENCE

About 210 AD, a religious leader named Mani was born in Persia. Mani combined features of different religions to create a new religion called Manichaeism.

Mani claimed to be the Paraclete promised in the *New Testament*, the Last Prophet, the Seal of the Prophets, completing a long line of prophets, which included Seth, Enoch, Noah, Shem, Abraham, Zoroaster, Hermes, Palto, Buddha and Jesus, accusing their followers of corrupting their teachings. Gifted as a child with a mystic temperament, Mani claimed to have been visited by a spirit.

His theology contained a dualistic, continual battle against evil. Mani went on evangelistic missionary journeys to India, Iran and Turkistan.

In the centuries prior to Mohammed's birth, Manichaeism became popular in Persia, Egypt, Syria, Palestine, Mesopotamia and the Middle East. A famous follower of Manichaeism was Augustine of Hippo (354-430 AD) before he rejected it and converted to Christianity. (*The Confessions of Saint Augustine*, 397 AD)

⊷

QUR'AN: ZOROASTRIAN INFLUENCE

Like Mani, Mohammed was aware of many faiths:

As for the true believers, the Jews, the Sabeans, the Christians, the Zoroastrians, and the pagans, Allah will judge them on the day of Resurrection. Allah bears witness to all things. (Sura 22:17)

The Zoroastrians or Magians of Persia believed in one uncreated Creator, with seven heavens and seven hells.

The old *Pahlavi Book of Arta Viraf* had a story of the priest Arta Viraf flying on a journey through seven heavens, similar to Mohammed's "Mi'raj" a purported miraculous night journey to the 7th heaven. (Sura 17:1, *Hadith Sahih al-Bukhari*, Vol. 1, No. 345)

Zoroastrians had the concept of jihad, a continual struggle of dualism-good fighting evil, and focused on ritual cleanliness. Mohammed adopted the Zoroastrian term for demon called "Jinn" or "Genie." (Sura 72 Al-Jinn)

Zoroastrians believed there was a tree in Paradise called "humaya,' similar to Islam's lote-tree "sidrah."

Zoroastrian Paradise was sensual with wine and women called "Faries" or "Houris."

The Pahlavi name "Houris" is used several times in the *Qur'an*'s sensual description of Paradise, referring to "bashful virgins," "fair as coral and ruby," "dark eyed youths," "high bosomed maidens":

> We shall join them to fair women with beautiful, big, and lustrous eyes. (Sura 44:54)

> Reclining on ranged couches. And we wed them unto fair ones with wide, lovely eyes. (Sura 52:20)

> In them will be (Maidens), chaste, restraining their glances, whom no man or Jinn before them has touched. (Sura 55:56)

> There will be Companions with beautiful, big, and lustrous eyes,-Like unto Pearls well-guarded. (Sura 56:22-23)

> Verily for the Righteous there will be a fulfillment of (the heart's) desires; Gardens enclosed, and grapevines; And voluptuous women of equal age; And a cup full (to the brim). (Sura 78:32-34)

Some Muslims considered Zoroaster (Zarathustra), founder of Zoroastrianism, as one of Allah's prophets.

⚜

QUR'AN: ARAB PAGAN INFLUENCE

Each pagan Arabian tribe called its main local deity "allah," which simply meant "the god."

In Mecca, the pagans worshipped as many as 360 deities, represented by stones believed to have fallen from the sun, moon, stars.

The most senior deity was the moon god Hubal, whose idol was brought to Mecca from Moab. Hafiz Ghulam Sarwar, author of *Muhammed The Holy Prophet* (Sh. Muhammad Ashraf, Lahore, Pakistan, 1969) wrote:

> About four hundred years before the birth of Muhammed...Amr ibn Luhayy had put an idol called Hubal on the roof of the Ka'aba. This was one of the chief deities of the Quraysh (tribe) before Islam.

Perhaps influenced by Canaanites, who worshipped Baal and his three daughters, pre-Islamic Mecca revered three female daughter goddesses:

> 1) "al-Lat," worshipped as a square stone;
> 2) "al-Uzzah," worshipped as a granite slab on the road to al-Talf;
> 3) "Manat," worshipped as a black stone on the road to Medina.

Mohammed referred to these goddesses:

> Have ye thought upon al-Lat and al-Uzza. And another, the third goddess, Manat? Are yours the males and His the females? That indeed were an unfair division. They are but the names which ye have named, ye and your fathers, for which Allah hath revealed no warrant. (Sura 53:19-23)

Hisham ibn Al-Kalbi (ca. 819) was an Arab historian raised in Baghdad. He wrote in *Kitab al-Asnam* (*Book of Idols*, translated by Nabih Amin Faris in 1952):

> They then adopted al-Lat as their goddess. Al-Lat stood in al-Ta'if and was more recent that Manah. She was a cubic rock beside which a certain Jew used to prepare his barley porridge. Her custody was in the hands of the

banu-'Attab ibn-Malik of the Thagif (tribe), who had built an edifice over her.

The Quraysh, as well as all the Arabs, were wont to venerate al-Lat. They also used to name their children after her, calling them Zayd-al-Lat and Taym-al-Lat. She stood in the place of the left-hand side minaret of the present day mosque of al-Ta'if.

She is the idol which God mentioned when He said, "Have you seen al-Lat and al-Uzza?"

...Al-Lat continued to be venerated until the Thaqif (tribe) embraced Islam.

Arab pagans walked in circles around the square edifice called the Ka'aba and went inside it to kiss the Black Stone, a 12-inch in diameter meteor rock or impact glass from a meteor crater.

Arab pagans prayed five times a day towards the Ka'aba in Mecca and fasted part of a day for an entire month, as Muslims do at Ramadan. The symbol of the crescent moon, which pre-Islamic Turks also venerated, is atop every mosque and on many Islamic countries' flags. Islam adopted the Lunar calendar, starting their months with the sighting of the first crescent of a New Moon.

∽

QUR'AN: CHRISTIAN INFLUENCE

Encyclopedia Britannica stated of Mohammed:

The gospel was known to him chiefly through apocryphal and heretical sources. (15:648)

In Mohammed's day, there were complicated Christian schisms, mostly over the nature of Christ.

Orthodox Christianity repeatedly confirmed the doctrine of Jesus' nature being the only-begotten Son "of one substance with the Father" at the First Council of Nicea, 325 AD; First Council of Constantinople, 381 AD; Council of Ephesus, 431 AD; Council of Chalcedon,

451 AD; Second Council of Constantinople, 553; and the Third Council of Constantinople, 680 AD.

QUR'AN & CHRISTIAN SCHISMS

Christian schisms in Mohammed's day were over the nature of Christ. This confusion is reflected in Islam:

-Nestorianism believed Jesus had two natures, man and Logos, which were unmingled yet eternally united;
-Monophysitism believed Jesus had two natures united and joined in one body;
-Docetism believed Jesus had one nature, which was all God, and only appeared human;
-Arianism believed Jesus had a special nature, a special creation by God for man's salvation;
-Ebionites believed Jesus was not of divine nature, but was still the Messiah.

Studying Jesus' nature raises the question, "who is his father?" Science reveals the human genome has 46 chromosomes, 23 from the mother and 23 from the father.

Islam allows a nonrational mental disconnect, teaching that Jesus did not have a "human" father, being conceived in Mary's womb by the will of God, yet Islam claims that God was not Jesus' father, that Jesus is not the son of God. This belief is blasphemy, punishable by death.

A possible origin for this incongruity in Islam may be due to the two different Arabic words for son:

"walad"- son from a sexual union; and
"ibn" - son in the widest sense, similar to the Hebrew word "ben"- builder of the family name.

In verses which say Allah did not have a son, the Arabic word used for "son" is "walad"- son of a sexual union, not "ibn"- son in the widest sense:

Allah is one Allah: Glory be to Him (far exalted is He) above having a son (walad) (Sura 4:17);

It is not befitting to (the majesty of) Allah that He should beget a son (walad). Glory be to Him when He determines a matter, He only says to it 'Be,' and it is. (Sura 19:35)

In this sense, Muslims and Christians agree that God did not have a sexual union with Mary.

"Behold" the angels said: "O Mary! Allah giveth thee glad tidings of a Word from Him: his name will be **Christ (Messiah) Jesus**, the Son of Mary, held in honor in this world and the Hereafter and of (the company) of those nearest Allah. He shall speak to the people in childhood and in maturity and he shall be (of the company) of the righteous."
She said "O my Lord! How shall I have a son when no man hath touched me?" He said: "Even so: Allah createth what He willeth; when He hath decreed a plan He but saith it to it 'Be' and it is!" (Sura 3:45-51)

He said "Mary, I am only a messenger from the Lord to announce to thee the gift of a HOLY SON."
She said "How shall I have a son, seeing that no man has touched me, and I am not unchaste?"
He said "So it will be: thy Lord saith, 'that is easy for me. And we wish to appoint Him as a sign unto men and a Mercy from us. It is a matter so decreed.'"
So she conceived him, and retired with him to a remote place. (Sura 19:16-22)

Another translation renders Sura 19:19:

I am only a messenger of thy Lord that I may bestow on thee **a faultless son.** (Arabic word for "faultless" is "zakkiyya" meaning totally without sin.)

The *Hadith,* sayings of Mohammed remembered by his wives, warriors and companions, stated:

> The Prophet said, "When any human being is born, Satan touches him at both sides of the body with his two fingers, **except Jesus, the son of Mary, whom Satan tried to touch but failed,** for he touched the placenta-cover instead." *(Hadith Sahih al-Bukhari,* Vol. 4, No. 506, narrated by Abu Huraira)

In *Hadith Sahih al-Bukhari* (Vol. 4, No. 641), narrated by Said bin al-Musaiyab:

> Abu Huraira said, "I heard Allah's Apostle saying, 'There is none born among the offspring of Adam, but Satan touches it.' A child therefore, cries loudly at the time of birth because of the touch of Satan, **except Mary and her child.**"

QUR'AN: **JESUS & THE** *GOSPEL*

The *Qur'an* acknowledges Jesus and the *Gospel,* though it does not explain what the *Gospel* is:

> Subsequent to them, we sent Jesus, the son of Mary, confirming the previous scripture, the Torah. We gave him **the Gospel**, containing guidance and light, and confirming the previous scriptures, the Torah, and augmenting its guidance and light, and to enlighten the righteous.
>
> The people of **the Gospel** shall rule in accordance with Allah's revelations therein.
>
> Those who do not rule in accordance with Allah's revelations are the wicked. (Sura 5:46-7)

> Allah will say, "O Jesus, son of Mary, remember My blessings upon you and your mother. I supported you with the Holy Spirit, to enable you to speak to the people from the crib, as well as an adult.

I taught you the scripture, wisdom, the Torah, and **the Gospel**. Recall that you created from clay the shape of a bird by My leave, then blew into it, and it became a live bird by My leave.

You healed the blind and the leprous by My leave, and revived the dead by My leave.

Recall that I protected you from the Children of Israel who wanted to hurt you, despite the profound miracles you had shown them. "

The disbelievers among them said, "This is obviously magic." (Sura 5:110; see Sura 57:27)

QUR'AN: JESUS' DEATH & RESURRECTION

The views of different Christian heresies are reflected in the *Qur'an*'s treatment of Jesus' death, resurrection and his role in judgment at the last day.

Islam teaches that the Jews did not kill Jesus, which is factually true, as during the Roman occupation of Israel only Romans had the power to carry out a death sentence.

It is an Islamic teaching that Jesus did not die, citing a rebuke to a false charge of the Jews in Sura 4:156-159:

And for their unbelief, and their uttering against Mary a grave false charge, and for their saying, "We killed the Messiah, Jesus, son of Mary, the Messiah of God"...yet they did not slay him, neither crucified him, only a likeness of that was shown to them.

Those who are at variance concerning him are surely in doubt the following of conjecture; and they did not kill him of certainty...no indeed; God raised him up to Him; God is Almighty, Allwise.

There is not one of the people of the book but will assuredly believe him before his death, and on the Resurrection Day he will be a witness against them.

The *Qur'an* gives it as a "statement of truth" that Jesus said "I shall die," Sura 19:30-35:

Jesus said, "I am a servant of Allah. He has given me the Book, and has made me a Prophet, And He has made me blessed wheresoever I may be, and has enjoined upon me Prayer and almsgiving so long as I live;

And He has made me dutiful towards my mother, and has not made me arrogant and graceless

And peace was on me the day I was born, and peace will be on me **the day I shall die**, and **the day I shall be raised up to life again.**" Such was Jesus, son of Mary. It is a statement of truth.

Sura 3:55 states that Jesus was raised up:

"Behold!" Allah said: "O Jesus! I will take thee and raise thee to Myself and clear thee (of the falsehoods) of those who blaspheme; I will make those who follow thee superior to those who reject faith, to the Day of Resurrection."

QUR'AN: CONFUSION OVER TRINITY

The Father, Son and Holy Spirit being three distinct, co-eternal persons sharing one indivisible Divine essence is the orthodox Christian understanding of the Trinity. A study of prepositions in the New Testament reveal their relationship: "from" and "to" the Father; "by" and "through" Jesus; and "in" and "with" the Holy Spirit.

Perhaps due to being illiterate, Mohammed mistakenly thought Christians worshipped three gods - a male god, a female goddess and a child god, as idols were worshiped for centuries in Arabia and Persia, i.e.: Sumerian god Dumuzi & goddess Ianna; Babylonian god Tammuz & goddess Ishtar; Egyptian god Osiris & goddess Isis and son, Horus; Greek god Cronus & goddess Rhea and son, Zeus.

Mohammed confused pagan beliefs with what Christians believed regarding the Father, Mary and Jesus:

Allah will say, "O Jesus, son of Mary, did you say to the people, 'Make me and my mother idols beside Allah?'
He will say, "Be You glorified. I could not utter what was not right." (Sura 5:116)

In the *Hadith*, narrated Abu Said al-Khudri:

Afterwards the Christians will be called upon and it will be said to them, "Who do you use to worship?" They will say, "We used to worship Jesus, the son of Allah." It will be said to them, "You are liars, for Allah has never taken anyone as a wife or a son," (Vol. 6, Book 60, No. 105)

Over a century before Mohammed, the Council of Ephesus (431AD) gave Mary the title of "Theotokos" (Mother of God), which may have contributed to his misunderstanding the concept of the Trinity.

Hilaire Belloc, President of the Oxford Union and a Member of the British Parliament, wrote in *The Great Heresies* (1938):

Mohammedism was a perversion of Christian doctrine...He eliminated the Trinity ...He was content to accept all that appealed to him...and to reject all that seemed to him too complicated...He was born a pagan, living among pagans, and never baptized. He adopted Christian doctrines...and dropped those that did not suit him...The success of Mohammedanism...was an extreme simplicity which pleased the unintelligent masses.

Bishop Fulton J. Sheen wrote in *The World's First Love* (McGraw-Hill, 1952):

Because it had its origins in the 7th century under Mohammed, it was possible to unite within Islam some elements of Christianity and of Judaism, along with particular customs of Arabia...

Misunderstanding the notion of the Trinity, Mohammed made Christ a prophet announcing himself (Mohammed).

<8

QUR'AN: JEWISH INFLUENCE

In Mohammed's day, Jewish scriptures were hand-copied, protected in synagogues, and unavailable to common people. What Mohammed knew of Judaism was from Jewish law oral commentaries called *Midrash,* and oral traditions called *Talmud, Mishnah* and *Gemara,* with stories like *The Book of Enoch* and *The Apocalypse of Abraham.*

Mohammed's *Qur'an* mentioned Old and New Testament characters, like Adam, Noah, Abraham, Moses, David, the angel Gabriel and Jesus, but the story line is changed from the promise of forgiveness and redemption to building a case that when Allah's prophets are rejected, Allah will punish those who reject the prophet.

QUR'AN: CONFUSED JEWISH BELIEFS

British scholar Edward Carpenter in his book *Pagan and Christian Creeds: Their Origin and Meaning* (1920; reprinted 1998), wrote that the child of the mother goddess in Arabia and Persia was called "Aben Ezra."

Mohammed imputed this pagan belief to the Jews when he said Jews believed "Ezra" was the "son of God," as written in the *Hadith,* narrated Abu Said Al-Khudri:

Then the Jews will be called upon and it will be said to them, "Who do you use to worship?"

They will say, "We used to worship Ezra, the son of Allah."

It will be said to them, "You are liars, for Allah has never taken anyone as a wife or a son. What do you want now?"

They will say, "Our Lord! We are thirsty, so give us something to drink."

They will be directed and addressed thus,
"Will you drink,"
Whereupon they will be gathered unto
Hell (Fire) which will look like a mirage whose
different sides will be destroying each other.
(Vol. 6, Bk. 60, No. 105)

The Arabic spelling of Ezra is "Uzair." Sura 9:30-31 revealed Mohammed was inadvertently imputing this pagan belief in "Aben Ezra" to Jews.

The Jews call Uzair a son of Allah, and the
Christians call Christ the son of Allah. That is a
saying from their mouth, (in this) they but
imitate what the unbelievers of old used to say.

✒ QUR'AN: APOCRYPHAL INFLUENCE

Many apocryphal and heretical stories that Mohammed heard were reflected in the *Qur'an*.

The *Qur'an's* description of Hell is very similar to the *Homilies of Ephraim*, a Nestorian Christian preacher of the 6th century (John Bagot Glubb, *The Life and Times of Mohammed*, 1970, page 36).

QUR'AN & INFANCY GOSPEL

Another influence on the *Qur'an* is the *Infancy Gospel of Thomas*, a non-canonical, questionable Gnostic text written by someone, (definitely not the apostle Thomas) who knew little of Jewish life. Written centuries after Christ, it is not taken seriously by Biblical scholars, considered simply as Christian fiction.

The online encyclopedia *Wikipedia.com* stated:

An Arabic text, *Injilu 't Tufuliyyah*,
translated from a Coptic original, gives some
parallels to the episodes, 'recorded in the
book of Josephus the Chief Priest, who was
in the time of Christ': Jesus speaking from

the cradle and the episode of the swallows made of clay found their way into the *Qur'an*.

INFANCY GOSPEL - SPEAKING FROM CRADLE

The apocryphal *Infancy Gospel of Thomas* has Jesus speaking while still an infant:

A teacher named Zacchaeus overheard everything Jesus said to Joseph and marveled, saying to himself, "As just a child, he utters these things." (*Infancy Gospel of Thomas* 6:1-2)

This story made it into the *Qur'an*:

He shall speak to the people in cradle and in maturity. (Sura 5:110)

But Mary pointed to the baby. They said "How can we talk to one who is a child in the cradle?"
Jesus said: "I am indeed a servant of Allah; He hath given me revelation and made me a prophet." (Sura 19:29-33)

Eth-Thalabi, a leading commentator of Islamic traditions, recounted the story:

Then Mary told them to talk to Jesus, and they grew angry and said, "How can we speak to him who is in the cradle, a little child?"
Wahab says that then Zachariah came to her, when she showed herself to the Jews, and said to Jesus, "Speak up, and give us your argument if you are so commanded."
And at that instant Jesus and He was only forty days old, said,
"Verily, I am a servant of Allah to whom He has given a wonderful Book."

INFANCY GOSPEL - CLAY BIRDS FLY

The apocryphal *Infancy Gospel of Thomas* says Jesus made clay birds, clapped and they flew away:

> When the boy Jesus was five years old, he was playing in a narrow part of a rushing stream...and after he had made clay, he molded twelve sparrows from it. And it was the Sabbath when he did these things...
>
> Then, a certain Jew saw what Jesus was doing while playing on the Sabbath.
>
> Immediately, he departed and reported to Jesus' father, Joseph,
>
> "Look, your child is in the stream and he took clay and formed twelve birds and profaned the Sabbath?"
>
> And Joseph went to the area and when he saw him, he shouted, "Why are you doing things that are not permitted on the Sabbath?"
>
> Jesus, however, clapped his hands and shouted to the sparrows, "Depart, fly..." and the sparrows departed. (*Infancy Gospel* 2:1-7)

This story was referred to in the *Qur'an*:

> I make for you out of clay as it were the figure of a bird and breathe into it and it becomes a bird. (Sura 3:49)

> Thou makest out of clay as it were the figure of a bird...and thou breathest into it and it becometh a bird. (Sura 5:110)

INFANCY GOSPEL - RESURRECTING PLAYMATE

The apocryphal *Infancy Gospel of Thomas* says one of Jesus' playmates died and Jesus raised him up.

> Jesus was up on a roof of a house. And one of the children playing with him died after falling off the roof.
>
> And when the other children saw, they fled and Jesus was left standing alone.

When the parents of the one who had died came, they accused Jesus, "Troublemaker, you threw him down."

But Jesus replied, "I did not throw him down, rather he threw himself down.

When he was not acting carefully, he leaped off the roof and died.

Jesus leaped off the roof and stood by the corpse of the boy and cried out with a loud voice and said, "Zeno," -for that was his name- "rise up, talk to me, did I throw you down?" and rising up immediately, he said

"No, Lord, you did not throw me down, but you did raise me up." (*Infancy Gospel of Thomas* 9:1-5)

A like story is in Islam's *Kusus al-Anbiah* by Imam Eth-Thalabi:

Said Wahab. While Jesus was playing with his playmates, one of them jumped upon another and kicked him with his feet till he died.

So they threw him between the arms of Jesus and He was covered with blood, and when the people came upon them, they took notice of it and carried him to the Kadi of Egypt, and said to him, 'This boy has killed the other.'

So the Kadi asked Him, and Jesus said, 'I do not know who killed him, and I am not his companion.'

They desired to fall upon Jesus and He said to them, "Bring me the boy who was killed," and they said, "What do you wish to do with him?"

He said "I wish to ask him who killed him." Said they, "How can he speak to you when he is dead?"

They took Jesus and brought Him to the place where the boy was killed, and when Jesus offered a prayer, Allah raised him from the dead, and Jesus said to him,

"Who killed you?" The boy said, "So and so." (Cairo edition, pages 241-255)

∽

IS THE *BIBLE* CORRUPTED?

Most Muslims do not read the *Bible*, claiming it has been corrupted, but when was it corrupted? The *Bible*, or "the Book," must not have been corrupted in 610 AD when Allah told Mohammed:

> If thou (Mohammed) art in doubt concerning that which We reveal unto thee, **then question those who read the Book that was before thee.** Verily the Truth from thy Lord hath come unto thee. (Sura 10:94)

The *Qur'an* mentions "the Book" over 200 times, such as Sura 3:3:

> It is He Who sent down to thee (step by step), in truth, the Book confirming what went before it; and He sent down the **Taurat (Torah-Law of Moses) and the Injeel (Evangel-Gospel of Jesus)** before this, as a guide to mankind, and He sent down the criterion (of judgment between right and wrong). (*Yusifali Translation*)

Archeological discoveries, Dead Sea Scrolls and critical scholarship have confirmed that the *Law, Psalms, Prophets* and *Gospels* have remained virtually unchanged. Fouad Masri examined this in *Is the Injeel Corrupted?-My Search for the Truth About the New Testament* (CrescentProject.org, Box 50986, Indianapolis, IN 46250)

Dr. Gary R. Habermas, author of *The Historical Jesus-Ancient Evidence For The Life Of Christ*, (College Press Publishing, 1996) cites that documents like the *Dead Sea Scrolls* confirm the accuracy of the *Old Testament*, and over 5,000 complete and partial ancient texts confirm the accuracy of the *New Testament*, **making the *Bible* the most thoroughly documented piece of ancient literature.**

Events contained in the *Gospel* are also confirmed by ancient non-biblical and extra-biblical sources, such as: Tacitus (ca. 56-ca. 117 AD), Suetonius (ca. 69-ca. 130 AD), Josephus (37-ca. 100 AD), Thallus (ca. 50-ca. 170 AD), Pliny the Younger (ca. 61-ca. 113 AD), Trajan (53-117), Hadrian (76-138 AD), Lucian (ca. 125-ca. 180 AD), Mara Bar Serapion (prior ca. 73-no later than ca. 200 AD), Phlegon (ca. 100-ca. 199 AD), Justin Martyr (100-165 AD), and Tertullian (ca. 155-230 AD).

Robert M. Bowman, Jr., author of eleven books, including *Faith Has Its Reasons-An Apologetics Handbook* (Paternoster, 2006), explains that most variances between ancient *New Testament* texts are mostly in the category of spelling and punctuation. When all texts and versions are examined together, there is virtually no theological difference between the first century and today.

Muslim scholars explain the understanding that "text" of the *Law of Moses* and *Gospels* were NOT corrupted, only the "interpretation" of them. Therefore the *Law of Moses* and *Gospels* should be read by Muslims, as one of the six articles of Islamic faith requires belief in the *Scriptures:* the *Law of Moses-Torah* (*Taurat-Tawrat*), the *Psalms of David* (*Zabur*) and the *Gospels of Jesus* (*Injeel-Injil*):

> Say (O Muslims): **We believe in** Allah and that which is revealed unto us and **that which was revealed unto Abraham (Ibrahim) and Ishmael (Ismail) and Isaac (Ishaq), and Jacob (Yaqoub), and the tribes, and that which Moses (Musa) and Jesus (Isa) received**. (Sura 2: 136 *Pickthal Translation;* see also Sura 5:68)

Those who think the *Law of Moses* and *Gospels* were corrupted cannot explain which verses were corrupted, when they were corrupted or by whom. If the *Law of Moses* and *Gospels* could be corrupted by mortal man, then so could the *Qur'an*. (Indeed, some scholars speculate about verses Caliph Uthman may have chosen not to include when he compiled the first *Qur'an* in 651 AD.)

❧

MOHAMMED'S FIRST MARRIAGE

At age 22, Mohammed began working for a wealthy Christian woman named Khadijah, who had been widowed twice. In 595 AD, when Mohammed was 25 years old, he married Khadijah, who was 40 years old. Presiding over the ceremony was her cousin, Waraqah Ibn Nawfal, who was a monk in the heretical Christian Ebionite sect, and who was reputed to have translated the *Bible* from Hebrew into Arabic.

⛧

MOHAMMED BEGINS THE *QUR'AN*

At this time in Egypt, there were Christian hermits, ascetics and monks who in stoic self-discipline, would go out in the wilderness and find a cave to fast and pray. Attempting to follow the example of Elijah and John the Baptist, these individuals were known as "Desert Fathers."

In 610 AD, Mohammed went to a cave near Mecca and began spending time in prayer. He claimed an angel appeared to him and squeezed him, forcing him "recite." The word *Qur'an* means "recitation." The *Qur'an* and *Hadith Sahih al-Bukhari* record:

> After that, solitude became dear to him and he would go to the cave, Hira, to engage in devotion there for a certain number of nights before returning to his family, and then he would return for provisions for a similar stay.
>
> At length, unexpectedly, the Truth (the angel) came to him and said, "Read." "I cannot read," he said. The Prophet described: "Then he took me and squeezed me vehemently and then let me go and repeated the order 'Read.' 'I cannot read' said I, and once again he squeezed me and let me till I was exhausted.
>
> Then he said, 'Read.' I said, 'I cannot read.' He squeezed me for a third time and then let me go and said 'Read! In the name of thy Lord that createth. Createth man from a clot.'" (Sura 96:1-3)

Mohammed was greatly disturbed, so he returned home. He feared he had been tormented by an evil spirit called a "Jinni" or "Genie." This spiritual encounter was different from Biblical stories where a visit from an angel of the Lord would bring a greeting of "Fear not."

> Then Allah's Apostle returned with the Inspiration, his neck muscles twitching with terror till he entered upon Khadija and said, "Cover me! Cover me!" They covered him till his fear was over and then he said,
> "O Khadija, what is wrong with me?"
> (*Hadith Sahih al-Bukhari,* Vol. 9, No. 111)

> "O Khadija, I see light and hear sounds and I fear I am mad." (Ibn Sa'd, d. 852 A.D., *Kitab al-Tabaqat al-Kabir, Book of the Major Classes*, p. 225, S.Moinul Haq, Pakistan Historical Society)

The Hadith describes that sometimes during the "wahy" or inspiration, Mohammed would hear ringing of bells, buzzing of bees, sweat profusely, his face would be perturbed, he would shiver and swoon, his mouth would foam, he would roar like a camel and have tremendous headaches. Mohammed's wife, Khadijah, tried to test the spirit by removing her veils and "disclosing her form." She took him to her Ebionite Christian cousin, Waraqah Ibn Nawfal. Described as "a blind, old man," he suggested this was the angel that visited Moses. A few days later, Waraqah died.

> But after a few days Waraqa died and the Divine Inspiration was also paused for a while and the Prophet became so sad as we have heard that he intended several times to throw himself from the tops of high mountains and every time he went up to the top of a mountain in order to throw himself down, Gabriel would appear before him and say,
> "O Mohammed! You are indeed Allah's Apostle in truth" whereupon his heart would

become quiet and he would calm down and would return home.

And whenever the period of the coming of the inspiration used to become long, he would do as before, but when he used to reach the top of a mountain, Gabriel would appear before him and say to him what he had said before. (*Hadith Sahih al-Bukhari,* Vol. 9, No. 111)

So I read it, and he departed from me. And I awoke from my sleep, and it was though these words were written on my heart.

Tabari: Now none of Allah's creatures was more hateful to me than an (ecstatic) poet or a man possessed: I could not even look at them. I thought, Woe is me poet or possessed-Never shall Quraysh say this of me! I will go to the top of the mountain and throw myself down that I may kill myself and gain rest.

So I went forth to do so and then when I was midway on the mountain, I heard a voice from heaven saying "O Mohammed! thou are the apostle of Allah and I am Gabriel." (Ibn Ishaq, d. 782, *Sirat Rasulallah,* compiled by A. Guillaume, *The Life of Mohammed,* p. 106, Oxford, London, 1955)

Mohammed spent the next 23 years with this spirit appearing to him and giving him sayings, which he would memorize as he was illiterate. The word *Qur'an* means "recitations." Purportedly given in Arabic, recent scholarship suggests Syro-Aramaic, the trade language of the area. The verses had a rhyme to them which helped followers recite them, similar to rap music today. Later, Mohammed's son-in-law, Caliph Uthman, had Zayd ibn Thabit compile the verses, though disputes arose immediately from Mohammed's companion, Abdullah ibn Mas'ud, and Mohammed's best reciter, Ubai ibn Ka'b. Caliph Uthman ordered variant verses burned.

Muslims are taught the *Qur'an* was word-for-word from Allah: "It is We (Allah) Who have sent down the

Qur'an to thee (Mohammed) by stages" (Sura 76:23), but an upheaval occurred Jan. 12, 2008, when the *Wall Street Journal* article "The Lost Archive," reported a pre-Uthman *Qur'an* was found in Yemen with potentially variant verses. Photographed by a German Arabic scholar in 1944, the film is in the Berlin-Brandenburg Academy of Science.

∽

MOHAMMED'S FIRST CONVERTS

Mohammed's biography, written 100 years after his death, listed his first converts as his aging wife Khadijah, his slave/adopted son Zayd, his daughter Fatima, his 10-year-old cousin/future son-in-law Ali ibn Abu Talib and his future father-in-law Abu Bakr.

As a **religious leader,** Mohammed only converted 150 people. Islam did not rapidly expand till Mohammed fled to Medina and became a **political/military** leader, stating (*Hadith al-Bukhari,* Vol. 9, Bk. 84, No. 57):

> Mohammed said, "Whoever changes his Islamic religion, kill him." (*Mu'atta Imam Malik's Hadith* "break his neck," and Sura 2:217)

Shaykh 'Abd-Allaah ibn Jibreen stated:

> If your wife leaves Islam and if she does not repent then the ruling of Allah should be carried out on her, which is execution, because the Prophet (peace and blessings of Allah be upon him) said: "Whoever changes his religion [leaves Islam], execute him."

Muslims are not encouraged to critically examine Islam's origins, as they could be accused of doubting and punished by death. The University of Southern California's web page for searching the *Qur'an* stated: "Warning (especially for Muslims)...There is a real danger that Muslims...We would like to warn you..." www.usc.edu/schools/college/crcc/engagement/resources/texts/muslim/reference/searchquran.html

～

MOHAMMED'S WIVES

Mohammed's first wife, Khadijah, financed him while he prayed. After her death in 619 AD, Mohammed, in addition to concubines, consorts and slave-mistresses (*Hadith al-Tabari* vol. 9), had at least 11 wives: Sawda, Aisha (Abu Bakr's daughter), Hafsa (Umar's daughter), Zainab and Umm Salama (whose husbands died in battle), Zainab (Zayd's former wife), Juwariya (beautiful captive), Umm Habiba Ramlah (whose husband became Christian), Rayhana and Safia (captive Jews whose husbands were beheaded), Maria (captive Coptic Christian), Fatimah, Hend, Habla, Asma, Umm Sharik, Maymuna, Maymuna of Hareth, Zainab (third), Khawla and Duba.

Mohammed claimed a fifth of the women taken as war booty, as later did the Caliphs and Sultans. "Prophet, we have made lawful to you...the slave girls who Allah has given you as booty." (Sura 33:50) The *Qur'an* made it permissible to rape women captured in war, "women their right hands possess." (Sura 23:5-6; 33:52; 4:24; 70:29-30).

Mohammed's wives were obedient:

O Consorts of the Prophet if any of you were guilty of evident unseemly conduct, the punishment would be doubled to her, and that is easy for Allah. (Sura 33:30)

In the *Hadith*, Mohammed said:

Woman can be married for religion, her fortune, or her beauty. So marry one for the religion (*Abu Issa al-Tarmidi, Sunan al-Tarmidi, Medina* n.d., p.275, B: 4, H:1092)

Mohammed's youngest wife was Aisha:

The Prophet engaged me when I was a girl of six...Later...my mother, Um Ruman, came to me while I was playing in a swing with some of my girl friends...

She took some water and rubbed my face...Some women said "Allah's Blessing and good luck"...Allah's Apostle came to me in the forenoon and my mother handed me over to him, and at that time I was a girl of nine years of age. (*Bukhari* Vol 5, Bk 58, N 234; Vol 8, Bk 73, N 151)

After Mohammed died, a division arose in Islam:

●Sunni Muslims believe Aisha's father, Abu Bakr, inherited Mohammed's authority and became the first Caliph.
●Shi'a Muslims believe Mohammed's cousin and son-in-law, Ali Ibn Abi Talib, who was married to Mohammed's daughter Fatima, was the rightful Caliph

ॐ

ZAYD'S WIFE

Mohammed once visited Zayd, his former slave and adopted, and saw Zayd's wife, Zainab, scantily clothed. Mohammed desired her, even though she was also his cousin. Circumstances mounted till Zayd divorced her so that Mohammed could have her.

Mohammed later abolished the practice of adoption so he could no longer be accused of the abhorrent practice of a man having intercourse with the same woman as his son.

A verse was then revealed to Mohammed:

Fear Allah. Then when Zayd had dissolved his marriage with her (Zainab) we joined her in marriage to thee: in order that there may be no difficulty to the believers in the matter of marriage of the wives of their adopted sons.... (Sura 33:37)

The *Hadith Sahih al-Bukhari* recorded:

When the Qur'anic verse that allows Mohammed to postpone the turn [in bed] of any wife was revealed, and when Mohammed said that Allah allowed him to marry his adopted son's wife, Aisha (one of his wives) told him,

"O Allah's Apostle I do not see but that your Lord hurries in pleasing you."
(*Hadith Sahih al-Bukhari*, Vol. 7, No. 48)

The *Hadith Sahih al-Bukhari* recorded:

Anas said, "The prophet used to visit all his wives in an hour round, during the day and night and they were eleven in number."
I asked Anas, "Had the prophet the strength for it?" Anas replied, "We used to say that the prophet was given the strength of thirty (men)." (*Hadith al-Bukhari*, Vol. 1, Bk. 5, No. 268)

⚜

"RPM" - RELIGIOUS - POLITICAL - MILITARY

Beginning in 610 AD, at age 40, Mohammed tried to convert those who came to worship Mecca's 360 different pagan gods. Though hoping his faith would be embraced by Jews, Christians, Zoroastrians and Pagans, as it had elements of each, he only converted around 150.

His initial "MECCAN" verses were revealed to him while in Mecca. These "weak" verses were respectful of Christians and Jews-"people of the Book," even instructing followers to pray toward the Jewish Temple site in Jerusalem as Solomon did when he dedicated the Temple (1 Kings 8:26-49, 2 Chron. 6:17-39) and as Daniel did while exiled in Babylon. (Daniel 6:10).

If you are in doubt about the revelation I am giving you ask those who read the *Bible* before you. (Sura 10:94)

And if you (Mohammed) art in doubt concerning that which We reveal unto thee, then question those who read the Scripture (that was) before thee. (Sura 10:94, Pickthal Trans.)

There is no compulsion in religion. (Sura 2:256)

In 622 AD, at age 52, Mohammed was rejected in Mecca and fled to Medina. This is called "the Flight" (Hegira), and is Year One in Islam's calendar. Here he received "MEDINA" or "strong" verses, which canceled out the "weak" verses and advocated coercion, robbing, killing and enslaving of infidels. Mohammed transitioned from a **RELIGIOUS** leader to also being a **POLITICAL** and **MILITARY** leader.

Islam is not just a religion. In the same way the word "light" has **3 meanings:** a NOUN -a source of illumination; an ADJECTIVE -the opposite of heavy or dark; and a VERB -to ignite, ie. light a match or a stove, similarly the word "Islam" has **3 meanings**: a RELIGIOUS system, a POLITICAL system and a MILITARY system.

∽

CHANGED DIRECTION OF BOWING

Mohammed then changed the direction of bowing away from the Jewish Temple site in Jerusalem to Mecca. (The name "Jerusalem" does not appear in the *Qur'an*.) The *Hadith* narrated Bara' bin 'Azib stated that the "qibla" or "direction" toward which Mohammed originally prayed was facing the Jewish Temple site in Jerusalem, called the "Baitul-Maqdis" or "the House of the Holiness."

Mohammed made the new direction of prayer toward the black meteorite stone in the square building in Mecca called the Ka'aba, which pagan Arabs had previously bowed to for centuries in association with the moon god, believing the stone to have fallen from the sky:

> Allah's Apostle prayed facing Baitul-Maqdis for sixteen or seventeen months but he loved to face the Ka'ba (at Mecca) so Allah revealed: "Verily, We have seen the turning of your face to the heaven!" (Sura 2:144)

> So the Prophet faced the Ka'ba and the fools amongst the people namely "the Jews" said, "What has turned them from their qibla (Baitul-

Maqdis) which they formerly observed" (Allah revealed): "Say: 'To Allah belongs the East and the West. He guides whom he will to a straight path.'" (Sura 2:142)

A man prayed with the Prophet (facing the Ka'ba) and went out. He saw some of the Ansar praying the 'Asr prayer with their faces towards Baitul-Maqdis [Temple site in Jerusalem], he said,

"I bear witness that I prayed with Allah's Apostle facing the Ka'ba." So all the people turned their faces towards the Ka'ba. (*Hadith Sahih al-Bukhari*, Vol. 1, Book 8, No. 392)

∽

MOHAMMED & THE JEWS

When Mohammed first fled as an **immigrant** to Medina, his followers were few. He made a treaty with the pagans and the three Jewish tribes living there: Banu Qaynuqa, Banu Nadir and Banu Qurayza. As his followers increased, Mohammed became a **political leader**. When converts in Mecca threatened the city's peace, they were chased out.

Fleeing to Medina, Mohammed allowed them to retaliate by robbing caravans headed to Mecca: "Permission is given unto those who fight because they have been wronged." (Sura 22:39)

In 624, Mohammed became a **military leader.** With just 300 men he defeated 1,000 Meccans guarding their caravan at Badr. He found reason to void his treaty with Medina's first Jewish tribe, Banu Qaynuqa, drove them out and confiscated their property. This gave rise to the concept in Islam that when you are weak you make treaties until you are strong enough to disregard them.

Mecca was feeling the pain of their caravans being robbed, so in 625 they sent an army of 3,000 and defeated Mohammed at the *Battle of Uhud,* though they mistakenly failed to pursue Mohammed. Medina's second Jewish tribe, Banu Nadir, sent a leader to Mecca begging for help, but he was assassinated. Mohammed then expelled that tribe and confiscated their property.

≪

MOHAMMED BEHEADS 700 JEWS

In 627, Mecca sent a coalition 10,000 to stop Mohammed in Medina, but Mohammed dug trenches around the city, rendering the Meccan cavalry useless.

Anas Ibn Malik reported:

Abu Talhah was a good marksman with arrows. When he threw his arrows at the unbelievers, the Prophet would look up to see what they hit. (*Hadith Sahih al-Bukhari*)

When the Meccans withdrew, Mohammed attacked the neighborhood of Medina's third Jewish tribe, Banu Qurayza. After 25 days they surrendered. Ibn Ishaq described what followed:

They surrendered, and the apostle confined them in Medina in the quarter of the d. al-Harith...The apostle went out to the market of Medina (which is still its market today) and dug trenches in it. Then he sent for them and struck off their heads in those trenches as they were brought out to him in batches...

There were 600 or 700 in all, though some put the figure as high as 800 or 900. As they were being taken out in batches to the apostle they asked Ka'b what he thought would be done with them.

He replied, "Will you never understand? Don't you see that the summoner never stops and those who are taken away do not return? By Allah it is death!" This went on until the apostle made an end of them.

Ibn Hisham recorded:

Zoheir, an aged Jew, who had saved some of Mohammed's allies of the Bani Aws in the *Battle of Boath*, Thabit interceded and procured a pardon, including the restoration of his family and his property.

"But what hath become of all our chiefs, - of Kab, of Huwey, of Ozzal Ibn Samuel?" asked the old man. As one after another he named the leading chiefs of his tribe, he received to each inquiry the same reply; - they had all been slain already. -"Then of what use is life to me any longer? Slay me also, that I may go and join those that have preceded me."

When this was told to Mohammed, he said, "Yea, he shall join them, in the fire of Hell?" and he too was beheaded." (Ibn Hisham p. 301)

Jewish women and children were divided among his warriors, and Mohammed reserved a fifth for himself.

∽

MOHAMMED "TOOK" A JEWISH WIFE

The expelled Jews of Medina fled north to the fortified Jewish oasis of Khaybar, but Mohammed conquered it in 628 AD. *The Life of Mahomet*, another spelling for Mohammed, records his tender side in taking the wife of the Jewish chief he had beheaded:

After this defeat, the fortress of Camuss surrendered, on condition that the inhabitants were free to leave the country, but that they should give up all their property to the conqueror.

With the rest, came forth Kinana, chief of the Jews of Khaybar, and his cousin. Mahomet accused them both of keeping back, in contravention of the compact, a portion of their riches, especially the treasures of the Bani Nadhir, which Kinana had obtained as a marriage portion with his wife, the daughter of the chief of that tribe.

"Where are the vessels of gold," he asked, "which ye used to lend to the people of Mecca?" They protested that they no longer possessed them. "If ye conceal anything from me," continued Mahomet, "and I should gain knowledge of it, then your lives and the lives of your families shall be at my disposal."

They answered that it should be so. A traitorous Jew, having divulged to Mahomet the place in which a part of their wealth was deposited, he sent and fetched it.

On the discovery of this attempt at imposition, Kinana was subjected to cruel torture, — "fire being placed upon his breast till his breath had almost departed," -in the hope that he would confess where the rest of his treasures were concealed.

Mahomet then gave command, and the heads of the two chiefs were severed from their bodies. The scene of torture and bloodshed was hardly ended, when Mahomet sent Bilal [Mahomet's African slave] to fetch the wife of Kinana, whose beauty was probably well known at Medina.

Bilal speedily performed his errand. Finding with Safia another damsel, her cousin, he brought them both straight across the battlefield strewed with the dead, and close by the corpses of Kinana and his cousin.

At the ghastly sight of their headless trunks, the companion of Safia screamed wildly, beating her face, and casting dust upon her head.

"Take that she-devil hence;" said Mahomet angrily: but aside he chided Bilal for his want of consideration in bringing the women so near the bodies of their relatives.

"Truly," said Bilal, "I did it designedly; I wished to see their grief and anger stirred up."

But Mahomet was moved by tenderer emotions; — turning complacently towards Safia, he cast his mantle around her, in token that she was to be his own.

∽

MOHAMMED'S ENEMY BEHEADED

The Life of Mahomet, with Introductory Chapters on the Original Sources for the Biography of Mahomet, Vol. IV (Bengal Civil Service, William Muir, Esq., 1861), stated:

That same year, after suffering many raids and killings by Muslims, the Arab tribes of Bani Layhan met with their chief Sofyan Ibn Khalid to discuss attacking Medina to stop the raids.

Mahomet's spies discovered their plan, so Mahomet sent Abdullah Ibn Oneis to use diplomacy to gain an opportunity to assassinate Sofyan. Abdullah went forth, pretending to be on his Sofyan's side, and when the moment was right, cut off his head.

He carried it to Mahomet, who was in the Mosque in Medina. Mahomet was so gratified, he gave the assassin his staff, saying:

"This shall be a token betwixt you and me on the day of resurrection. Verily, few on that day shall have anything to lean upon."

∽

MOHAMMED ORDERED EXECUTIONS

In 630 AD, Mohammed marched on Mecca with 10,000 warriors and it peacefully surrendered. Upon entering the city, he ordered 10 personal enemies to be murdered. Ibn Sa'd Tabaqat reported:

The apostle of Allah entered through Adhakhir, [into Mecca], and prohibited fighting. He ordered 6 men and 4 women to be killed, they were (1) Ikrimah Ibn Abi Jahl,

(2) Habbar Ibn al-Aswad, (3) Abd Allah Ibn Sa'd Ibn Abi Sarh, (4) Miqyas Ibn Sababah al-Laythi, (5) al-Huwayrith Ibn Nuqaydh, (6) Abd Abbah Ibn Hilal Ibn Khatal al-Adrami, (7) Hind Bint Utbah, (8) Sarah, the mawlat (enfranchised girl) of Amr Ibn Hashim, (9) Fartana and (10) Qaribah. (*Tabaqat*, Vol 2, page 168.)

Anas Ibn Malik recorded:

The Prophet entered Makkah on the day when it was taken over, wearing a helmet. When he took it off, a man came and said: 'Ibn Khatal is holding to the covering of the Ka'aba.' The Prophet ordered him to be killed. (*Hadith al-Bukhari,* Vol. 3, Bk. 29, No. 32; Vol. 5, Bk. 59, No. 582; *Hadith Muslim* Bk. 007, No. 3145; *Hadith Malik's Muwatta*, Bk. 20, No. 20.76.256; *Abu Dawood, Al-Nassaie and Ibn Majah*.)

The *Hadith* recorded:

Abdullah Ibn Khatal...had two slave girls who used to sing for him and for his companions songs full of abuse of the Prophet. The Prophet's instructions specified that the two slave girls should also be killed.

In 631 AD, Mohammed "invited" the Christians of Najran to accept that Jesus was not divine, but a prophet of Islam. When they refused, Mohammed forced them to pay the annual jizyah tribute or be killed.

❧

JIZYAH "PROTECTION MONEY"

Fight those who believe not in Allah, nor the Last Day, nor hold that forbidden which hath been forbidden by Allah and His Messenger, nor acknowledge the religion of Truth, (even if they are) of the People of the Book, **until they pay the jizya with willing submission, and feel themselves subdued.** (Sura 9:29)

"Jizyah" can best be described to the western mind as "protection money" or extortion, typically 80% of one's income in times of tolerance and 150% during oppression.

In cities like New York or Chicago, gang members were notorious for entering a storefront business and offering to "protect" the store for a fee. If the business owner declined, they would soon find their store broken into and vandalized. After this, the store owners would pay the "protection money," with willing submission, when gang members would visit.

∽

JIHAD IS THE PATH OF ALLAH

In the *Qur'an* and in other Muslim usage the word "jihad" is followed by "fi sabil Illah," meaning "in the path of Allah." All 199 references to jihad in the *Hadith Sahih al-Bukhari* assume warfare.

The *Hadith Sahih al-Bukhari* recorded:

> Mohammed said, "The person who participates in (Holy battles) in Allah's cause and nothing compels him to do so except belief in Allah and His Apostle, will be recompensed by Allah either with a reward, or booty (if he survives) or will be admitted to paradise (if he is killed)." (*Hadith Sahih al-Bukhari,* Vol. 1, No. 35)

Raymond Ibrahim, in his *The Al Qaeda Reader* (Doubleday, 2007), explained how **terrorists today are inspired by the example of Mohammed, who used a catapult to besiege the city of Ta'if (Elta'el).**

When informed that catapults were killing women and children, Mohammed continued the siege, saying: "They are from among them [infidels]."

Hadith Sahih al-Bukhari recorded:

> Mohammed said, "No Muslim should be killed for killing a Kafir (infidel)." (*Hadith Sahih al-Bukhari,* Vol. 9, No. 50)

Some modern Muslims promote the idea of jihad as simply a personal inner struggle, which, coincidentally, is the name of Adolph Hitler's book, *Mein Kampf,* (My Struggle). In the struggle to be a better Muslim, one must ask, who was the best Muslim? Obviously, Mohammed. So it follows that as Mohammed was a religious, political and military leader, those following his example imitate him religiously, politically and militarily.

The effort to promote a more politically correct version of "jihad" is incongruous with imams and clerics issuing fatwahs and calling for violence on Israel and infidels. The 1400-year historical record leaves little confusion over the interpretation of jihad held by Mohammed, the "rightly guided" Caliphs and the Sultans who conquered large areas of the world for Allah.

Mohammed received the verses:

O Prophet! Struggle against the unbelievers and hypocrites and be harsh with them. (Sura 9:73)

Then, when the sacred months have passed, slay the idolaters wherever ye find them, and take them (captive), and besiege them, and prepare for them each ambush. But if they repent and establish worship and pay the poor-due, then leave their way free. (Sura 9:5)

They desire that you should disbelieve as they have disbelieved, so that you might be (all) alike; therefore take not from among them friends until they fly (their homes) in Allah's way; but if they turn back, then seize them and kill them wherever you find them, and take not from among them a friend or a helper. (Sura 4:89)

Hadith Sahih Bukhari, narrated Abdullah bin Masud, stated:

I asked Allah's Apostle, "O Allah's Apostle! What is the best deed?"

He replied, "To offer the prayers at their early stated fixed times."

I asked, "What is next in goodness?"

He replied, "To be good and dutiful to your parents."

I further asked, what is next in goodness?"

He replied, "To participate in Jihad in Allah's Cause."

I did not ask Allah's Apostle anymore and if I had asked him more, he would have told me more. (Vol. 4, Bk 52, No. 41)

Hadith Malik's Muwatta (Bk. 21, No. 3, 11) reads:

It has been passed down to us that when the Messenger of Allah, may Allah bless him and grant him peace, sent out a raiding party, he would say to them,

"Make your raids in the name of Allah in the way of Allah. Fight whoever denies Allah. Do not steal from the booty, and do not act treacherously. Do not mutilate and do not kill children."

Say the same to your armies and raiding parties, Allah willing. Peace be upon you.

&

FIGHTING IS OBLIGATORY FOR YOU

"Labor to keep alive in your Breast that
little Spark of Celestial fire called Conscience."
-George Washington

Humans have an innate feeling that lying, raping and killing is wrong. This is referred to as conscience. Mohammed instructed his followers to deny their conscience and kill in obedience to Allah:

Fighting is obligatory for you, as much as you dislike it. (Sura 2:216)

The *Yusufali Translation* of that verse states:

Fighting is prescribed for you, and ye dislike it. But it is possible that ye dislike a thing which is good for you, and that ye love a thing which is bad for you. But Allah knoweth, and ye know not.

The *Pickthal Translation* states:

Warfare is ordained for you, though it is hateful unto you; but it may happen that ye hate a thing which is good for you, and it may happen that ye love a thing which is bad for you. Allah knoweth, ye know not.

The *Shakir Translation* states:

Fighting is enjoined on you, and it is an object of dislike to you; and it may be that you dislike a thing while it is good for you, and it may be that you love a thing while it is evil for you, and Allah knows, while you do not know.

Mohammed fought in 66 battles/raids, including:

624 AD *Battle of Badr*
625 AD *Battle of Uhud* & *Expulsion of Banu Nadir*
626 AD *Attack on Banu Mustaliq*
627 AD *Battle of the Trench* & *Killing/Enslaving Banu Quraiza*
628 AD *Battle of Khaybar*
629 AD *Battle of Mu'tah*
630 AD *Conquest of Mecca, Battle of Hunayn, Battle of Auras* & *Siege of al-Ta'if* (where Mohammed used a catapult)
631 AD *Battle of Tabouk, Subjugation of Banu Thaqif* (Yemen) & *Subjugation of Ghassanids* (Arab Christians)

It is difficult to separate the political/military aspect of Islam from the religious aspect, as Mohammed led religiously, politically and militarily.

MOHAMMED - GHAZI WARRIOR

"It is not fitting for any prophet to have prisoners until he has made a great slaughter in the land." (Sura 8:57)

Wikipedia.com online encyclopedia defines "ghazi":

Ghazi...an Arabic term initially referring to the battles in which the Muslim prophet Mohammed personally participated. It has since evolved into the term for...warrior for the faith...in later battles.

The definition continues:

Ghazi (Arabic) is an originally Arabic word, from ghaz (contracted from ghazawa) "he raided" or "he made war," and was also adopted by such languages as Turkish for Muslims vowed to combat non-believers. As such it is essentially equivalent to Mujahideen: waging jihad bin-saif, i.e. holy war.

The Cambridge History of Islam, edited by P. M. Holt, Ann K. S. Lambton and Bernard Lewis (Cambridge University Press, 1977, page 283) stated:

For the ghazis in the marches, it was a religious duty to ravage the countries of the infidels who resisted Islam, and to force them into subjection.

Rudolph Peters, in *Jihad in Classical and Modern Islam: A Reader* (Princeton Series on the Middle East, 1996, page 3) explained:

quote> After the conquests had come to an end, the legal specialists laid down that the Caliph had to raid enemy territory at least once a year in order to keep the idea of jihad alive.

Wikipedia.com continues:

> Ghazi warriors depended upon plunder for their livelihood, and were prone to brigandage [highway robbery from caravans] and sedition in times of peace...
> In the west, Turkic ghazis made continual incursions along the Byzantine frontier zone...
> After the *Battle of Manzikert* these incursions intensified, and the region's people would see the ghazi corporations coalesce into semi-chivalric fraternities, with the white cap and the club as their emblems.
> The height of the organizations would come during the Mongol conquest when many of them fled from Persia and Turkistan into Anatolia...

Bernard Lewis, in *The Political Language of Islam*, (Exxon Lecture Series, 1991, pp. 147-148) wrote:

> The Ottoman poet Ahmedi, writing ca. 1402, defines a ghazi as "the instruments of God's religion, a servant of God who cleanses the earth from the filth of polytheism...the sword of God."

Muslim rulers vied amongst themselves for preeminence in the ghazi, with Ottoman Sultans acknowledged as excelling all others in this feat.

The Cambridge History of Islam, edited by P. M. Holt, Ann K. S. Lambton and Bernard Lewis (Cambridge University Press, 1977, page 290) stated:

> For political reasons the Ottoman Sultans—also being the last dynasty of Caliphs—attached

the greatest importance to safeguarding and strengthening the reputation which they enjoyed as ghazis in the Muslim world.

When they won victories in the Balkans, the ghazi used to send accounts of them as well as slaves and booty to eastern Muslim potentates.

Christian knights captured by Bayezid I at his victory over the Crusaders at Nicopolis in 1396, and sent to Cairo, Baghdad and Tabriz were paraded through the streets, and occasioned great demonstrations in favor of the Ottomans.

∾

STIRRUP & THE SPREAD OF ISLAM

The stirrup for riding horses is a small device which made a great impact. It is a classic example of whoever gets military technology first can rule the world.

In the 2nd century B.C., nomadic Asian tribes, such as the Scythians, rode horses barefoot and used a looped fabric for their big toe to help them keep balance.

By the 5th century A.D., the Chinese enlarged the fabric loop with a metal brace to hold a rider's whole foot. In the 6th century this device migrated west along trade routes to Persia where wooden blocks were used to support the feet, allowing a rider to effectively fight on horseback.

Now the full power of a galloping horse could be put behind a curved sword, called a "scimitar," enabling a charging ghazi warrior to literally slice a person in half. Mohammed's "raids" were the first instance of lightning attacks with this new device. The stirrup allowed a relatively small band of raiders to quickly subdue large areas.

∾

SUDDEN ATTACKS TO TERRORIZE

The *Wikipedia.com* definition of "ghazi" continues:

When performed within the context of Islamic jihad warfare, the ghazi's function was to weaken the enemy's defenses in preparation for his eventual conquest and subjugation.

Because the typical ghazi raiding party often did not have the size or strength to seize military or territorial objectives, this usually meant sudden attacks on weakly defended targets (e.g. villages) with the intent of terrorizing/demoralizing their inhabitants and destroying material which could support the enemy's military forces.

Though rules of war in Islam offered protection to non-combatants such as women, monastics and peasants (in that, generally speaking, they could not be slain), their property could still be looted or destroyed, and they themselves could be abducted and enslaved (*Cambridge History of Islam*, p. 269)

Edited by P. M. Holt, Ann K. S. Lambton and Bernard Lewis, *The Cambridge History of Islam* (Cambridge University Press, 1977, page 285) stated:

The only way of avoiding the onslaughts of the ghazis was to become subjects of the Islamic state. Non-Muslims could then enjoy the status of dhimmis, living under its protection...

Faced with the terrifying onslaught of the ghazis, the population living outside the confines of the empire, in the 'abode of war', often renounced the ineffective protection of Christian states, and sought refuge in subjection to the Ottoman empire.

The *Hadith*, narrated by Abu Huraira, stated:

A man came to Allah's Apostle and said, "Instruct me as to such a deed as equals Jihad (in reward)."

He replied, "I do not find such a deed." Then he added, "Can you, while the Muslim fighter is in the battlefield, enter your mosque

to perform prayers without cease and fast and never break your fast?"
The man said, "But who can do that?"
Abu- Huraira added, "The Mujahid (i.e. Muslim fighter) is rewarded even for the footsteps of his horse while it wanders about (for grazing) tied in a long rope." (*Hadith,* Vol. 4, Book 52, No. 44)

The *Hadith,* narrated by Abu Huraira, stated:

I heard Allah's Apostle saying, "The example of a Mujahid in Allah's Cause - and Allah knows better who really strives in His Cause - is like a person who fasts and prays continuously.

Allah guarantees that He will admit the Mujahid in His Cause into Paradise if he is killed, otherwise He will return him to his home safely with rewards and war booty." (*Hadith*, Vol. 4, Book 52, No. 46)

∽

MOHAMMED WAS WHITE

Hadith al-Bukhari, Volume 1, Book 3, No. 63:

While we were sitting with the Prophet in the mosque, a man came riding on a camel. He made his camel kneel...then said: "Who amongst you is Muhammad?" At that time the Prophet was sitting amongst us (his companions) leaning on his arm. We replied, "This **white man** reclining on his arm."

Hadith al-Bukhari, Volume 4, Book 56, Number 744:

"I saw the Prophet, and Al-Hasan bin Ali resembled him." I said to Abu-Juhaifa, "Describe him for me." He said, "**He was white** and his beard was black with some white hair."

Hadith al-Bukhari, Volume 2, Book 17, Number 141:

The Prophet never raised his hands for any invocation except for that of Istisqa' and he used to raise them so much that the **whiteness of his armpits** became visible.

Hadith al-Bukhari, Volume 1, Book 8, Number 367:

'When Allah's Apostle invaded Khaibar, we offered the Fajr prayer there yearly in the morning when it was still dark. The Prophet rode and Abu Talha rode too and I was riding behind Abu Talha. The Prophet passed through the lane of Khaibar quickly and my knee was touching the thigh of the Prophet. He uncovered his thigh and I saw the **whiteness of the thigh of the Prophet.**

Hadith al-Bukhari, Volume 2, Book 17, Number 122:

"I heard Ibn 'Umar reciting the poetic verses of Abu Talib: And a **white (person) (i.e. the Prophet)** who is requested to pray for rain."

MOHAMMED OWNED AFRICAN SLAVES

Hadith al-Bukhari, Volume 9, Book 91, Number 368:

"I came and behold, Allah's Apostle was staying on a Mashroba (attic room) and a **black slave** of Allah's Apostle was at the top of its stairs. I said to him, "(Tell the Prophet) that here is 'Umar bin Al-Khattab (asking for permission to enter)." Then he admitted me.

Syrian Islamic jurist, Ibn Qayyim al Jawiyya (1292-1293), wrote in Zad al-Ma'ad (part 1, page 114, 116, 160), of Mohammed's BLACK SLAVES, Bilal, Abu Hurairah, Usamah Ebn Zaayed, Rabbah, and stated:

"Muhammad had many male and female slaves. He used to buy and sell them, but he purchased more than he sold, especially after God empowered him by his message, as well as after his immigration from Mecca. He once sold one **black slave** for two. His name was Jacob al-Mudbir."

Hadith al-Bukhari, Volume 9, Book 89, Number 256:

Allah's Apostle said, "You should listen to and obey, your ruler even if he was an **Ethiopian (black) slave** whose head looks like a raisin."

Hadith al-Bukhari, Volume 4, Book 52, No. 137:

"The Prophet said, 'Let the **black slave** of Dinar perish. And if he is pierced with a thorn, let him not find anyone to take it out for him...If he [the **black slave**] asks for anything it shall not be granted, and if he needs intercession [to get into paradise], his intercession will be denied.'"

∽

MOHAMMED'S DEATH

At the age of 63, suffering the effects of one of his wives poisoning his food, Mohammed died in 632 AD. He had conquered from the southern Arabian Peninsula to the frontiers of Byzantium. *Hadith Sahih Bukhari*, narrated by Abu Huraira, recorded his dying words:

Allah's Apostle said, "I have been sent with the shortest expressions bearing the widest meanings, and I have been made victorious with terror (cast in the hearts of the enemy), and while I was sleeping, the keys of the treasures of the world were brought to me and put in my hand."

Abu Huraira added: "Allah's Apostle has left the world and now you, people, are bringing out those treasures." (*Hadith Sahih Bukhari*, Vol. 4, Book 52, No. 220)

Mohammed's sword was passed down by Caliphs and Sultans through the centuries and is kept the Topkapi Museum in Istanbul, Turkey. Within a 100 years of his death, followers conquered Arabia, Damascus, Syria, Persia, North Africa, the Holy Land, Spain and assaulted Constantinople, capital of the Byzantine Roman Empire. Mohammed did not know his fate (*Hadith* 5:266):

By Allah, though I am the Apostle of Allah, yet I do not know what Allah will do to me."

∿

SUNNI & SHI'A

Just as Christians use the letters WWJD to remind them "What Would Jesus Do," Muslims strive to imitate Mohammed's example, called the way, or "SUNNA." Jewish and Christian theology has a fall and redemption theme: sin is atoned by the sacrifice of a lamb; breaking God's Law is forgiven through the shed blood of Jesus- "the lamb of God." Pope John Paul wrote in *Crossing the Threshold of Hope* (1995):

Islam is not a religion of redemption. There is no room for the Cross and the Resurrection...**Redemption is completely absent**...The God of the Koran is outside of the world, a God who is only Majesty, never Emmanuel, God-with-us...
Not only the theology, but also the anthropology of Islam is very distant from Christianity.

In Islam, the concept of sin is not following Mohammed's example. What Mohammed permitted is "Halal"; what Mohammed did not permit is "Haram." For example, Mohammed liked cats, so they are halal. Mohammed did not like dogs, so they are haram. In Islam, lying, stealing, raping and murdering are not always wrong. Mohammed shows when they are permitted and when they are not. What advances Islam is good; what does not, is bad.

When Mohammed died in 632 AD, he had not designated a successor, so family infighting began over who would succeed him as "Caliph." A period of murders followed in a desert gangland Mafia-Soprano style struggle over who would be, in a sense, the next godfather. Sunni, who make up about 90 percent of all Muslims, believe that Mohammed's father-in-law, Abu Bakr, was the rightful heir. Abu Bakr was Mohammed's first adult male convert and the father of Mohammed's 6 year-old wife, Aisha. Abu Bakr fought in all the battles (ghazi) that Mohammed led.

Abu Bakr declared that those who did not recognize him as Caliph were apostate and would be killed. He waged the Apostasy "Ridda" Wars, murdering many who opposed him. He died two years after Mohammed in 634 AD from a rumored poisoning.

The next Caliph was Umar, who fought alongside Mohammed and whose daughter Hafsa was one of Mohammed's wives. Waging jihad, Umar conquered Mesopotamia, parts of Persia, Egypt, Palestine, Syria, North Africa, Armenia, Damascus and Jerusalem.

The world's oldest library was in Alexandria, Egypt. Persian traveler, Abd-Al-Latif Al Baghdadi and Syrian prelate Bar Hebraeus related when Caliph Umar invaded in 641 AD, he told his commander Amr bin al-Ass:

> Touching the books you mention, if what is written in them agrees with the *Qur'an*, they are not required; if it disagrees, they are not desired. Destroy them therefore.

The story continues that the books were burned to heat the city's bath-houses for six months, similar to Muslim destroying the Buddhist statues in Afghanistan, or Ayotollah Khomeini attempts to destroy the ancient palace of Cyrus at Persepolis.

After Caliph Umar was assassinated with a dagger in 644 AD, Uthman became the next Caliph.

Uthman, fought alongside Mohammed in many battles and married two of Mohammed's daughters,

Ruqayyah and Umm Khulthum. Uthman conquered Iran, most of North Africa, the Caucasus region and Cyprus. He formed a committee to compile the *Qur'an*, commanding any variant texts to be destroyed. Suras were arranged in order of length, the longest being first.

Uthman was assassinated in 656 AD while at prayer. Rioters wanted to mutilate his body, so it was kept hidden in his house for several days until it could be secretly carried out at night. He was hurriedly buried without ceremony in the same clothes he was assassinated in.

After Uthman, Ali took the title of Caliph. Mohammed's wife, Aisha led an army against Ali, but was defeated at the *Battle of the Camel* in 656 AD. Ali finally succeeded in being recognized as Caliph by all Muslims.

Shi'a or Shi'ite is an abbreviation for "Shiat Ali" or party of Ali, the cousin and son-in-law of Mohammed. Shi'a believe that Ali was Mohammed's first male convert, though just a child when converted. Shi'a comprise about 10 percent of all Muslims and are mostly in Iran. Shi'a believe that since Ali married Mohammed's daughter Fatima, their descendants were of the direct blood line of Mohammed and therefore the rightful heirs of his religious, political and military power.

Islam believes in the duty of revenge. Since Ali did not take revenge on those who killed Uthman, Uthman's cousin, Muawiyah I, exercised revenge against Ali. Muawiyah's soldiers attacked Ali at the *Battle of Suffin.*

Muawiyah I had his soldiers put verses of the *Qur'an* on the ends of the spears, which resulted in Ali's supporters refusing to fight them. Ali was then assassinated in 661 AD. With Ali dead, Muawiyah I declared himself the new Caliph and arranged for Ali's eldest son, Hassan, to be poisoned by his own wife.

When Muawiyah I died in 680 AD, his son Yazid made himself the next Caliph, beheading Ali's younger son, Hussein at the *Battle of Karbala*, marking the official split between the Shi'a and Sunni. The anniversary of Hussein's death is called "Ashura." Hussein's infant son, Ali, survived and was able to continue his family's blood line, which Shi'a believe were the rightful spiritual descendants, or Imams, of Mohammed.

Ali's blood line ended in 878 AD with the mysterious disappearance of the 4-year-old descendant, referred to by Shi'a as the 12th "Hidden" Imam, or Mahdi, who will return to conquer the world. Yazid began the hereditary Ummayad dynasty, which conquered Spain and southern France. After another era of infighting, or Fitna (civil war), Yazid and his son Muawiyah II met an untimely death in 683 AD.

Ibn al-Zubayr became the next Caliph, but he faced uprisings in Iran and Iraq by Shi'a wanting to avenge the death of Ali's son. Ibn al-Zubayr was killed in 685 AD by the next person to claim to be Caliph, Abd al-Malik Ibn Marwan.

The Ummayad dynasty was replaced in 758 AD by the Abbasid dynasty, followed by numerous other splits, until the Ottoman dynasty in 1258.

SHI'A & SUNNI THEOLOGY

When the mysterious 12th Imam never returned after several centuries, **Shi'a** spiritual authority passed to the "ulema," a council of twelve scholars who elected a supreme Imam, such as the late Ayatollah Khomeini.

Approximately 10 percent of Muslims are **Shi'a** and live predominately in Iran, Iraq, Yemen, parts of India, the east coast of Saudi Arabia and Lebanon. The **Shi'a** Imam is considered to have Pope-like infallibility and the **Shi'a** religious hierarchy is similar in structure to that of the Catholic Church. **Shi'a** theology focuses on the death of Ali and has a strong theme of martyrdom.

The **Shi'a** terrorist group in Lebanon is called Hezbollah (Party of Allah). Hezbollah is known for the 1983 bombing of the U.S. Embassy and Marine barracks which killed 258 Americans. Hezbollah, an umbrella group over numerous terrorist organizations, has not disarmed or renounced violence.

Since 1975, **Shi'a** Muslims have used the democratic process to transition Lebanon from a majority

Christian nation (Maronite, Orthodox, Greek Catholic and Protestant) into a majority Muslim nation, with Hezbollah holding 23 seats in the Lebanese parliament in 2006.

In contrast, **Sunni** Islam resembles the innumerable independent churches of Protestantism. **Sunni**, which means "well trodden path," has no hierarchy of clergy, just scholars and jurists who make nonbinding, yet considered inerrant, opinions interpreting Islamic law and traditions.

The world's Muslims are approximately 90 percent **Sunni**. There are at least 40 Sunni terrorist groups, the most well-known being Hamas and al-Qaida.

Though both the **Sunni** and **Shi'a** agree on the Five Pillars of Islam, they each have a different call to prayer, varying times of prayer, perform their bowing differently, and prefer different *Hadiths*.

Shi'a Islam permits Mu'tah – temporary marriages for pleasure, as did Mohammed, but Sunnis do not.

᭞

PERMISSION TO FIGHT

Wikipedia.com, the online encyclopedia, stated:

Through raids, sieges, and diplomacy, Mohammed and his followers allied with or subdued most of the tribes and cities of the Arabian Peninsula in their struggle with the powerful Banu Quraysh of Mecca. They also sent out raiding parties against Arabic-speaking communities under Byzantine rulership. Mohammed was believed by the Muslims to be divinely chosen to spread the religion of Allah and warfare was one aspect of this struggle.

Mohammed proclaimed in the *Qur'an*:

Fight and slay the Pagans wherever ye find them, and seize them, beleaguer them, and lie in wait for them in every stratagem (of war). (Sura 9:5 Yusufali Translation)

Permission to fight is given to those who are fought against. (Sura 22:39-40)

O Prophet! urge the believers to war. (Sura 8:65 *Shakir Translation*)

Fight them, and Allah will punish them by your hands, cover them with shame. (Sura 9:14 *Yusufali Translation*)

Fight those of the unbelievers who are near to you and let them find in you hardness. (Sura 9:123 *Shakir Translation*)

When ye meet the Unbelievers (in fight), smite at their necks...Allah lets you fight in order to test you. (Sura 47:4 *Yusufali Translation*)

Certainly Allah helped you in many battlefields. (Sura 9:25 *Shakir Translation*)

∽

ISLAMIC DIPLOMACY

Muslim "diplomacy" involves the concept known as "al-Taqiyya" ("al-Takeyya") which literally means to conceal or disguise one's beliefs, convictions, ideas, feelings, opinions, intentions or strategies, thus preventing or guarding against your enemy.

It is permissible in Islam to speak falsehoods for the sake of Allah, to promote the cause of Islam, to prevent denigration of Islam, or to protect oneself by pretending to be friends with an infidel. This is less of a premeditated act of deceit than a cultural habit, similar to haggling over prices in the marketplace.

Mohammed spoke of this concept in the *Qur'an:*

Let not the believers take disbelievers for their friends in preference to believers. Whoso doeth that hath no connection with Allah unless (it be) that ye but guard (Takeyya) yourselves against them, taking (as it were) security. Allah biddeth you beware (only) of Himself. Unto Allah is the journeying. (Sura 3:28, *Pickthal Translation*)

Let not the believers Take for friends or helpers Unbelievers...(Sura 3:28, *Yusufali Trans.*)

Let not the believers take the unbelievers for friends... (Sura 3:28 *Shakir Translation*)

᭟

HOLY LYING

The *Qur'an* has Suras like: "Truly Allah guides not one who transgresses and lies," (Sura 40:28) and the *Hadith*: "Be honest because honesty leads to goodness, and goodness leads to Paradise. Beware of falsehood because it leads to immorality, and immorality leads to Hell."

However, the Muslim scholar Afif A. Tabbarah wrote in his book, *The Spirit of Islam* (Intl Book Centre; 2nd Rev. ed., 1988, page 247):

Lying is not always bad, to be sure; there are times when telling a lie is more profitable and better for the general welfare, and for the settlement of conciliation among people, than telling the truth. To this effect, the Prophet says: "He is not a false person who (through lies) settles conciliation among people, supports good or says what is good."

Mohammed's daughter, Umm Kulthum, who married Caliph Uthman, testified that she had never heard the Apostle of Allah condone lying, except in three situations: **For reconciliation among Muslims, in war, and amongst wives, to keep peace in the family.**

Hadith Sahih Muslim (No. 6303-05) and *Hadith Sahih al-Bukhari*, (Vol. 3, No. 857), stated:

Humaid b. 'Abd al-Rahman b. 'Auf reported that his mother Umm Kulthum daughter of 'Uqba b. Abu Mu'ait, and she was one amongst the first emigrants who pledged allegiance to Allah's Apostle (may peace be upon him), as saying that she heard Allah's Messenger (may peace be upon him) as saying:

"A liar is not one who tries to bring reconciliation amongst people and speaks good (in order to avert dispute), or he conveys good."

Ibn Shihab said he did not hear that exemption was granted in anything what the people speak as lie but in three cases:

In battle, for bringing reconciliation amongst persons and the narration of the words of the husband to his wife, and the narration of the words of a wife to her husband (in a twisted form in order to bring reconciliation between them).

&

WAR IS DECEPTION

In the *Hadith*, Mohammed said:

The sons of Adam are accountable for all lies with the exception of those spoken to reconcile two (Muslim) men that are quarreling, for a man to appease his wife, and in war, because war necessitates deception.

Considering that Islam defines the entire non-Muslim world as the House of War (dar al-harb), it is acceptable to always lie and deceive non-Muslims.

In *Hadith Sahih al-Bukhari*, Mohammed said:

"Who is willing to kill Ka'b bin al-Ashraf who has hurt Allah and His Apostle?"

Thereupon Mohammed bin Maslama got up saying, "O Allah's Apostle! Would you like that I kill him?" The Prophet said, "Yes."

Mohammed bin Maslama said, "Then allow me to say a (false) thing (i.e. to deceive Kab)."

The Prophet said, "You may say it." (*al-Bukhari*, Vol. 5, No. 369, cf. Ka'b bin al-Ashraf.)

> Allah will not call you to account for thoughtlessness in your oaths, but for the intention in your hearts; and He is Oft-forgiving, Most Forbearing. (Sura 2:225)

The Islamic commentator, al-Tabary, told how Ammar Ibn Yasser was kidnapped by the Banu Moghera tribe and forced to deny his faith in Mohammed. When he got free and returned, Mohammed forgave him and said "If they turned, you turn," meaning, if they again capture you, you are allowed to deny me again.

Mohammed received a *Qur'an* verse:

> Any one who, after accepting faith in Allah, utters Unbelief - except under compulsion, his heart remaining firm in Faith - but such as open their breast to Unbelief, on them is Wrath from Allah, and theirs will be a dreadful Penalty. (Sura 16:106, *Yusufali Translation*)

> Whoso disbelieveth in Allah after his belief - save him who is forced thereto and whose heart is still content with the Faith - but whoso findeth ease in disbelief: On them is wrath from Allah. Theirs will be an awful doom. (Sura 16:106, *Pickthal Translation*)

> He who disbelieves in Allah after his having believed, not he who is compelled while his heart is at rest on account of faith, but he who opens (his) breast to disbelief— on these is the wrath of Allah, and they shall have a grievous chastisement. (Sura 16:106, *Shakir Translation*)

∾

TREATIES - HUDNA

The Muslims concept for treaty is "Hudna" or "cease-fire." Mohammed set the example that when Muslim armies are weak, they should seek truces and when they are strong, they should fight without mercy.

Kaab Ibn al-Ashrf was a member of the Jewish tribe, Banu al-Nudair. It was reported that Kaab had supported the Quraishites in their battle against Mohammed. Mohammed was also infuriated because he heard Kaab had recited amorous poetry to Muslim women. Mohammed asked for volunteers to rid him of Kaab Ibn al-Ashraf, saying Kaab had "harmed Allah and His Apostle."

On November 5, 2009, a fundamentalist Muslim, Major Malik Nabal Hasan killed 14 and wounded 30 at the largest U.S. Army base, Fort Hood, TX.

This has roots in Islamic tradition. When pagan leader Kaab Ibn al-Ashraf was preparing to fight Mohammed, his tribe was strong and it was not easy to gain access to him. Mohammed granted permission for his warrior, Ibn Muslima, to lie in order to infiltrate Kaab's camp and murder him. Ibn Muslima went to Kaab, saying he was no longer loyal to Mohammed, thus gaining Kaab's trust. Ibn Muslima said he wanted to talk privately and lured Kaab away from his other soldiers, then murdered him under cover of darkness.

Another story is of Shaaban Ibn Khalid al-Hazly, who was rumored to be gathering an army to stop Mohammed. Mohammed retaliated by ordering Abdullah Ibn Anis to murder Shaaban by telling a lie, saying he was a member of the Khazaa clan. When Shaaban saw Abdullah coming, he asked him, "From what tribe are you?" Abdullah answered, "From Khazaa...I have heard that you are gathering an army to fight Mohammed and I came to join you."

Abdullah started walking with Shaaban telling him how Mohammed was a heretic of Islam and complained how Mohammed badmouthed the Arab patriarchs. They continued talking until they reached Shaaban's tent. Shaaban's companions departed and Shaaban invited Abdullah into his tent to rest. Abdullah stayed there until everyone was asleep. Abdullah then severed Shaaban's head and carried it to Mohammed.

Mohammed was jubilant and shouted, "Your face has been triumphant (Aflaha al-wajho)." Abdullah responded, "It is your face, Apostle of Allah, who has been triumphant. (Aflaha wajhoka, ye rasoul Allah)."

Winston Churchill described this as a "**system of ethics, which regards treachery and violence as virtues rather than vices.**" (Stanely Kurtz, "Tribes of Terror," Claremont Review, Winter 2007/2008, p. 39, Akbar S. Ahmed's *Resistance & Control in Pakistan,* Routledge, 2004).

John Quincy Adams wrote in his "Essay on Turks" that to Muslims, "**treachery and violence are taught as principles of religion.**" (See pages 158-168)

༅

PERSIA

In 634 AD, Muslims invaded the Sassanid Persian Empire, which, next to the Byzantine, was the most powerful empire in the world. Muslim General Khalid ibn al-Walid, the "Drawn Sword of Allah," was undefeated in nearly 100 battles. He lured the Persians into the desert, where their horses were at a disadvantage, and defeated them at the *Battle of Namraq*. Persians tried to regroup at Kasker. As Muslim hordes neared Ctesiphon, Persian Emperor Yazdgard sent an emissary, saying:

> Our emperor asks if you would be agreeable to peace on the condition that the Tigris should be the boundary between you and us, so that whatever is with us on the eastern side of the Tigris remains ours and whatever you have gained on the western side is yours.
>
> And if this does not satisfy your land hunger, then nothing would satisfy you.
>
> The Muslim commander, Saad Ibn Wagas, responded that the Muslims were not hungry for land; and that they were fighting to convert the Persians to Islam. He added that if the Persian emperor wanted peace it was open to him to accept Islam, or to pay Jizya.

If both the alternatives were not acceptable then peace was out of question, and only the sword could decide the issue between them.

In 1007, the Persian poet Ferdowsi completed his epic poem "Shahnameh," which contained the lines:

Damn this world, damn this time, damn this fate, That uncivilized Arabs have come to make me Muslim.

<∽

SYRIA

As related by Peter BetBasoo, Assyria was first ruled by Sargon of Akkad in 2371 BC. The ancient Assyrian city of Nineveh (near present-day Mosul) had become a religious/cultural center by 1800 BC. The Old Testament prophet Jonah preached there circa 760 BC and Nineveh repented. King Shalmaneser V ruled Assyria 727-721 BC and carried Israel's the ten northern tribes into captivity. King Sennacherib, 705-681 BC, made Nineveh one of the most magnificent capitals in the world.

The word "Arab" is actually an Assyrian word meaning "westerner," first used by King Sennacherib in telling his conquest of the "ma'rabayeh"–westerners. Assyrians and Babylonians laid down the fundamental basis of mathematics, the Pythagorean Theorem, and the concept of zero. For centuries prior to Islam, Assyrians designed parabolic domes and arches.

In 33 AD, the Assyrian Christian Church was founded by Saint Thomas, Saint Bartholemew and Saint Thaddeus, and by the year 265 AD, Assyria was one of the first nations to be completely Christian.

In the 4th, 5th and 6th centuries, Christian Assyrians began a systematic translation into Arabic of Greek works in religion, science, philosophy (Socrates, Plato and Aristotle) and medicine (Galen). These Arabic translations were later taken by the Moors into Spain, where they were translated into Latin and spread into Europe, laying groundwork for the Renaissance.

One of the greatest Christian Assyrian achievements of the 4th century was the founding of the first university in the world, the School of Nisibis. It had three departments, theology, philosophy and medicine, and became a center of intellectual development in the Middle East. The statutes of the School of Nisibis became the model for the first Italian university.

The book, *How Greek Science Passed to the Arabs*, documented the work of 22 scholars, 20 of which were Assyrians, 1 was Persian and 1 was Arab. Saint John of Damascus in Syria, the Patriarch of Jerusalem, was one of the greatest scholars in the 8th century.

The Christian Assyrian Bakhteesho family had nine generations of physicians and founded the great medical school at Gundeshapur (Iran). Assyrian Hunayn ibn-Ishaq's textbook on ophthalmology in 950 AD remained the authoritative source until 1800 AD. Assyrian philosopher Job of Edessa developed a physical theory of the universe rivaling Aristotle's. The literary output of the Assyrians and Jews was vast. After Latin and Greek, the 3rd largest corpus of Christian writing is Assyrian (also called "Syriac.")

Assyrian missionaries brought Nestorian "Syriac" Christianity to Mesopotamia, the Persian Sassanid Empire (including parts of what is now Iran and Iraq), India, Central Asia, the Uyghurs, the Tang Dynasty of China, Korea, Japan, and the Philippines.

When Marco Polo traveled to China in 1271 AD, he wrote of Assyrian Christian missionaries who had converted tens of thousands to Christianity in China and India. Even the influential mother of Kublai Khan, Sorghaghtani Beki, was a Nestorian Christian. The first Mongolian system of writing used the Assyrian "Aramaic" alphabet, with the name "Tora Bora" being an Assyrian phrase meaning "arid mountain."

In 630 AD, Muslims began sweeping through the Middle East. The hundreds of years of rich, highly developed Assyrian Christian civilization was expropriated into the Arab Muslim culture. Chaldean and Babylonian astronomers were forcibly Islamized till they eventually disappeared. As Muslims conquered trade routes to the east, they co-opted advances made by other civilizations, claiming them as their own. As the heavy burdens of the "dhimmi" status and intermittent persecutions caused the Assyrian Christian community to declined, the so-called "Golden Age of Islam" also declined.

Nestorian Christianity declined in China when the Ming Dynasty forced out Mongolian and foreign influences, and Nestorian Christianity was eradicated from Persia and Central Asia by the Muslim crusader Tamerlane, who massacred an estimated 17 million.

Since the invasion of Islam in 630 AD, the Assyrian Church of the East, the Syriac Orthodox Church, the Syriac Catholic Church, the Maronite Church, and the Chaldean Catholic Church, quietly suffered 33 major genocides, averaging one every 40 years. During World War I, Turks and Kurds killed 750,000 Assyrians. When Iraq gained its independence from the British mandate in 1932, one of its first governmental acts was to massacre 3,000 Assyrians in the village of Simmele. The recent War on Terror and the current "Arab Spring" has renewed the persecution.

⚜

JERUSALEM

In 638 AD, Muslims conquered Byzantine Christian Jerusalem, largely because these areas were weakened by a recent costly war with the Zoroastrians of Persia, 614-629 AD, who had damaged every church in the Holy Land, except the one in Bethlehem, as it had a mural of the Magi who visited baby Jesus. After Muslim besieged Jerusalem for four bloody months, the Byzantine Patriarch, Sophronius, surrendered.

Caliph Umar received the submission of the citizens and formally set their rights and obligations in the Pact or Covenant of Umar (Ahd Umar), which is the foundation of the "dhimmi" or second-class status of Christians and Jews in Muslim dominated lands.

❧

DHIMMI STATUS - JIM CROW LAWS

After America's Civil War, Democrats in the southern States passed "Black Codes" or "Jim Crow Laws," requiring African Americans to sit on the back of the bus, use different drinking fountains, live in different neighborhoods, not own firearms or carry knives, and, in short, live as second-class citizens. As long as they did not try to be equal, there was peace.

This is the way Christians and Jews, called in the *Qur'an* "People of the Book," are treated in Muslim lands. They can avoid death or slavery if they submit to being humiliated as "dhimmi," without complaining and pay protection money, called "jizyah," to their Muslim masters. In the 13th century, dhimmi rules were:

(1) they are not to build any new places of worship;

(2) they are not to repair any old places of worship which have been destroyed by the Muslims;

(3) they are not to prevent Muslim travelers from staying in their places of worship;

(4) they are to entertain for three days any Muslim who wants to stay in their homes, and for a longer period if the Muslim falls ill;

(5) they are not to harbor any hostility towards the Islamic state, or give any aid and comfort to hostile elements;

(6) they are not to prevent any one of them from getting converted to Islam;

(7) they have to show respect towards every Muslim;

(8) they have to allow Muslims to participate in their private meetings;

(9) they are not to dress like Muslims;

(10) they are not to name themselves with Muslim names;

(11) they are not to ride on horses with saddle and bridle;

(12) they are not to possess arms;

(13) they are not to wear signet rings or seals on their fingers;

(14) they are not to sell or drink liquor openly;

(15) they are to wear a distinctive dress which shows their inferior status, and which separates them from the Muslims;

(16) they are not to propagate their customs and usages amongst the Muslims;

(17) they are not to build their houses in the neighborhood of Muslims;

(18) they are not to bring their dead near the graveyards of the Muslims;

(19) they are not to observe their religious practices publicly, or mourn their dead loudly;

(20) they are not to buy Muslim slaves.

Saudi Sheikh Marzouq Salem al-Ghamdi summarized what is taught in the major schools of Islamic jurisprudence in a television sermon in 2002:

If the infidels live among the Muslims, in accordance with the conditions set out by the Prophet - there is nothing wrong with it provided they pay the jizya (tolerance tax) to the Islamic treasury. Other conditions are...that they do not renovate a church or monastery, do not rebuild ones that were destroyed, that they feed for three days any Muslim who passes by their homes...that they rise when a Muslim wishes to sit, that they do not imitate Muslims in dress or speech, nor ride horses, nor own swords, nor arm themselves with any kind of weapon; that they do not sell wine, do not show the cross, do not ring church bells, do not raise their voices during prayer, they shave their hair in front so as to make them

easily identifiable, do not incite anyone against the Muslims, and do not strike a Muslim...
If they violate these conditions, they have no protection.

Muslims treated Christians and Jews, "People of the Book," harshly, but through the centuries Muslims treated polytheistic Hindus in India worse.

ᦗ
EGYPT & NORTH AFRICA

In 639, Muslim General Amr ibn al-As began conquering Egypt and North Africa, taking advantage of the weakness following the Persian invasions and dissension between Coptic, Catholic and Byzantine Christians. Over 250 Catholic dioceses were abolished.

Coptic Christians, who first welcomed the Muslim invasion to free them from the Byzantines, were soon reduced to dhimmi status, having to pay the jizya.

Sultans later cut out the tongues of Egyptian caught speaking the "Coptic" language, rather than Arabic. North Africa previously had been a stronghold of Christianity for centuries:

Philip, one of seven deacons in the early church, baptized a cabinet member of Queen Candace of Ethiopia, who evangelized in Eastern Africa (Acts 8:26-40). Simeon, one of the teachers in the early church, was from Niger in west Africa (Acts 13:1).

Mark, writer of the *Gospel*, preached in Egypt, founding the Coptic (Egyptian) Orthodox Church. Mark was martyred and buried in Alexandria in 68 AD. In 828 AD, his remains were packed under pork and smuggled to Venice where they were placed in St. Mark's Basilica, because Mohammed said (Vol 2, Book 23, No. 414): "Allah cursed the Jews and the Christians because they took the graves of their Prophets as places for praying," and "Do not leave an image without obliterating it, or a high grave without leveling it." *(Hadith Sahih Muslim,* 2115)

North Africa was home of Tertullian (155-220 AD) and the Christian Montanist sect. Saints Perpetua and Felicitas were martyred in Carthage, North Africa, in 203 AD, when Roman Emperor Septimius Severus commanded that no imperial subjects could become Christians or Jews. Cyprian, the Christian Bishop of Carthage, North Africa, was martyred in the persecution by Roman Emperor Valerian in 258 AD.

In 297 AD, Nobatae was the King of Lower Nubia's Christian African Nobatia Kingdom.

Roman Emperors Diocletian and Maximian persecuted Christians in the 3rd and 4th centuries, forcing Bishops to hand over copies of the *Holy Scriptures* to be destroyed. Many Christians denied their faith in order not to be killed. In 313 AD, when Emperor Constantine granted toleration to Christians, a bitter controversy arose by a group called Donatists who did not want to admit back into the church those who had denied the faith during the persecution. This division went on for nearly a century.

In 328 AD, Saint Frumentius of Abyssinia was sent to Ethiopia by Saint Athanasius after the Council of Nicea. Called "Abuna" or "the father" of Ethiopia, Frumentius was the first bishop of Ethiopia.

In 330 AD, Ezana ruled Northeast Africa's Christian Asksumite (Ethiopian) Empire.

Saint Moses the Black from Egypt was an Ethiopian bandit taken in by monks who converted and became an apostle of non-violence (330-407 AD). In the 5th century, nine Syrian Monks translated into the Ethiopian language of Geez many Greek, Hebrew, and Syriac works. They organized monastic orders and schools, some of which are still in existence.

Saint Augustine of Hippo, born in 354 AD was from the present-day area of Algeria, North Africa. Saint Augustine died in 430 AD when the Vandals, who had become Arian Christians, invaded North Africa and attacked Catholic and Donatist Christians. Vandals were defeated by Byzantine Christians in 533

AD, but the divisions within Christianity in North Africa weakened its defenses against later Islamic invasions.

In 697 AD, Merkurios ruled Africa's Christian Nubian Makuria Kingdom. Saint Takla Haimanot lived in the 13th century and is considered the national Saint of Ethiopia. As Patriarch of the Ethiopian Orthodox Church, Takla Haimanot was instrumental in his country resisting Islamic invasion.

DOME OF THE ROCK

In 691 AD, after seeing the magnificent Christian cathedral of the Church of the Holy Sepulchre, Caliph Abd al-Malik built a mosque of equal splendor over the rock in Jerusalem believed to be where Abraham was about to sacrifice his son Isaac. Christian pilgrims were harassed, massacred and crucified. In the 8th century, Christians were banned from giving religious instruction to their children and displays of the cross were banned in Jerusalem. In 772 AD, Caliph al Mansur ordered Jews and Christians to be branded on the hand.

QASIM CONQUERS PAKISTAN

In 710 AD, the 17-year-old Governor of Persia, Muhammad bin Qasim, led an army to conquer the Sindh and Punjab regions of Pakistan.

After each battle, Qasim executed every captured enemy soldier, an estimated 44,000, as Qasim wrote to his commander, Hajjaj:

> My ruling is given: Kill anyone belonging
> to the combatants (ahl-i-harb) arrest their sons
> and daughters for hostages and imprison them.

Four-fifths of the slaves were divided among the soldiers, and one-fifth, 60,000 slaves, went to Caliph Walid.

MUSLIM INVASION OF EUROPE

In 711 AD, the Muslim Umayyad dynasty invaded Spain and Portugal with a powerful cavalry 80,000 strong. An unidentified Muslim commented they "went through all places like a desolating storm." Possessing the advanced military technology of the stirrup, the Muslim cavalry charged at lightning speed with lances and scimitar swords, slicing Europeans who fought only on foot. *The Mozarabic Chronicle*, 754, recorded that churches were burned and: "God alone knows the number of the slain."

Muslims, also called Moors, suffered a setback at the *Battle of Covadonga*, 718 AD, which was symbolic as the first victory of Christians over the invading Moors. It is considered the start of the Reconquista (Reconquest). Muslims crossed the Pyrenees Mountains, experienced a defeat at the *Battle of Toulouse*, 721 AD, but went on to occupy Nimes, southern France by 725 AD.

In 731, Duke Eudo's army was butchered by Muslim cavalry, monasteries were raided and the city of Bordeaux was put to the sword. In just 100 years after Mohammed's death, millions were killed and an estimated 3,200 churches destroyed. The Islamic invasion of Europe was only halted by the *Battle of Tours/Poitiers* in 732 AD.

∽

CHARLES MARTEL - *BATTLE OF TOURS*

Pope Gregory III called all soldiers of Europe to join Frankish King Charles Martel (Martel - "the Hammer"), who possibly took his name from Judas Maccabeus ("the Hammerer") who drove Syrians from Judah.

Charles Martel, who was the grandfather of Charlemagne ("Charles the Great"), assembled 30,000 soldiers. There was no other army this large in all the rest of Europe, so if Martel did not stop the Islamic invasion, all Europe would have soon become Muslim.

With no armor or horses, just spears, swords and axes, Martel's fur clad men, secretly marched on back trails to a wooded hill up from the Muslim camp. The next day, the surprised Muslim commander, Abdul Rahman, ordered an attack. His heavy cavalry, covered with chainmaille armor, attacked with 20 foot-long lances, and his light cavalry wielded bows and scimitar swords.

Abdul Rahman's warriors found it difficult to charge up the tree-covered hill. On top, they met the Frankish infantry arranged in a disciplined tight square, which was difficult for Muslim cavalry to charge through.

The Arab battle account was (*Medieval Source Book*):

> And in the shock of the battle the men of the North [Franks] seemed like a sea that cannot be moved. Firmly they stood, one close to another, forming as it were a bulwark of ice; and with great blows of their swords they hewed down the Arabs.
>
> Drawn up in a band around their chief, the people of the Austrasians carried all before them. Their tireless hands drove their swords down to the breasts of the foe.

At the height of the battle, Charles Martel had prearranged for some of his men to steal into the undefended Muslim camp and free the prisoners.

When the Muslim warriors learned of this, they feared the loss of their plunder and retreated back to the camp. The Muslim commander, Abdul Rahman, tried to rally his warriors, but was distracted, surrounded and killed.

The next morning, Charles Martel waited for hours for the attack to resume, but nothing happened. Martel thought it was a trick to lure him onto the open plain. Finally, after sending out scouts, it was found the Muslim camp was abandoned.

The Muslim account was that when they discovered their leader Abdul Rahman was killed, confusion arose as to who would replace him. Concerned with protecting their plunder, they abandoned the fight.

Had Charles Martel not won the *Battle of Tours*, Muslims would have overrun France and all of Europe.

Europeans quickly adopted the Muslim military tactic of fighting on horseback with stirrups, which led to the development of their knights of chivalry. Since Muslims lost this military advantage, Europeans were eventually successful in their Reconquista, the 700 year effort to drive the Muslim invaders from the Continent.

In 778, Charlemagne fought the Muslims at Saragossa. On his return, part of his army was wiped out in the Pass of Roncesvalles, as retold in the *Song of Roland*.

&

CONSTANTINOPLE

In 704 AD, Caliph Walid tricked Armenian nobles to meet in St. Gregory's Church in Naxcawan and Church of Xram on the Araxis River and burned them to death.

Muslims attacked Constantinople, the capital port of the Byzantine Roman Empire, but were stopped in 678 AD and again in 717 AD. They were repulsed by a superior military technology the Byzantines called "Greek Fire."

Greek Fire was a complicated process in which oil was mixed with sawdust to thicken it, put in brass containers, pumped to high pressure, then sprayed through a brass nozzle fitted on a ship's deck, being lit on fire as it spewed forth, like napalm, on the enemies' ships and sails.

&

ISLAM WILL CONQUER LATER

After being repulsed at Constantinople in 717 AD, the Muslims pushed no further west for almost 400 years. They settled to ruling the "House of Islam," leaving the "House of War" to be conquered later. A revised theology developed that Islam will conquer the world, but it may have to wait till later or the last days.

&

ISLAM SPREADS IN ASIA

In the next several hundred years, Muslims conquered east into Persia, Afghanistan, a large part of India, China, Indonesia, Java, Borneo, and eventually into the Philippines. By 1400, the Muslim-influenced Malacca state became dominant in Southeast Asia.

ISLAM SPREADS IN AFRICA

Seven centuries of Greco-Roman civilization was swept away as Muslims subjugated large parts of North, East and West Africa. Seemingly unstoppable, they conquered into Egypt, Tripoli, Tunis, Algeria, Morocco, Eritrea, Sudan, Senegambia Niger, Abyssinia, Kamerun, Nigeria, Dahomey, Ivory Coast, Liberia, Sierra Leone, Guinea, Somaliland, Uganda, Togoland, Gambia, Senegal, Zanzibar, Rhodesia and the Congo.

From 650 AD to 1950 AD, over 100 million Africans were enslaved by Muslims, with many male slaves being castrated "level with the abdomen." (Ronald Segal, *Islam's Black Slaves: The Other Black Diaspora,* NY: Farrar, Straus & Giroux, 2002; Suzy Hansen, 04-05-01, Salon.com)

After World War I, many Muslim lands were pressured by Britain and France to limit slavery, though it continues in areas like Sudan and Mauritania. In 2003, Shaykh Salih al-Fawzan, imam of Prince Mitaeb Mosque in Riyadh and member of Saudi Arabia's highest religious body Senior Council of Clerics, stated:

> Islam has affirmed slavery. It will continue as long as jihad in the path of Allah exists.
> (*Taming a Neo-Qutubite Fanatic*, Part I , p. 24, www.salafipublications.com/sps/downloads/ pdf/GRV070005.pdf

In 1050, the Islamic Berber dynasty began in Sahel, northwest Africa. In 1033, Muslims killed 6,000 Jews in Fez, Morocco. In 1230, the Muslim Ghanaian Empire replaced by Mali, centered in Timbuktu. In 1493, the Muslim Songhai Empire reached its height under Sonni Ali. In 1592, Moors conquered the African Songhai Empire.

ISLAM TRIED TO CONVERT RUSSIA

The Primary Chronicle is a history of ancient Russia from 850 AD to 1110 AD, compiled in Kiev in 1113. It tells how in 986 AD, Prince Vladimir was visited by some Bulgar Muslims from Khwarezm, inviting him to adopt Islam. Originally a pagan, Vladimir asked them to explain their religion:

They replied that they believed in Allah, and that Mohammed instructed them to practice circumcision, to eat no pork, to drink no wine, and after death, promised them complete fulfillment of their carnal desires.

"Mohammed," they asserted, "will give each man 70 fair women. He may choose one fair one, and upon that woman will Mohammed confer the charms of them all, and she shall be his wife. Mohammed promises that one may then satisfy every desire.

But whoever is poor in this world will be no different in the next."

They also spoke other false things (which out of modesty may not be written down).

Vladimir listened to them, for he was fond of women and indulgence, regarding which he heard with pleasure. But circumcision and abstinence from pork and wine were disagreeable to him. "Drinking," said he, "is the joy of the Russes. We cannot exist without that pleasure."

Prince Vladimir was also visited by Germans from the Latin Church and Jewish Khazars.

Finally Vladimir was visited by Greeks from the Eastern Orthodox Church, whose beautiful Hagia Sophia Cathedral in Constantinople was the largest and most ornate church in the world for over a thousand years. After hearing an explanation of the *Gospel* and that the *New Testament* had been written in Greek, Vladimir converted to Eastern Orthodox Christianity and ordered all pagan idols in Russia cast into the Dnieper River. Vladimir also adopted the Eastern Orthodox Saint Nicholas as the Patron Saint of Russia. There is, perhaps, not a single city in Russia without a church named after Saint Nicholas.

◈

MONGOLS & TURKS

In the 11th and 12th centuries, the Mongols began expanding their empire west by attacking other tribes, one of which was a distantly related tribe called the Oguz Turks, a semi-savage nomadic people. This caused them to migrate further west from Mongolia and settle in the regions of west Turkestan.

A tribe within the Oguz Turks were the Seljuks. The Seljuks moved still further west toward Persia and Babylon. Noted for their warlike tendencies, they were hired as mercenaries by the caliphs of Baghdad. It never occurred to Turks to force those they defeated to change religions, so in time, the Turks became exposed to Islam.

When Turks realized that this new faith allowed them to continue their nomadic warfare of killing, plundering, and taking women, only now with the blessing of Allah, they became Muslim.

◈

TURKS & VIOLENT ISLAM

Once the Turks converted to Islam, they began to spread westward, breathing new energy into Islam, which by this time had largely settled into a more moderate form.

In 1055, Seljuk Turks captured Baghdad.

They took control of Persia and eventually most of the Arabic Muslim world. This began the conquest of Asia Minor and Constantinople, and eventually subjugated Greece, Romania, Bulgaria, coming up to the gates of Vienna, Austria, invading Russia, Serbia, Poland, and threatening Germany.

In 923, Muslims began destroying churches in Jerusalem and on Palm Sunday in 937, Muslims plundered the Church of Calvary and the Church of the Resurrection. In 1004, Caliph al-Hakim began a ten year persecution where thousands were forced to convert or die and 30,000 churches were destroyed, including the Church of the Holy Sepulchre.

ISLAM INVADES ASIA MINOR

Greek civilization flourished in Asia Minor for 3,000 years. In 330 AD, Constantine founded Constantinople, which began the Byzantine Roman Empire.

Within the Byzantine Empire was Armenia, the first nation to officially declare itself Christian in 301 A.D. during the Roman era. The Armenian alphabet is derived from Greek and Aramaic, the language Jesus spoke.

Armenia flourished in art and commerce with its capital Ani called the "city of a thousand and one churches."

The seven churches mentioned in the last book of the *Bible*, "Revelation," were all in Asia Minor.

In the 11th century, a wave of Seljuk Turks began invading. The Turkish king, Alp Arslan (1063-1072), had united the different Seljuk factions, invaded Armenia, and sacked its capital of Ani in 1064.

The Muslim Seljuk Turks defeated the Byzantine forces at the pivotal *Battle of Manzikert* in 1071, giving them a foothold into Byzantine Asia Minor.

In 1075, the Muslim Seljuk Turks captured Jerusalem from Muslim Arabs.

Gregory Bar-Hebraeus (1226-1286), a Syrian Orthodox Church leader, wrote how Muslims initially treated Christian subjects tolerably, then changed to intense hatred:

> And having seen very much modesty and other habits of this kind among Christian people, certainly the Mongols loved them greatly at the beginning of their kingdom, a time ago somewhat short.

But their love hath turned to such intense hatred that they cannot even see them with their eyes approvingly, because they have all alike become Muslims, myriads of people and peoples.

In 1097, Muslims set up their capital in Iconium, named the Sultanate of Rum (Kingdom of Rome).

✧

SANTA CLAUS

In 1087 AD, Muslim Seljuk Turks invaded Asia Minor, killing Christians, turning Byzantine churches into mosques and desecrating the graves of Saints. The city of Myra was concerned over the remains of Saint Nicholas, the most famous saint in the Eastern Orthodox Church.

Venetian merchants took Bishop Nicholas' remains from the cathedral in Myra and shipped them to the city of Bari in southern Italy, thus introducing Western Europe to this generous Saint Nicholas and the traditions of gift-giving on the anniversary of his death, December 6th.

Over centuries, these traditions spread across Europe and eventually, by immigrants, to America. The Dutch settlers pronounced Saint Nicholas "Sant Nicklaus," which was embellished into the modern Santa Claus.

Saint Nicholas' remains are still located in the Catedral de San Nicolás de Bari, in southern Italy, though in 2003, Muslims of Demre (Turkish name for Myra) demanded the remains be returned for a tourist attraction.

✧

SPAIN

In 1011, Muslims killed about 2,000 in Cordoba, Spain. Muslims massacred every one of the 5000 Jews living in Granada, Spain, December 30, 1066. The Kingdom of Castile freed Toledo from the Muslims in 1085, and the Spanish knight Rodrigo Diaz, called "El Cid," drove the Muslims out of Valencia in 1094. (The movie, *El Cid*, starred Charlton Heston in 1961). In 1119, the Spanish

Kingdom of Aragon freed the city of Zaragoza from the Moors. In 1189, Muslims raided Libson, Portugal, and enslaved 3,000 women and children. In 1191, Muslims attacked Silves, Portugal, and enslaved 3,000. The Catholic Order of Montjoie, later joining the Order of Calatrava, was organized in 1180 to ransom back Christian slaves.

∽

FIRST CRUSADE 1095-1099

By most numbering, there were nine major Crusades and numerous minor ones, continuing from 1095 till 1291 when Acre was finally captured by the Muslims. Origins can be traced to 1009 when Fatimid Caliph al-Hakim bi-Amr Allah ordered the Church of the Holy Sepulchre in Jerusalem destroyed.

Pilgrims returning from the Holy Land shared reports of Muslim persecution and cruelty toward "dhimmi" Christians.

Following the defeat of the Christian lands of Syria, Lebanon, Palestine and Egypt, the Muslims conquered Sicily. Italian city-states of Pisa, Genoa and Catalonia fought the Muslims who were raiding Majorca, Sardinia, Catalonia and the coasts of Italy. In 1057, the Norman adventurer Robert Guiscard took control of Calabria in the "toe of Italy" and fought against the Muslims of Sicily.

In 1071, the Muslims delivered a major defeat to the Byzantine Christians at the *Battle of Manzikert* and took control of all but the coastlands of Asia Minor. In desperation, the Byzantine Emperor Alexius I Comnenus humbled himself and sent ambassadors to the Council of Piacenza in March of 1095, appealing for help from his religious rival, the Roman Catholic Pope.

The seriousness of this appeal is underscored since it occurred after the beginning of the Great East-West Schism between the Roman Catholic Church and the Byzantine Church which began in 1054.

With Spain exuberant after driving the Muslims from Toledo and Leon by 1085, Pope Urban II gave an impassioned plea at the Council of Clermont in 1095 for Western leaders to help their Byzantine Christians brethren, whom Muslims "compel to extend their necks and then, attacking them with naked swords, attempt to cut through the neck with a single blow." (Robert the Monk, *Medieval Sourcebook*, Fordham University.)

The First Crusade began in 1097, led by Godfrey of Bouillon. It freed Iconium from the Muslims, though it was later taken back. The First Crusade defeated Turkish forces at Dorylaeum and Antioch, and captured Jerusalem in 1099, holding it for nearly 100 years.

෴

2ND CRUSADE 1145-1149

After the Muslims conquered Edessa, another crusade was called for by Bernard of Clairvaux in 1147. It was made up of French and German armies, led by King Louis VII and Conrad II.

In 1148, Muslim leader, Nur ed-Din, slaughtered every Christian in Aleppo. The Second Crusade failed to take Damascus and returned to Europe in 1150. Bernard of Clairvaux was disturbed by reports of misdirected violence, especially toward Jewish populations.

෴

3RD CRUSADE 1189-1192
ROBIN HOOD & MAGNA CARTA

In 1190, Pope Gregory VIII called for a Third Crusade. It was led by German King Frederick I, called Frederick Barbarossa (meaning Redbeard), who was the Emperor of the Holy Roman Empire. He was joined by Philip II of France and Richard I of England.

Frederick led 100,000 soldiers across Byzantium, driving out Muslims and temporarily freeing Iconium. He most likely would have freed Jerusalem and the surrounding area from Muslim domination had he not fallen off his horse while crossing the Göksu River in Cilicia, Asia Minor. Being 67 years old and weighted down with heavy armor, he drowned in waist deep water and the Crusade went into confusion.

Richard the Lionheart assumed leadership of the Crusade and captured Acre. Due to disagreements, Philip II returned to France in 1191. Richard's troops came within sight of Jerusalem in 1192, but narrowly failed to drive out Saladin (1138-1193). Western resolve for the war diminished and political unrest back home increased from King Phillip II of France and from Richard's ambitious brother John, who ruled England in his absence, as chronicled in the legends of Robin Hood.

This situation put Richard in the position of having to negotiate a hurried truce with Saladin, who, it was later discovered, was on the verge of defeat.

Saladin captured Crusaders at Hattim, July 4, 1187, and ordered their mass execution. Saladin allowed Christians to leave Jerusalem only if they paid a ransom, but according to Imad al-Din, approximately 7,000 men and 8,000 women could not make their ransom and were enslaved.

The vessel Richard sailed away on was shipwrecked, so he decided to travel with a party across Europe in disguise. He was recognized near Vienna and captured by Duke Leopold V of Austria.

The Holy Roman Emperor, Henry VI, imprisoned Richard at Dumstein. England had to place burdensome taxes on its populace to raise the "king's ransom."

In 1197, Henry VI, the Holy Roman Emperor, was preparing for another crusade but died due to malaria.

Once Richard was back in England, he ruled only a few years before being shot with an arrow during the siege of a castle. His brother became the oppressive King John, who lost Britain's claim to French lands.

This caused England's noblemen to surround John on the plains of Runymeade in 1215 and force him to sign the Magna Carta, a document which began the long process of limiting the arbitrary power of monarchs and guaranteeing rights of citizens.

∽

NOTORIOUS 4TH CRUSADE 1201-1204

The Great Schism between the Eastern Orthodox Church and the Western Roman Catholic Church over the wording of the Nicene Creed resulted in the Pope excommunicating the Patriarch of Constantinople in 1054. The following centuries saw a continual deterioration in the relationship between the East and West.

By the time of the 4th Crusade in 1206, the situation had become so grave that instead of coming to the aid of the Byzantines by fighting the Muslims, the Crusade was diverted by the 80 year-old Venetian Doge (Duke) Enrico Dandolo, who was in debt.

The Fourth Crusade ended up sacking the Byzantine capital of Constantinople and plundering its wealth.

Constantinople was the richest city in the world, having been built by Emperor Constantine nearly a thousand years earlier at the crossroads of world trade. The western European Crusaders stripped the city of its ornate treasures in what has been described as one of the worst travesties in world history.

The Italians ruled the city till 1261, and in that 57 years they outsourced in a globalist fashion much of the Byzantine Empire's trade and business. The Italian merchants of Venice and Genoa made immense fortunes, but left the Byzantine Empire's economy so devastated that it never recovered.

In the centuries following, despite exorbitant taxes levied by the Byzantine Emperor, there were never enough funds to repair Constantinople's aging defenses, and in the face of increasing Muslim terrorist attacks, the city's eventual downfall was fated.

&

5TH CRUSADE 1217-1221

In 1215, the Fourth Council of the Lateran proposed a 5th Crusade, with a force from Hungary and Austria joining the king of Jerusalem and the prince of Antioch to take back Jerusalem. In 1219, the Crusaders captured Damietta, Egypt, but made the mistake of attacking Cairo. Sultan Melek-el-Kamil, brother of Saladin, opened the dams of the Nile, forcing the Crusaders to retreat.

∽

SAINT FRANCIS OF ASSISI

In 1218, the Order of Our Lady of Ransom was founded to ransom Christian slaves from Islam.

In 1219, Francis of Assisi (1181-1226) went to Egypt, crossed the battle lines and was received by Sultan Melek-el-Kamil. Francis challenged the Muslim scholars that whoever could walk through fire unhurt, his religion the Sultan would recognize.

When Francis proposed to walk first, the Muslim scholars retreated. The Sultan was so impressed, he let Francis preach to his subjects.

According to *Historia Occidentalis, De Ordine et Praedicatione Fratrum Minorum*, written in 1221 by Jacques de Vitry, Bishop of Acre, the Sultan's departing words to Francis were "Pray for me that God may deign to reveal to me that law and faith which is most pleasing to Him."

∽

6TH CRUSADE 1228-1229

In 1228, Emperor Frederick II was excommunicated by the Pope for not fulfilling his vow to join the crusade. He finally set sail from Brindisi, landed in Palestine and through diplomacy gained control over Jerusalem, Nazareth, and Bethlehem for ten years. This was the first crusade that was initiated by a king and not the Pope.

In 1228, the Catholic Order of Trinitarians, also called Mathurins, was founder by St. John of Math, a doctor of the University of Paris.

The sole purpose of the Order, stated in its Latin title "Ordo S. Trinitatis et de Redemptione Captivorum," was to raise money from across

Europe to ransom thousands of Christian prisoners and slaves from the Mussulmen (Muslims).

In 1230, the Catholic Order of Mercedarians was organized in Spain for same purpose, ransoming Christian captives from the Moors (Muslims). The head of the Order had the title "Ransomer."

⌁

7TH CRUSADE 1248-1254 SAINT LOUIS

The Templars fought in Egypt in 1243, and in the following year a Khwarezmian force stormed Jerusalem. Drawn into battle at La Forbie in Gaza, the crusader army was defeated by Baibars' force of Khwarezmian tribesmen.

King Louis IX ruled the wealthiest kingdom in Europe and commanded the most powerful army. Reigning in the tradition of Frankish King Charles Martel, who stopped the Muslims in France in 732, the pious King Louis IX led a crusade from 1248 to 1254 against Egypt, with plans to proceed to Jerusalem.

Leaving from his newly constructed port of Aigues-Mortes in southern France, he achieved initial success, followed by defeat. Louis spent much time at the crusader kingdom in Acre. In the midst of this time there was an unorganized Shepherds' Crusade in 1251.

Sadly, during the era of the crusades, Egypt's Coptic Christian population was caught in the middle, being mistreated by crusaders as heretics and being persecuted and killed by Muslims as traitors.

⌁

8TH CRUSADE 1270 SAINT LOUIS

In 1268, Mamluk Sultan Baybars slaughtered all the Christian and Jewish men of Antioch, sold the women into slavery, smashed church crosses, burned Bibles, desecrated graves, and dragged every priest, deacon and monk to the altar and slit their throats. He destroyed the Church of St. Paul and the Cathedral of St. Peter.

In 1270, King Louis IX led another Crusade, setting sail from Aigues-Mortes. The crusade's original purpose was to come to the aid of the Christian states in Syria, but it was diverted to Tunis where they suffered defeat. Louis was in Tunis only two months before dying of the plague or dysentery.

∽

9TH CRUSADE 1271-1272

In 1271, the future King of England, Edward I, undertook an expedition. He accomplished very little in Syria and made a truce the following year. Antioch fell to the Muslims in 1268, Tripoli fell in 1289 and Acre fell in 1291, thus ending the last traces of Christian rule in Syria

∽

GENGHIS KHAN

In 1206, shortly after the Italians captured Constantinople, something happened 4,000 miles east.

Genghis Khan (1162-1227), King of Mongols (Tatars), started his conquest. By 1226, the Mongols invaded Poland, and by 1241, the Mongols invaded Russia and Central Europe.

With an army of 700,000 warriors, the Mongols developed a new military technology called the composite bow. It was as powerful as the English longbow, but half its size, enabling Mongols to shoot from the saddle of a horse and hit a target 300 yards away.

The Mongolian Empire became the largest contiguous land empire in history. It included Mongolia, China, Manchuria, Korea, North India, Java, Indonesia, Persia (Iran), Mesopotamia (Iraq), the Middle East, Pakistan, Afghanistan, Uzbekistan, Kazakhstan, Kyrgyzstan, Tajikistan, Turkmenistan, Moldova, South Korea, and Kuwait, Georgia, Azerbaijan, Turkey, Armenia, Russia and Hungary.

Genghis Khan's years of ruthless Mongolian raids caused other tribes to migrate westward, including the

Bulgars and Turks, who eventually crossed the borders into the Persian and Byzantine Empires.

In 1250, Genghis Khan's grandson, Hulegu Khan, destroyed the Muslim Caliphate in Baghdad. He also made a preemptive strike against the Muslim cult of the Assassins, to prevent them from sending out assassins against him, as it was rumored they sent out 400 assassins to kill his brother Mongke Khan.

⤳

SAINT THOMAS AQUINAS ON ISLAM

In 1258, Saint Thomas Aquinas wrote in *Summa contra Gentiles*, Book 1, Chapter 6 (translated by Anton C. Pegis, University of Notre Dame Press, 1975, pp. 73-75):

> Mohammed...seduced the people by promises of carnal pleasure to which the concupiscence of the flesh goads us...and he gave free reign to carnal pleasure. In all this, as is not unexpected, he was obeyed by carnal men.
>
> As for proofs of the truth of his doctrine, he brought forward only such as could be grasped by the natural ability of anyone with a very modest wisdom. Indeed, the truths that he taught he mingled with many fables and doctrines of the greatest falsity. He did not bring forth any signs produced in a supernatural way, which alone fittingly gives witness to divine inspiration...
>
> Mohammed said that he was sent in the power of his arms - which are signs not lacking even to robbers and tyrants...Those who believed in him were brutal men and desert wanderers, utterly ignorant of all divine teaching, through whose numbers Mohammed forced others to become his followers by the violence of his arms...
>
> He perverts almost all the testimonies of the *Old* and *New Testaments* by making them

into fabrications of his own, as can be seen by anyone who examines his law. It was, therefore, a shrewd decision on his part to forbid his followers to read the *Old* and *New Testaments*, lest these books convict him of falsity.

It is thus clear that those who place any faith in his words believe foolishly.

◈

MARCO POLO

In 1259, Venetian traders Niccolo and Matteo Polo settled on the Black Sea, in an area conquered a few years earlier by Genghis Khan. From there, the Polos traveled east and were received by the new ruler of the Mongols, Kublai Khan (1215-1294), grandson of Genghis Khan.

Kublai Khan sent Niccolo and Matteo Polo back to the Pope requesting 100 teachers of the Christian faith and a flask of oil from Christ's tomb in Jerusalem. When they reached Rome, they found Pope Clement IV had died and Pope Gregory X, who had just been elected, was facing wars in Europe. Because of the unsettled situation, only two preaching friars accompanied the Polo's on their return to China. Niccolo brought along his teenage son, Marco Polo. As they crossed a warring area of Turkey, the friars became afraid and turned back, leaving only speculation as to how history would have been different had they continued the journey.

Kublai Khan received the flask of oil from Jerusalem and was impressed with Marco Polo and employed him as an envoy for 17 years, during which time Polo learned several Asian languages. Marco Polo wrote that Kublai Khan tolerated various religions so as to prevent conflicts within his empire. He requested the Christian *Bible* be brought to him for Easter and Christmas, which he would kiss.

Marco Polo noted that he also honored Saracen (Muslim), Jewish and Buddhist feast days. When asked why he did this, not understanding the incompatibility of differing beliefs, he responded: "I respect and honor all four great Prophets: Jesus Christ, Mohammed, Moses and Buddha, so that I can appeal to any one of them in heaven."

Returning to Venice in 1294, Marco Polo was captured and imprisoned at Genoa. He dictated his travels, mentioning China's technological advances: coal, gunpowder, spaghetti, silk, pinata, porcelain dishes, ice cream, recurve bow, printed paper currency and an imperial "pony-express" style postal system

Genoa was to be the birthplace, 157 years later, of another explorer who wanted to travel to India and China - Christopher Columbus. As Muslims raided the caravans along the China Silk Road, trade diminished, finally ending when Muslims conquered Constantinople in 1453.

∽

ASSASSINS

The word "Assassin" is an 11th century Arabic word "Hashshashin," which was a militant sect of Ismaili Muslims, led by Hassan-i-Sabah (1034-1124). They also called themselves "fedayeen" which means one who is willing to sacrifice his life for the cause.

As a youth, Hassan-i-Sabah was friends with the Persian poet and mathematician Omar Khayyam (1048-1123), who wrote the *Rubaiyat of Omar Khayyam*.

Hassan-i-Sabah's militant religious sect specialized in terrorizing their enemies in fearlessly executed, politically motivated assassinations. They would approach their unsuspecting victim in disguise, often in public or in a mosque, and kill them with a dagger.

Marco Polo, who visited the Hashshashim's mountain fortress of Alamut after it was conquered by the Mongols in the 13th century, brought back one of the many accounts of how Hassan-i-Sabah recruited assassins.

A future assassin was made to feel he was in danger of being killed, but then, without his knowledge, he was drugged with opium or "hashish" and made to think he had died. He would awake in an altered state-of-mind in a garden filled with wine, beautiful women and sumptuous feasting. After he was convinced he was in paradise, he would be carried back to where he had been kidnapped from. Once he regained consciousness, he was told that he had just visited paradise and that if he died obeying Hassan-i-Sabah orders to assassinate someone, he would go back to paradise.

SPAIN

Back in Spain, the Christian armies of León, Castile, Navarre and Aragon defeated the Muslim Almohads in the decisive *Battle of Navas de Tolosa*, a mountain pass that guaranteed Christian forces passage into Southern Spain. In 1236, Christians won Cordoba, and in 1266, retook Lorca, Murcia, Purchena and Segura.

ISLAM IN ASIA MINOR 2ND WAVE

As mentioned earlier, Genghis Khan's raids on Turkistan forced the Turks to migrate further west. These Turks, under their leader Suleyman (Arabic for Solomon) adopted Islam and attempted to settle in eastern Asia Minor, but were resisted by the Armenians and Kurds.

Moving south, they attempted to cross the Euphrates River in 1227, but their leader Suleyman drowned. His grandson was Osman, who founded the Muslim Ottoman Empire.

OSMAN – GHAZI WARRIOR

Osman (1259-1326) took the title of Sultan. A form of his name, "Ottoman," was given to the Turkish people. Osman realized that since his tribe was small, it would be difficult to control occupied lands and at the same time conquer more, so he declared his entire tribe to be completely "ghazi" warriors of the Islamic faith bound to declare jihad on all nonbelievers.

He attracted those who would fight to spread Islam as well as those who fought for the spoils of war. His grandson was Murat I.

~

SEVEN CHURCHES OF REVELATION

In the last book of the *Bible*, the Apostle John wrote to seven churches in Asia Minor, all of which were eventually destroyed by invading Muslims: "What thou seest, write in a book, and send it unto the seven churches which are in Asia, unto Ephesus and unto Smyrna, and unto Pergamos, and unto Thyatira and unto Sardis and unto Philadelphia and unto Laodicea."

~

MURAT I & THE DEVSHIRMEH

The conquest of Byzantine Asia Minor was under five Sultans: Murat I (1319-1389); his son, Bayezid I (1354-1403); his son, Mehmet I (1389-1421); his son, Murat II (1404-1451); and his son, Mehmet II (1432-1481).

Sultan Murat I began attacking cities in Asia Minor in 1359. He would give inhabitants three options: resist and be killed; surrender and become Muslims; or surrender and become second-class citizens called "dhimmi" and pay the jizyah tax.

Christians who kept their faith were not only made "dhimmi," but Sultan Murat I forced upon them the "devshirmeh" or children tax. This was the practice of forcibly taking young Christian boys, ages 7 to 14, away from their families. These boys were put into Muslim homes as slaves where they would learn the Turkish language. They were purposely treated harshly to prepare them for the rigors of military life.

This emotional trauma was intended as a form of brainwashing to get them to forget their Greek, Armenian, Bulgarian, Albanian and Serbian Christian families. The boys were indoctrinated to become Muslims and told the Sultan was their only father. They were taught if they died in battle they would go to paradise.

∽

MUSLIM PEDERASTY

If boys were delicate, the Sultan would use them in what was an accepted Muslim practice of pederasty. When the Ottoman Turks conquered areas of Armenia, Greece and the Balkans, they would consider young boys spoils of war. In 1475, Muslims conquered Crimea and sailed away with a galleon of 150 young boys destined for "the filthy sodomy of the whoring Turk."

Boys used for this were never Muslim, but were levied or captured from Christian families. Pederasty existed in Muslim countries from Spain to India. In Turkey it was called kocek and it became a central element of Ottoman culture, akin to an entertainment industry or beauty pageants, as owners of boys would have them compete in lustful dances.

Reaching its height of popularity in the 17th to 19th centuries, many Muslim poets wrote sensual poems of desire for beautiful boys. It was publicly ended in Turkey in 1856 by Sultan Abd-ul-Mejid I after a riot broke out at one of the competitions. Though outwardly prohibited in Sharia Law, differing Islamic theologians accommodated pederasty as a "private behavior" as long as it did not disturb public order, in which case a person needed to be caught in the act witnessed by four Muslim men or eight Muslim women. (Sharia law does not allow a Christian to testify against a Muslim.)

∽

JANISSARIES

The boys taken from Christian homes and forced into Murat I's Muslim army were called "Janissaries" which meant "new soldier." This was similar to the slave-soldiers of Baghdad and Egypt called Mamluks, who belonged to the Muslim Caliphs.

As other Muslim warriors would return home when there was no fighting, the Janissaries were never allowed to return to their families, thus making them a full-time army, the first permanent standing army in Europe since Roman times.

Janissaries were not allowed to marry, partly because Turks wanted to ethnically eliminate non-Turks. To make sure they did not assimilate, the Sultan made them easily identifiable by only allowing them to grow mustaches, whereas Muslims wore full beards. In battle, Janissaries wore white, conical hats. Continually trained in the art of war, Janissaries were considered the fiercest troops. The Sultan would put them on the front lines when attacking the next Christian city. They evolved into the Sultan's personal bodyguard, similar to the Roman Emperor's "Praetorian Guard," not distracted by the competing political factions of other warriors.

For centuries, the Janissaries were a significant force within the Ottoman military, only being allowed to marry in 1566. They grew to dominate Turkish government and resisted several attempts to be disbanded, until they were destroyed in a coup in 1826. With the help of the Janissaries, Sultan Murat I conquered the Christian Balkans, including Bulgaria, Macedonia, Serbia, and into Hungary.

Murat I was killed in his tent after he won the *Battle of Kosovo* on June 15, 1389, by Serbian Knight Milos Obilic, who with other knights formed the Order of the Dragon of Saint George. Like the ancient story of Saint George slaying the dragon, these knights had dedicated themselves to slaying the dragon Murat I.

✆ TAMERLANE

While Murat I was attacking west into Europe, a new Muslim warlord arose in the east by the name of Tamerlane (1336-1405) whose name in Turkish is "Timur" meaning "iron." Related to Genghis Khan's family, he combined Genghis Khan's Mongolian barbarity with Islamic fanaticism and killed millions, conquering from the Black Sea to Moscow, India to Damascus, Persia to parts of Turkey.

In 1382, Tamerlane captured Moscow. In 1383, he conquered the Afghan city of Isfizar, building a tower with bricks, mortar and 2,000 prisoners cemented alive into it. In 1386, he destroyed the city of Kartid, and in 1387, he massacred 70,000 in the Persian city of Ishfahan.

In 1391, Tamerlane led 100,000 Muslim warriors 1,500 miles to fight Tokhtamysh near the Volga River. Tokhtamysh, also a descendant of Genghis Khan, was the Mongolian leader of the White, Blue and Golden Hordes, which controlled most of Russia. Tamerlane's insistence on maintaining the Islamic prayer schedule on this long march even brought complaints from his Muslim soldiers.

In a second campaign, Tamerlane attacked and defeated Tokhtamysh by crossing through the Caucasus Mountains. Tamerlane destroyed the Golden Horde's capital of Sarai Berke, which was one of the largest cities in the world with a population of 600,000. It was almost a century later, in 1481, that Russians finally defeated the Muslim Mongols.

TAMERLANE – GHAZI WARRIOR

An autobiographical memoir of Tamerlane, titled Malfuzat-i-Timuri, was composed in the Chaghatai Mongol language and translated into Persian by Abu Talib Husaini, dedicated to the Persian Emperor Shah Jahan (1592-1666). Tamerlane wrote:

About this time there arose in my heart the desire to lead an expedition against the infidels, and to become a ghazi, for it had reached my ears that the slayer of infidels is a ghazi, and if he is slain he becomes a martyr.

It was on this account that I formed this resolution, but I was undetermined in my mind whether I should direct my expedition against the infidels of China or against the infidels and polytheists of India.

In this matter I sought an omen from the *Qur'an*, and the verse I opened upon [Sura 66:9] was this, "O Prophet, make war upon infidels and unbelievers, and treat them with severity."

My great officers told me that the inhabitants of Hindustan were infidels and unbelievers. In obedience to the order of Almighty Allah I ordered an expedition against them.

In 1398, Tamerlane conquered Delhi, India, and slaughtered 100,000 people, leaving hundreds of "pyramids of skulls."

The Malfuza-i-Timuri recorded that at Hardwar, Tamerlane's Muslim troops:

> Displayed great courage and daring; they made their swords their banners, and exerted themselves in slaying the foe (during a bathing festival on the bank of the Ganges).
>
> They slaughtered many of the infidels, and pursued those who fled to the mountains.
>
> So many of them were killed that their blood ran down the mountains and plain, and thus (nearly) all were sent to hell.
>
> The few who escaped, wounded, weary, and half dead, sought refuge in the defiles of the hills. Their property and goods, which exceeded all computation, and their countless cows and buffaloes, fell as spoil into the hands of my victorious soldiers.

Marching into Syria, Tamerlane took control of Aleppo and Damascus, where he was shown the grave sites of Mohammed's wives, Umm Selma and Umm Habiba. Seeing they had been neglected, he ravaged and plundered the city, leaving 20 towers of skulls.

Tamerlane conquered Nakhichevan, a region near Azerbaijan credited by tradition to have been founded by Noah. He bombarded the Christian city of Smyrna, mentioned in the Book of Revelation, with decapitated heads of its fallen defending knights. Tamerlane declared a jihad on the Christians of Georgia, destroying churches, slaying thousands of inhabitants and burying alive 4,000 captured Christian soldiers. He forced the Christian King of Georgia, Bagrat V, to convert to Islam at sword point.

French historian and member of the French Academy, Rene' Grousset (1885-1952) published major works on Asiatic and Oriental civilizations. In his original edition of *L'Empire Des Steppes*, page 513, Grousset recounted how in 1403, Tamerlane slaughtered the inhabitants and destroyed all the Christian churches in Georgia's capital of Tiflis:

> It has been noted that the Jenghiz-Khanite Mongol invasion of the thirteenth century was less cruel, for the Mongols were mere barbarians who killed simply because for centuries this had been the instinctive behavior of nomad herdsmen toward sedentary farmers.
>
> To this ferocity Tamerlane added a taste for religious murder. He killed from Qur'anic piety. ("Il tuait par piete coranique")
>
> He represents a synthesis, probably unprecedented in history, of Mongol barbarity and Muslim fanaticism, and symbolizes that advanced form of primitive slaughter which is murder committed for the sake of an abstract ideology, as a duty and a sacred mission.

In Muslim on Muslim violence, Tamerlane, a Sunni Muslim, attacked Baghdad, the capital of the Muslim world and center of Islamic learning, in 1393. He massacred 20,000 Shi'a Muslims. In 1401, after another revolt, Tamerlane returned to Baghdad and ordered each of his soldiers to bring back two decapitated heads from the city. The Tigris flowed red and vultures feasted on 90,000 corpses and 120 pyramids of severed heads.

Tamerlane had planned on invading China to reestablish Mongolian control but died and was buried in Uzbekistan. A pious Muslim, Tamerlane had erected a grand mosque at his capital at Samarkand and reportedly had his court calligrapher make a *Qur'an* so large it had to be transported in a wheelbarrow.

In 1526, Babar, a descendent of Tamerlane, founded the Muslim Mughal (Mogul) Empire in India.

∽

BAYEZID I

While Tamerlane was conquering Asia, Sultan Bayezid I (1354-1403) crossed the Danube and attacked Romania, but was repulsed. He laid siege to Constantinople from 1391 until 1401, but had to break off the siege to defeat the Christian allies of the west, led by the King of Hungary, Sigismund, in 1396.

Bayezid I fought Tamerlane, was captured by him and, it was rumored, was kept in a cage till he died.

∽

POPE BENEDICT'S SPEECH

While the Turkish Muslim, Bayezid I, was laying siege to Constantinople, the Byzantine Emperor Manuel Paleologus II (1350-1425) had a series of written correspondences with a Persian Muslim. Pope Benedict XVI, in an address at the University of Regensburg, September 12, 2006, referred to these:

> I read the edition by Professor Theodore Khoury (Münster) of part of the dialogue carried on — perhaps in 1391 in the winter barracks near Ankara - the erudite Byzantine Emperor Manuel II Paleologus and an educated Persian on the subject of **Christianity and Islam,** and the truth of both.

It was probably the emperor himself who set down this dialogue, during the siege of Constantinople between 1394 and 1402...

The dialogue ranges widely over the structures of faith contained in **the Bible and in the Qur'an,** and deals especially with the **image of God** and of man, while necessarily returning repeatedly to the relationship of the "three Laws": the *Old Testament,* the *New Testament* and the *Qur'an.*

In this lecture I would like to discuss only one point...the issue of **"faith and reason."**

FAITH OF MIND & HEART, NOT BODY

Pope Benedict continued:

In the seventh conversation...edited by professor Khoury, the emperor touches on the theme of the **jihad.** The emperor must have known that Sura 2:256 reads: "There is no compulsion in religion." It is one of the Suras of the early period when Mohammed was still powerless and under [threat].

But naturally the emperor also knew **the instructions developed later and recorded in the Qur'an concerning holy war.**

Without descending to details, such as the difference in treatment accorded to those who have the "Book" and the "infidels," he turns to his interlocutor somewhat brusquely with the central question on **the relationship between religion and violence** in general, in these words:

"Show me just what Mohammed brought that was new, and there you will find things only evil and inhuman, such as **his command to spread by the sword the faith he preached."**

The emperor goes on to explain in detail the reasons why spreading the faith through

violence is something unreasonable. Violence is incompatible with the nature of God and the nature of the soul:

"God is not pleased by blood, and not acting reasonably ("syn logo") is contrary to God's nature. **Faith is born of the soul, not the body.** Whoever would lead someone to faith needs the ability to speak well and to reason properly, without violence and threats...

To convince a reasonable soul, one does not need a strong arm, or weapons of any kind, or any other means of threatening a person with death..."

The decisive statement in this argument against violent conversion is this: "Not to act in accordance with reason is contrary to God's nature."

Pope Benedict explained:

The editor, Theodore Khoury, observes: For the emperor, as a Byzantine shaped by Greek philosophy, this statement is self-evident.

But for Muslim teaching, God is absolutely transcendent. His will is not bound up with any of our categories, **even that of rationality.**

Here Khoury quotes a work of the noted French Islamist R. Arnaldez, who points out that **Ibn Hazm went so far as to state that God is not bound even by his own word, and that nothing would oblige him to reveal the truth to us. Were it God's will, we would even have to practice idolatry...**

GREEK LOGIC VS ISLAMIC OBEDIENCE

Pope Benedict XVI continued:

I believe that here we can see the profound harmony between what is Greek in the best sense of the word and the biblical understanding of faith in God. Modifying the first verse of the *Book of Genesis*, John began the prologue of his *Gospel* with the words: "In the beginning was the 'logos.'"

This is the very word used by the emperor: **God acts with logos. Logos means both reason and word** — a reason which is creative and capable of self-communication, precisely as reason.

John thus spoke the final word on the biblical concept of God, and in this word all the often toilsome and tortuous threads of biblical faith find their culmination and synthesis.

In the beginning was the logos, and the logos is God, says the Evangelist. **The encounter between the biblical message and Greek thought did not happen by chance.**

Pope Benedict said God had a purpose for the *Scriptures* to be written in the Greek language:

The vision of St. Paul, who saw the roads to Asia barred and in a dream saw a Macedonian man plead with him:

"Come over to Macedonia and help us!" (cf. Acts 16:6-10) — this vision can be interpreted as a "distillation" of the intrinsic necessity of a rapprochement between **biblical faith and Greek inquiry...**

Within the *Old Testament*, the process which started at the burning bush came to new maturity at the time of the Exile, when the God of Israel, an Israel now deprived of its land and worship, was proclaimed as the God of heaven and earth and described in a simple formula which echoes the words uttered at the burning bush: "I am."

This new understanding of God is accompanied by a kind of enlightenment, which finds stark expression in the mockery of gods who are merely the work of human hands (cf. Psalm 115)...

Biblical faith, in the Hellenistic period, encountered the best of Greek thought at a deep level, resulting in a mutual enrichment evident especially in the later wisdom literature...**We know that the Greek translation of the *Old Testament* produced at Alexandria—the Septuagint—is more than a simple translation of the Hebrew text:** It is an independent textual witness and a distinct and important step in the history of Revelation, one which brought about this encounter in a way that was decisive for the birth and spread of Christianity.

A profound encounter of faith and reason is taking place here, an encounter between genuine enlightenment and religion. From the very heart of Christian faith and, at the same time, the heart of Greek thought now joined to faith, Manuel II was able to say:

Not to act "with logos" is contrary to God's nature...**The *New Testament* was written in Greek and bears the imprint of the Greek spirit,** which had already come to maturity as the *Old Testament* developed...

We will succeed in doing so only if reason and faith come together in a new way...as inquiry into the rationality of faith.

POPE: DIALOGUE OF CULTURES

Concluding his remarks, Pope Benedict stated:

Only thus do we become capable of that genuine dialogue of cultures and religions so urgently needed today...

"Not to act reasonably (with logos) is contrary to the nature of God," said Manuel II, according to his Christian understanding of

God, in response to his Persian interlocutor. **It is to this great logos, to this breadth of reason, that we invite our partners in the dialogue of cultures.**

In response to Pope Benedict's invitation for there to be a dialogue of cultures based on reason, violent Muslims staged riots, burned the Pope in effigy and murdered a nun.

❧
MEHMET I

It was reported that Tamerlane put Sultan Bayezid I in a cage until he died in 1413. After this, his son Mehmet (Turkish for Mohammed) became the next Sultan.

Mehmet I (1389-1421) conquered parts of Albania, Candaroglu and the Christian Kingdom of Cilicia. He subjugated the lands around Constantinople, but did not attack the city, thereby honoring his alliance with the Byzantine Emperor, even referring to him as "father and overlord." He died at age 47, being succeeded by his son, Murat II.

❧
MURAT II -SIEGE OF CONSTANTINOPLE

In 1421, Murat II (1404-1451) laid siege to Constantinople, but called it off so he could kill his younger brother, Mustafa, who was posing a threat to his power.

In 1443, the Turkish advance west was stopped by a European federation in Hungary. In 1444, the King of Hungary, John Hunyadi (1387-1456) led a coalition of European powers to stop the Muslim invasion at the *Battle of Varna*, but was terribly defeated due to the betrayal of the Serbian prince George Brankovic.

❧
BITTER BYZANTINE POLITICS

Toward the end of the Byzantine Empire, there was much political strife. When Emperor Manuel Paleologus II died, he left his son John Paleologus VIII as Emperor. When John died suddenly, there was confusion as to which brother should replace him.

When Constantine XI was chosen, his brother Demetrius bitterly challenged him. Demetrius turned to the Muslims for help.

In the same way centuries earlier Herod the Great invited Roman troops into Israel to help establish his claim to the throne and once Roman Legions came, they never left, Demetrius invited Ottoman Turks to cross the Bosporus in 1442 and come up to the walls of Constantinople to try to force his brother Constantine XI to recognize his claims for royal power.

This was the beginning of the end for Constantinople, as it whet the appetite of the next Sultan, young Mehmet II, to conqueror the city.

∾

MEHMET II -FALL OF CONSTANTINOPLE

Murat II conquered the land surrounding Constantinople, cutting it off from Western Europe. He then retired and made his 12 year-old son, Mehmet II, the next Sultan. The nations of the west thought this would be the opportune time to come to Constantinople's rescue. Hungary, Poland, Bosnia, Serbia, Croatia, Bulgaria, and Romania united for one last attempt to push back the Muslim aggressors and keep a land route open to Constantinople.

Murat II came out of retirement, took back the Sultan leadership from his young son and defeated the combined western forces at the *Battle of Varna*. This setback dissolved the political will of the west to confront the Muslims anymore, and no major attempt was ever made after this to rescue Constantinople.

This once great city, with Christian roots going back to Emperor Constantine, who legalized Christianity in 313 AD., was left to its fate.

Mehmet II's two half brothers died suspiciously, leaving him the only heir, so when Murat II died in 1451, Mehmet II, now 19 years old, became the Sultan again.

Mehmet was spurred forward by a fanatical belief that he was fulfilling old Islamic prophecies, as well as by the glories of martyrdom. In *Hadith Sahih Muslim,* Mohammed spoke of conquering Constantinople:

> Abu Huraira reported Allah's Messenger saying...
> "They will then fight and a third (part) of the army would run away, whom Allah will never forgive. A third (part of the army) which would be constituted of excellent martyrs in Allah's eye, would be killed and the third who would never be put to trial would win and they would be conquerors of Constantinople."
> (*Kitab al-Fitan wa Ashrat As-Sa`ah, Pertaining to the Turmoil and Portents of the Last Hour"* Book 41, Chapter 9, Number 6924)

By age 21, Mehmet II amassed an army of 100,000 Muslim warriors and around 10,000 to 20,000 Janissaries, who had been taken from Christian homes as boys and forced into the Muslim army.

NUCLEAR POWER OF THE AGE

Mehmet was also determined to acquire the most advanced military technology of the era, one that could shoot a deadly bomb great distances. This was a new explosive more powerful than any the world had ever seen. It was "corned gunpowder."

The old technology of gunpowder was to mix the ingredients of sulfur, saltpeter and charcoal on the battlefield, resulting in an inferior product where the ingredients separated, burning was slow, inconsistent and susceptible to moisture. The new process of corned gunpowder was to mix the ingredients into a paste, let it dry, then break it into granules. This rendered gunpowder 30 percent more powerful and more resistant to moisture. The more powerful gunpowder necessitated stronger cannons forged in one piece, requiring a knowledge of metallurgy, the equivalent of nuclear technology for the age.

Mehmet obtained the services of a Hungarian cannon maker named Urban.

Urban had defected from Constantinople because they did not have money to pay him. Mehmet had Urban build the largest cannons in the world for that time, including one 27 feet long which could fire a 1,200 pound stone cannon ball over a mile.

The barrel was so large a man could crawl inside it. When it was fired, the explosion could be heard ten miles away. Ironically, this and other cannons were made from melted down church bells from the hundreds of churches Muslims destroyed. It took 140 days to move the cannons into location outside the walls.

The twelve miles of walls, which had been built by Constantine, Justinian and other Roman Emperors, were three tiered with a huge ditch in front of them. They had never been breached in a thousand years, but the new technology of corned gunpowder and forged cannons was about to change that.

Constantinople had 8,000 defenders along the walls, most being untrained in warfare.

In a scene which could have been from the final battle of J.R.R. Tolkien's *Lord of the Rings* trilogy, the 120,000 strong force of Mehmet II attacked Constantinople, only contrary to the movie, the attackers won.

DIVISIONS UNDERMINE DEFENSE

Leading up to this point, Constantinople had been plagued by religious divisions. Byzantine Christians were Greek Eastern Orthodox, living in the land where Apostles Paul and John preached, speaking the language of the *New Testament*. Western Europe was Roman Catholic and had the *Scriptures* translated into Latin.

In 1054, after centuries of religious disagreements, the Roman Catholic Pope excommunicated the Patriarch of Constantinople over the wording of the Nicene creed.

Some in Constantinople wanted to unite with the Roman Catholic Church for religious reasons. Others wanted to unite with the Roman Catholic Church for political reasons - thinking the west would then send military help, and still others thought that uniting would bring the curse of God on their city.

WESTERN HELP DIMINISHES

Constantinople was weakened by the Black Death or Bubonic Plague, which began in Asia around 1347 and followed land and sea trade routes after the Crusades back to Constantinople, Italy, Europe and England. It killed an estimated 25 million people - a third of Europe's population.

Doctors refused to visit the sick, parents abandoned children, entire households died, and there were not enough people to bury the dead. This resulted in social upheaval and devastated commerce as crops were left standing in the fields with no one to harvest them.

There were not enough priests to hear the confessions of the dying so Pope Clement VI granted remission of sin to all who died of the plague. This not only ravaged the already struggling Byzantine Empire, but significantly depopulated western Europe, preventing it from having spare soldiers to send to Constantinople's defense.

Mehmet II's great fear was that western Europe would come to the rescue of Constantinople, but Western Europe was preoccupied with its own problems:

> France and England were drained from the Hundred Years War (1337-1453), of which Joan of Arc played a part; Hungary and Poland had been defeated by Murat II; Spain was driving out the Muslims in its Reconquista; and the Papal Schism of competing Popes destabilized the German led Holy Roman Empire.

GLOBALISTS UNDERMINE DEFENSE

Wealthy merchants of Venice and Genoa were the globalists of their day. They were more interested in profits than preserving any nationality, religion or culture. From the Fourth Crusade on, they had been undercutting the Byzantine Empire's economy.

They viewed Constantinople as an old, inner city property surrounded by violent gangs and was not worth investing to save. In contrast, they saw their growing Italian city-states as the new upper class suburban developments.

Venetians and Genoese merchants wanted to stay neutral in Constantinople's fight against invading Muslims, as they traded with both side, even supplying military goods to Muslims.

The Venetians and Genoese did not trust each other. Since 1253, there were four major wars between Venice and Genoa and they sacked each other's cities. They constantly betrayed each other, and in the process, weakened Constantinople's defense.

WESTERN MEDIA HELPS ENEMY

Mehmet II listened with great interest to news accounts of dissension in the West and from within Constantinople, being greatly encouraged by the religious, economic and political disunity.

As western powers lost their resolve to help, Mehmet II was emboldened to go forward with his plan of attacking the thousand year old Christian city that had been the richest, most powerful city in the world.

ISOLATE & CONQUER WEAK FIRST

Mehmet II conquered the surrounding Christian cities first, not only requiring them to pay the jizyah and give up their young boys to the Muslim army, but he pressured them to participate in the siege on Constantinople, filling supportive roles, such as building boats, making roads and hauling supplies.

INVITATION TO ISLAM

Before the siege, Mehmet offered Islamic peace. He sent a detachment to the city gates with an invitation to surrender as required by Qur'anic law:

Nor do we punish until we have sent forth a messenger. When we resolve to raze a city, we first give warning to those its people who live in comfort. If they persist in sin, judgment is irrevocably passed, and we destroy it utterly.

Defenders knew their choices were: convert to Islam; surrender to being dhimmi and pay the annual jizyah tax; or hold out and anticipate three days of slaughter and plunder if they were defeated.

Desire for plunder and zeal for religion were the two great motivators of the Muslim army, though they were not aware that by this time most of the riches had long since departed Constantinople. Mehmet was skilled in effectively manipulating these motivations to keep his troops on the attack.

GLOBAL DISASTERS & PROPHECIES

Global disasters and strange weather were seen as apocalyptic portents. Roger Crowley, in *1453–The Holy War for Constantinople and the Clash of Islam and The West* (NY: Hyperion Books, 2005), described:

Sometime around the start of 1453, the volcanic island of Kuwae, 1,200 miles east of Australia, literally blew itself up.

Eight cubic miles of molten rock were blasted into the stratosphere with a force two millions times that of the Hiroshima bomb. It was the Krakatoa of the Middle Ages, an event that dimmed the world's weather.

Volcanic dust was propelled across the earth on global winds, lowering temperatures and blighting harvests from China to Sweden,

South of the Yangtze River, an area with a climate as mild as Florida, it snowed continuously for forty days.

Constantinople's cathedral is called Hagia Sophia (Saint Sophia). It is still considered one of the greatest buildings in the world, with its 102 foot in diameter dome resting over 180 feet above the ground.

Constructed with multicolored marble, it has over four acres of inlaid gold and ivory mosaics. It was the largest cathedral in the world for 1,000 years.

The seat of the Patriarch of Constantinople was as important to Eastern Orthodox Christians as the Vatican, the seat of the Pope, is to Roman Catholics in the West.

Atmospheric ash from the volcanic eruption of Kuwae caused a strange and ominous electrical phenomenon in the sky and on the dome of the Hagia Sophia Cathedral shortly before Mehmet II's final attack.

Roger Crowley writes:

> Toward evening the atmosphere seemed to grow even thicker and a "great darkness began to gather over the city." And something even stranger was witnessed.
>
> Initially the sentries on the walls observed Constantinople to be illuminated by lights as if the enemy were burning the city. Alarmed, people ran to see what was happening and cried aloud when they looked up at the dome of St. Sophia. A strange light was flickering on the roof.
>
> The excitable (Russian chronicler) Nestor-Iskander described what he saw: "at the top of the window, a large flame of fire issuing forth; it encircled the entire neck [dome] of the church for a long time.
>
> The flame gathered into one, its flame altered and there was an indescribable light. At once it took to the sky. Those who had seen it were benumbed; they began to wail and cry out in Greek: "Lord have mercy! The light itself

has gone up to heaven." It was clear to the faithful that the Lord had abandoned Constantinople...

When Mehmet saw the glow over the city he was initially troubled and sent for his mullahs to interpret the portents. They came and duly proclaimed the omens favorable to the Muslims cause: "This is a great sign. The city is doomed."

Roger Crowley continued in his book *1453*:

Lurid light effects after the Krakatoa eruption in 1883 similarly alarmed people in New York...They assumed huge fires were raging and sent forth the fire brigade.

Christians within the walls of Constantinople thought what was happening was the fulfillment of *Bible* prophecies of the end of the world and that Mehmet was the antichrist. They were disturbed by omens, such as the fact that the first and last leaders of the Western Roman Empire were both named Romulus, and that the first and last emperors of the Eastern Roman Empire were named Constantine.

Roger Crowley wrote in his book *1453–The Holy War for Constantinople and the Clash of Islam and The West* (NY: Hyperion Books, 2005):

Everything pointed to a belief that time was nearly completed. In the Monastery of St. George there was an oracular document, divided into squares, showing the succession of emperors, one emperor to each square: "in time the squares were all filled and they say that only one last square was still empty – the square to be occupied by Constantine XI."

This was like the *Prophecy of Saint Malachy*, who lived in 1143 and listed attributes of 112 Roman Catholic Popes that were to follow – there is only one remaining after Pope Benedict XVI.

END OF BYZANTINE CIVILIZATION

Niccolo Barbaro, in his *Diary of the Siege of Constantinople 1453*, translated by Professor John Melville-Jones (New York, 1969), related the horror of the sack of the city, scenes which were repeated all over central and southern Europe:

> On 29 May 1453, the Turks entered Constantinople at daybreak...The confusion of those Turks and of the Christians was so great that they met face to face, and so many died that the dead bodies would have filled twenty carts...
>
> The Turks put the city to sword as they came, and everyone they found in their way they slashed with their scimitars [curved swords], women and men, old and young, of every condition, and this slaughter continued from dawn until midday. Those Italian merchants who escaped hid in caves under the ground, but they were found by the Turks, and were all taken captive and sold as slaves.
>
> When those of the Turkish fleet saw with their own eyes that the Christians had lost Constantinople, that the flag of Sultan Mehmet had been hoisted over the highest tower in the city, and that the emperor's flags had been cut down and lowered, then all those in the seventy galleys went ashore...
>
> They sought out the convents and all the nuns were taken to the ships and abused and dishonored by the Turks, and they were all sold at auction as slaves to be taken to Turkey, and similarly the young women were all dishonored and sold at auction; some preferred to throw themselves into wells and drown.
>
> These Turks loaded their ships with people and a great treasure. They had this custom: when they entered a house, they would at once

raise a flag with their own device, and when other Turks saw such a flag raised, no other Turk would for the world enter that house but would go looking for a house that had no flag; it was the same with all the convents and churches.

As I understand it, it seems there were some two hundred thousand of these flags on the houses of Constantinople...these flags flew above the houses for the whole of that day, and for all of that day the Turks made a great slaughter of Christians in the city.

Blood flowed on the ground as though it were raining.

A Greek scholar recited the last minutes of the last Roman Emperor, Constantine XI, as he charged to fight the Muslim who had come in through an unlocked gate:

Although he clearly saw with his own eyes the danger that threatened the city, and had the opportunity to save himself - as well as many people encouraging him to do so - he refused, preferring to die with his country and his subjects.

Indeed, he chose to die first, so that he might avoid the sight of the city being taken and of its inhabitants being either savagely slaughtered or shamefully led away into slavery.

VATICAN TURNED INTO MOSQUE?

After his 53 day siege, Mehmet II conquered Constantinople and marched directly to the Hagia Sophia cathedral and turned it into a mosque.

This shocked Eastern Orthodox Christians in the same way Roman Catholic Christians would be if Muslims turned the Vatican into a mosque.

Mehmet II built an altar (Mihrab) inside along the east wall, the direction of Mecca, and a brick minaret on the southeast corner.

The cathedral's four acres of gold mosaics were plastered over and covered with *Qur'an* verses. The uniquely shaped dome was copied by Islamic architects for mosques around the world for over 500 years.

๛

FLEEING GREEKS SPREAD RENAISSANCE

Sultan Mehmet II's dominion extended from the Danube River to the Euphrates River. He attacked Hungary in 1456 but was repulsed at the Siege of Belgrade by King John Hunyadi and the courageous peasants led by Saint John of Capistrano. Injured in the thigh and forced to retreat, Mehmet II vented his anger by wounding a number of his generals with his own sword.

Islamic conquest of Byzantium caused Greeks to flee west to Italy, inspiring an interest in Greek art, architecture and philosophy known as the Renaissance, referred to by President Obama in Egypt, June 4, 2009: "It was Islam...paving the way for Europe's Renaissance."

In fact, the very concept of "Europe" was a result of Islamic invasion, for previously, Europe viewed itself as innumerable independent kingdoms. Additionally, as Greeks fled west with their ancient manuscripts, European scholars began translating the Bible from Greek - thus paving the way for the Reformation.

๛

COLUMBUS' NEW ROUTE-INDIA & CHINA

The capture of Constantinople by Sultan Mehmet II in 1453 effectively cut off land trade routes from Western Europe to India and China - routes that had been used since before Marco Polo. Europe now sought new routes.

In 1479, Spain's Kingdoms of Aragon and Castile were united by the marriage of Ferdinand and Isabella. Together, in 1492, they recaptured the last Muslim stronghold of Granada, forcing the Moorish King Abu 'abd Allah Muhammad XII to surrender.

JIHAD RESULTS IN COLUMBUS' VOYAGE

The jihad which conquered the Byzantine Empire and captured Constantinople led the Spanish Monarchs to support Christopher Columbus' idea of a new route to India and China by sailing west. Columbus thought the islands he discovered were around India, so he named inhabitants "Indians." He thought Haiti was Japan and Cuba was the tip of China. Though it was not till his fourth voyage that he admitted he had not found the Far East, the fact is, Columbus would have never set sail had it not been for Islamic jihad closing off the land trade routes east.

In 1492, Genoa born Christopher Columbus wrote to the King and Queen of Spain in his *Journal of the First Voyage* (*El Libro de la Primera Navegacion*), as recounted in the abstract of Bartolome' de Las Casas' and translated into English by Samuel Eliot Morison, (*Journals & Other Documents on the Life & Voyages of Christopher Columbus* NY: Heritage Press, 1963):

> In the Name of Our Lord Jesus Christ, Because, most Christian and very Exalted, Excellent and mighty Princes, King and Queen of the Spains and of the Islands of the Sea, our Lord and Lady, in this present year 1492,
>
> after **Your Highnesses had made an end to the war with the Moors who ruled in Europe,** and had concluded the war in the very great City of Granada, where in the present year, on the 2nd day of the month of January,
>
> I saw the Royal Standards of Your Highnesses placed by force of arms on the towers of the Alhambra (which is the citadel of the said city),
>
> **And I saw the Moorish King come forth to the gates of the city and kiss the Royal Hands of Your Highnesses** and the Prince of my Lord, and soon after in that same month, through

information that I had given to Your Highnesses concerning the lands of India, and of a Prince who is called Gran Can [Khan], which is to say in our vernacular "King of Kings,"

how many times he and his predecessors had sent to Rome to seek doctors in our Holy Faith to instruct him therein, and that never had the Holy Father provided them, and thus so many people were lost through lapsing into idolatries and receiving doctrines of perdition;

And Your Highnesses, as Catholic Christians and Princes devoted to the Holy Christian Faith and the propagators thereof, and **enemies of the sect of Mahomet and of all idolatries and heresies,**

resolved to send me, Christopher Columbus, to the said regions of India, to see the said princes and peoples and lands and the dispositions of them and of all, and the manner in which may be undertaken their conversion to our Holy Faith,

And ordained that I should not go by land (the usual way) to the Orient, but by the route of the Occident, by which no one to this day knows for sure that anyone has gone...

October 10, 1492, Columbus' Journal stated:

He had come to the Indies, and so had to continue until he found them, with the help of Our Lord.

Columbus thought he had reached India, so he named inhabitants "Indians." Native civilizations would have never been disrupted by Europeans had it not been for Muslims cutting off the land routes to the Orient.

In his *Libro de las profecias* (*Book of Prophecies*), written between his third and fourth voyages, Christopher Columbus stated:

Most Christian and very high Princes: My argument for **the restitution of the Holy Temple** to the Holy militant Church is the following:

At a very early age I went to sea and have continued navigating until today.

The art of sailing is favorable for anyone who wants to pursue knowledge of this world's secrets. I have already been at this business for forty years. I have sailed all the waters which, up to now, have been navigated.

I have had dealings and conversations with learned people - clergymen and laymen, Latins and Greeks, Jews and Moors, and with many others of other sects.

I found Our Lord very well-disposed toward this desire, and he gave me the spirit of intelligence for it.

He prospered me in seamanship and supplied me with the necessary tools for astrology, as well as geometry and arithmetic and ingenuity of intellect and of manual skill to draw spherical maps which show cities, rivers and mountains, islands and ports - everything in its proper place.

At this time I have seen and put in study to look into all the *Scriptures*, cosmography, histories, chronicles and philosophy and other arts, which our

Lord opened to my understanding (I could sense His hand upon me), so that it became clear to me that it was feasible **to navigate from here to the Indies;** and He unlocked within me the determination to execute the idea. And I came to your Highnesses with this ardor.

All those who heard about my enterprise rejected it with laughter, scoffing at me. Neither the sciences which I mentioned above, nor the authoritative citations from them, were of any avail. In only your Highnesses remained faith and constancy. Who doubts that this illumination was from the Holy Spirit?

I attest that He (the Spirit), with marvelous rays of light, consoled me through the holy and sacred *Scriptures*, a strong and clear testimony, with 44 books of the *Old Testament*, and 4 *Gospels* with 23 *Epistles* of those blessed Apostles, encouraging me to proceed, and, continually, without ceasing for a moment, they inflame me with a sense of great urgency...

The *Holy Scriptures* testify in the *Old Testament*, by the mouth of the prophets, and in the *New*, by our Savior Jesus Christ, that this world will come to an end...

St. Augustine says that the end of this world will occur in the seventh millennium following the Creation...

Our Savior said that before the consummation of this world, all that was written by the Prophets must be fulfilled...

I have already said that for the execution of the enterprise of the Indies, neither reason, nor mathematics, nor world maps were profitable to me; rather the prophecy of Isaiah was completely fulfilled...

I stated above that some of the prophecies remained yet to be fulfilled, and I say they are great things in the world...

The sign which convinces me that our Lord is hastening the end of the world is the preaching of the *Gospel* recently in so many lands.

᳕

ORDER OF DRACULA

Modeled after the Order of St. George the Dragon Slayer to stop the "dragon" Sultan Murat I in 1389, Sigismund (1368-1437), King of Hungary, formed the Order of the Dragon in 1408 to stop the Muslim invasion into Europe. The Order's members were leaders of Hungary, Poland, Austria, Serbia, Aragon, Naples, Lithuania, Bavaria, Denmark, Orzora, Transylvania, Saxony, Moldavia and Wallachia. Wallachia, which became part of Romania, was led by Vlad II (1390-1447). The Romanian word for "Dragon" was "Dracula."

In 1443, Sultan Murat II took Vlad II's two younger sons as hostages, Vlad III (1431-1476) and Radu (1439-1475). They were put in the dungeon of the fortress of Egrigöz in the forests of Anatolia, before being removed to the Ottoman capital of Edirne.

Three years earlier, the Sultan had taken the sons of the wealthy Prince George Brankovic of Serbia. When the sons were suspected of plotting an escape, the Sultan had them blinded with hot irons.

While a hostage, Vlad III's father was killed and his older brother was blinded and buried alive. Vlad III was cruelly whipped and tortured, while his handsome younger brother, Radu, attracted the attention of Ottoman heir Mehmet II, who forced him to engage in Muslim homosexual pederasty.

Mehmet II, who modeled himself after Alexander the Great, conquered Constantinople in 1453 and wanted to conquer all the former Roman Empire, including the City of Rome.

Vlad III eventually escaped through the Borgo Pass and in 1456 became ruler of Wallachia. Having learned torture and the use of terror from his Ottoman captors, Vlad III punished his enemies with impalement, a common form of Islamic execution, resulting in his name Vlad the Impaler.

Previously, in 1444, Vlad's father had failed to keep his oath to help Hungarian King John Hunyadi (1387-1456) at the *Battle of Varna* in 1444, which ended in a terrible defeat due to the betrayal of George Brankovic. Vlad III reconciled with John Hunyadi, who resisted Mehmet II at the Siege of Belgrade in 1456.

During this time George Kastrioti (1405-1468), also called Skanderbeg, "the Dragon of Albania," rebelled against the Sultan and led a guerrilla warfare to free Albania from Muslim control.

In 1459, Vlad III stopped paying the Sultan the annual tribute, which included 500 young boys. In 1461, Vlad crossed south of the Danube and won several victories near the Black Sea. In 1462, Mehmet II led 100,000 Muslims into Wallachia. In heated fighting, Vlad's soldiers killed 20,000 of the Sultan's men.

One night during the battle, Vlad, who knew the Turkish language, dressed as a Turkish officer and stole into the Sultan's tent to kill him. The Sultan, suspicious of an attempt on his life, had switched tents allowing another soldier to be stabbed in his place.

Outnumbered, Vlad retreated, poisoning the wells and burning his own villages so the invading Muslims would have no food and water. Vlad was forced from his throne and escaped only by nailing the horseshoes backwards on his horse's hooves so the Muslims thought he was riding towards his castle instead of away from it.

When Sultan Mehmet II finally reached the capital of Wallachia, his men lost the stomach to fight when they saw Vlad's attempt to out-terrorize them - a gruesome spectacle of 20,000 captives impaled in what became called the "Forest of the Impaled." The tactic worked and the Sultan retreated.

Victor Hugo, author of *Les Miserables* and *The Hunchback of Notre Dame*, made mention of Vlad and the Sultan in his *Legend of the Ages*, 1859-1883 (translated from French):

> From Aden [port in Yemen] and Erzeroum [port in Greece] he [Sultan] made broad pits,
> A mass grave of Modon [city in Greece] overcome, and three clusters of corpses of Aleppo, Bush and Damascus [piles of dead left by Muslims in cities of Anatolia and Syria];

One day, tie of the arc, he took his son for target,
And killed him; [Sultans would kill siblings and sometimes sons to eliminate rival claims to power.]
Mourad [Mehmet II-son of Murat] Sultan was invincible;
Vlad, boyard [feudal prince] of Tarvis, called Beelzebub,
Refused to pay to the Sultan his tribute,
Takes the Turkish embassy [300 soldiers] and all makes it perish
On thirty stakes, planted at the two edges of a road;
Mourad runs, extreme harvests, barns, attics,
The boyard beats, makes him twenty thousand prisoners,
Then, around one immense and black battle field,
Builds a very broad floor out of large stones,
And made in the crenels [openings in stone wall], full with dreadful plaintive cries,
To build and wall the twenty thousand prisoners,
Leaving holes by where one sees their eyes in the shade,
And leaves, after having written on their dark wall:
"Mourad, mason stone, with Vlad, grower of piles."
Mourad was believing, Mourad was pious;
He burned hundred convents of Christians in Euboea [second largest Greek Island],
Where by chance its lightning was one day fallen;
Mourad was forty years the bright murderer

Sabring [killing with a saber] the world,
having God under his clamp;
He had Rhamséion [tomb of Ramses in
Egypt] and Généralife [Moorish palace in
Granada, Spain];
He was the Pasha, the Emperor, the Caliph,
And the priests said: "Allah! Mourad is great."

After a time of imprisonment by a rival king,
Vlad reconquered Wallachia in 1476, but was soon
killed in battle with the Ottomans. His head was sent
to Constantinople, where Sultan Mehmet II had it
preserved in honey then displayed on a stake as proof
that Vlad the Impaler was dead.

◆

SAINT STEPHEN THE GREAT

A cousin of Vlad III was Stephen III of Moldavia
(1433-1504). He won the *Battle of Vaslui* in 1475, with 40,000
troops against 120,000 Muslim Ottomans, commanded
by Hadan Suleiman Pasha, under Sultan Mehmet II.
Pope Sixtus IV called Stephen "Athleta Christi"
(Champion of Christ). Polish chronicler Jan Dlugosz
(1415-1480) wrote: "He was the first contemporary
among the rulers of the world to score a decisive victory
against the Turks."

◆

MUSLIMS IN THE EAST

In 1502, the Islamic Shi'a sect developed under
Safavids of Persia. In 1514, a series of wars erupted
between the Sunni Muslim Turkish Empire and the
Shi'a Muslim Persian Empire.

◆

BARBAROSSA

In 1465, Muslims massacred the entire Jewish
population of Fez, Morocco. In 1516, the Muslim pirate
Barbarossa (Redbeard) killed the king of Algiers and

proclaimed himself king. Barbarossa notoriously pirated Spanish ships and raided Spanish, French and Italian coastal cities.

He allied himself with the Ottoman Sultan, Suleiman the Magnificent, and his ruthless piracy gave Muslims naval dominance of the Mediterranean Sea. For centuries, Algiers was a Barbary pirate haven where tens of thousands of captured Christian sailors and Christian men, women and children taken in raids were imprisoned in the dreaded, rat-infested dungeons of Bagnio. Held with large iron shackles, they were clothed in rags, fed rotten food, slept in crowded filth, tortured, sold as slaves and forced to work hard labor in the heat rebuilding Muslim fortifications.

In 1517, the Ottoman Turks conquered Egypt.

⤚

SULTAN SULEIMAN THE MAGNIFICENT

Islam teaches that world peace is when the whole world is brought to submit to the will of Allah. Towards this end, Sultan Suleiman the Magnificent defeated the Byzantines, Bulgars, Serbs, and in 1521, surrounded the city of Belgrade with 250,000 soldiers. He captured it by bombarding it from an island in the Danube River. Suleiman deported the entire Christian population to Istanbul as slaves. When Belgrade, one of Christendom's major cities, collapsed, fear spread throughout Europe.

In 1522, Suleiman attacked the Island of Rhodes with 400 ships and 100,000 troops. After a 5 month siege, the defenders capitulated and retreated to the Island of Malta.

In 1526, when Hungarians were defeated by the Turks at the *Battle of Mohacs*, and their King Louis II was killed, it was a moral defeat for all of Europe.

Islam advanced most where political and religious divisions existed. Protestant leaders in the Holy Roman Empire often refused to support Spain's King Charles V in his wars against the Turks as they saw Muslims as a check on Catholic power.

Suleiman attempted to take advantage of Europe's disunity during Luther's Reformation, Henry VIII's divorce, and Charles V's sacking of Rome, where he imprisoned Pope Clement VII for 6 months.

SULEIMAN TAXES CHRISTIANS

Suleiman the Magnificent, also called Suleiman the Lawgiver, compiled an entire set of laws for the Christians he conquered. These laws included paying the holders of the timars (lords of the fiefdom) a tenth of the produce from the ground, though often by abuse this was a higher proportion. Christians paid a poll tax and delivered up a tenth of their boys for the army.

Christians had to pay a whole series of rents and taxes which combined were a heavy burden. Taxes included: bride tax, hoof tax, pasture tax, bee tax, mill tax, herd tax, and meadow tax, compulsory or villein (serf tied to the land) service, and provisions for the army taking the field.

∽

MARTIN LUTHER & THE REFORMATION

In 1517, Martin Luther began the Reformation by posting *Ninety-Five Theses*, or debate questions, on the church door in Wittehberg, Saxony, Germany.

Luther first mentioned "the Turks" in his 1518 *Explanations of the Ninety-Five Theses*, as revealed by Robert O. Smith, Doctoral Fellow, Baylor University, in "Luther, the Turks, and Islam" (*Currents in Theology and Mission*, Lutheran School of Theology at Chicago, 10/1/07).

As recorded in *Luther's Works-American Edition, 55 volumes* (Philadelphia: Fortress; St. Louis: Concordia, 1955-1986), vol. 46:170-171, Martin Luther wrote:

> The Turk is the rod of the wrath of the Lord our God...If the Turk's god, the devil, is not beaten first, there is reason to fear that the Turk will not be so easy to beat...Christian weapons and power must do it...

[The fight against the Turks] must begin with repentance, and we must reform our lives, or we shall fight in vain. [The Church should] drive men to repentance by showing our great and numberless sins and our ingratitude, by which we have earned God's wrath and disfavor, so that He justly gives us into the hands of the devil and the Turk.

Luther wrote in Preface to *Book of Revelation*, 1530:

2nd woe...the 6th [evil] angel, the shameful Mohammed with his companions, the Saracens, who inflicted great plagues on Christendom, with his doctrine and with the sword.

In *On War Against the Turk*, 1529, Luther wrote:

The Turk is the very devil incarnate... The Turk fills heaven with Christians by murdering their bodies.

In *Luther's Works*, 3:121-122, Martin Luther wrote:

Yet it is more in accordance with the truth to say that the Turk is the Beast, because he is outside the church and openly persecutes Christ.

Luther wrote (*Tischreden*, 1532, Weimer, ed., 1, 330):

The Turk is the flesh of Antichrist...[which] slaughters bodily by the sword.

James M. Kittleson, in *Luther the Reformer: The Man and His Career* (Minn: Augsburg, 1986, p. 220), wrote that Archduke Ferdinand, under authority of Emperor Charles V, called for the Second Diet of Speyer in 1529:

With Vienna under siege, the Diet was to discuss both the Turkish threat and the religious controversy together. Ferdinand declared that the fact that the Turks were advancing up the

Danube had much to do with God's anger over the existence of heretics within the empire. Both Turks and Luther were to be dealt with summarily.

Eric W. Gritisch wrote in *Martin-God's Court Jester: Luther in Retrospect* (Philadelphia: Fortress, 1983, p. 69-70):

Afraid of losing the much-needed support of the German princes for the struggle against the Turkish threat from the south, Emperor Charles V agreed to a truce between Protestant and Catholic territories in Nuremberg in 1532...

Thus the Lutheran movement was, for the first time, officially tolerated and could enjoy a place in the political sun of the Holy Roman Empire.

✍

FIRST SIEGE OF VIENNA

In 1529, Suleiman laid siege to Vienna, Austria. Torrential rains caused 10,000 of his supply camels to slip in the mud and break their legs. Unsuccessful in sending suicide bombers at the gates and tunneling under the walls, Suleiman beheaded 4,000 Christian hostages and left. In 1532, he attacked Vienna again but was turned back.

In 1534, Suleiman led his Ottoman Turkish Sunni Muslims to conquer the Shi'a Muslims of Persia (Iran) and annexed most of the Middle East and huge areas of North Africa, including Barbary States of Tripoli, Tunisia, Algeria, and Morocco.

As the Protestant Reformation was spreading in Europe, King Charles V of Spain, head of the Holy Roman Empire, fought Suleiman's ships, which sailed from North Africa to raid the coast of Spain. In 1535, Charles won a victory against the Muslims at Tunis.

Like the political disunity in 1442 in the Byzantine Empire, where Demetrius allied himself with Muslim Sultan Murat II against his brother Constantine

XI, France allied itself with Muslim Sultan Suleiman against Spain's Charles V in 1536, and again in 1542.

In response, Charles V allied himself in 1543 with England's Henry VIII and together they forced France to sign the Truce of Crepy-en-Laonnois.

Nevertheless, Charles V was pressured to sign a humiliating treaty with the Ottomans. Muslim attacks continued against Spain from Muslim Barbary pirates of North Africa, resulting in the Muslim Ottoman Empire gaining naval dominance of the Mediterranean Sea.

Ohio State University Professor Robert C. Davis wrote *Christian Slaves, Muslim Masters: White Slavery in the Mediterranean, the Barbary Coast and Italy 1500-1800* (Palgrave Macmillian, 2003). In 1544, when Algerian pirates carried an enormous 7,000 into slavery from the Bay of Naples, it forced the price of a slave so low that one could "swap a Christian for an onion."

In 1554, Muslim pirates sacked Vieste in southern Italy and took 6,000 captives. In 1566, when an attack on Granada netted 4,000 men, women and children, it was said to be "raining Christians in Algiers." In the same year, Turks and Corsairs sailed up the Adriatic coast and landed at Fracaville, resulting in residents abandoning over 500 square miles.

∽

JOHN CALVIN

John Calvin wrote to Philip Melanthon, 1543 (*Selected Works of John Calvin: Tracts & Letters, I: 373*):

> I hear of the sad condition of your Germany!... The Turk again prepares to wage war with a larger force. Who will stand up to oppose his marching throughout the length and breadth of the land, at his mere will and pleasure?

Calvin wrote in *Commentary of 2nd Thessalonians*:

> Since Mohammed was an apostate, he turned his followers, the Turks, from

Christ...The sect of Mohammed was like a raging overflow, which in its violence tore away about half of the Church.

Calvin wrote in *Commentary on Daniel*:

Turks have spread far and wide, and the world is filled with impious despisers of God.

Calvin wrote in *Sermons on Timothy & Titus*:

The Turks at this day, can allege and say for themselves: 'We serve God from our ancestors!' - It is a good while since Mahomet gave them the cup of his devilish dreams to drink, and they got drunk with them. It is about a thousand years since cursed hellhounds were made drunk with their follies - Let us be wise and discreet! - For otherwise, we shall be like the Turks and Heathen.

⊰৯

INDIA

In 1556, Mughal leader Jalaluddin Muhammad Akbar controlled most of India. His son, Jahangir, who was infamous for drinking, was the first to grant permission to trade to the British East India Company.

⊰৯

BATTLE OF LEPANTO IN 1571

In 1565, during the *Great Siege of Malta*, 9,000 defenders, led by La Valette, repulsed 40,000 Muslim invaders for nearly two months. The Muslims finally gave up and sailed away on September 11, 1565.

This was followed in 1571 with the *Battle of Lepanto*, considered to be one of the most important naval battles in history, as it ended the westward drive of the Muslim Ottoman navy.

Earlier, in 1453, western European nations failed to come to the aid of Constantinople and it fell to invading Muslims. By 1571, the Muslim Ottoman navy dominated the eastern and southern Mediterranean Sea and was preparing to conquer Italy and the western Mediterranean.

Just two months before the *Battle of Lepanto*, the Island of Cyprus fell on August 3, 1571. The Ottoman navy ravaged the coasts and leveled towns in Sicily and southern Italy. Pope Pius V called on all Europe to pray as the City of Rome was in danger.

Spain, Venice, Genoa, Naples, Sicily, Tuscany, the Duchy of Savoy, the Papal States and the Knights of Malta joined in a Holy League to stop them.

They were led by Don John of Austria, the illegitimate son of Emperor Charles V and half brother of King Philip II of Spain. The Holy League fleet had 12,920 sailors, 43,000 rowers, and 28,000 Spanish, German and Italian fighting troops in 206 galleys and 6 galleasses.

The Ottoman Muslim fleet had over 30,000 sailors, including 2,500 Janissaries, in 230 galleys and 56 galliots. It was led by Ali Pasha, who served under Sultan Selim the Drunkard (1524-1574), the son of Suleiman the Magnificent who was notorious for his debauchery.

Ali Pasha was joined by the corsairs Chulouk Bey of Alexandria and Uluj Ali. The battle was on October 7, 1571, in the Gulf of Patras near western Greece. The five-hour battle, the last major sea battle in world history solely between rowing vessels, cost the Holy League 12 galleys and 13,000 men, but freed about 15,000 Christian galley-slaves from the Muslim ships.

The Ottomans lost 25,000 soldiers and 200 ships. In fact, the Ottomans lost all but 30 of their ships. With Ali Pasha killed, it was a crushing defeat for the Muslims, who had not lost a major naval battle since the fifteenth century.

Some historians consider it to be the most decisive naval battle since the *Battle of Actium* of 31 BC. Pope Pius V instituted a new Catholic feast day of Our Lady of Victory to commemorate the battle.

꿏

G.K. CHESTERTON'S POEM "LEPANTO"

The English author G.K. Chesterton portrayed the battle in his poem *Lepanto,* published in 1911:

...St. Michael's on his Mountain in the sea-roads of the north
(Don John of Austria is girt and going forth.)
Where the grey seas glitter and the sharp tides shift
And the sea-folk labour and the red sails lift.
He shakes his lance of iron and he claps his wings of stone;
The noise is gone through Normandy; the noise is gone alone...
Don John calling through the blast and the eclipse
Crying with the trumpet, with the trumpet of his lips,
Trumpet that sayeth ha!
Domino gloria!
Don John of Austria is shouting to the ships.
King Philip's in his closet with the Fleece about his neck
(Don John of Austria is armed upon the deck.)...
And death is in the phial and the end of noble work,
But Don John of Austria has fired upon the Turk...
Gun upon gun, ha! ha! Gun upon gun, hurrah!
Don John of Austria has loosed the cannonade
The Pope was in his chapel before day of battle broke,
(Don John of Austria is hidden in the smoke.)...
He sees as in a mirror on the monstrous twilight sea
The crescent of his cruel ships whose name is mystery;
They fling great shadows foe-wards, making Cross and Castle dark,
They veil the plumed lions on the galleys of St. Mark;

And above the ships are palaces of brown, black-bearded chiefs,

And below the ships are prisons, where with multitudinous griefs,

Christian captives sick and sunless, all a labouring race repines

Like a race in sunken cities, like a nation in the mines.

They are lost like slaves that swat, and in the skies of morning hung

The stairways of the tallest gods when tyranny was young.

They are countless, voiceless, hopeless as those fallen or fleeing on

Before the high Kings' horses in the granite of Babylon.

And many a one grows witless in his quiet room in hell

Where a yellow face looks inward through the lattice of his cell,

And he finds his God forgotten, and he seeks no more a sign -

But Don John of Austria has burst the battle-line!

Don John pounding from the slaughter-painted poop,

Purpling all the ocean like a bloody pirate's sloop,

Scarlet running over on the silvers and the golds,

Breaking of the hatches up and bursting of the holds,

Thronging of the thousands up that labour under sea

White for bliss and blind for sun and stunned for liberty.

Vivat Hispania! Domino Gloria!

Don John of Austria has set his people free!

Cervantes on his galley sets the sword back in the sheath

Don John of Austria rides homeward with a wreath.

And he sees across a weary land a straggling road in Spain,
Up which a lean and foolish knight forever rides in vain,
And he smiles, but not as Sultans smile, and settles back the blade...
But Don John of Austria rides home from the Crusade.

&

DON QUIXOTE

One of the better-known participants in the *Battle of Lepanto* was Spanish author Miguel de Cervantes (1547-1616), who was wounded in the battle and lost the use of his left hand.

Four years after the battle, Cervantes was captured by Muslim Barbary pirates on his return home. Cervantes spent five years in captivity as a slave in Algiers before being ransomed by the Trinitarian Order and returned to Madrid.

A contemporary of Shakespeare, Miguel de Cervantes is believed to have referenced his exploits in his novel *Don Quixote de La Mancha*, published in 1605, in the First Part, Chapters 39-41.

&

HOLY LEAGUE DISUNITY

After the massive defeat of the Muslims at Lepanto, the Holy League bickered amongst themselves and lost the opportunity to capitalize on the victory. They failed to free the Greek cities, islands, and Constantinople from Muslim domination.

Within six months, the Muslim Ottomans had rebuilt their navy and added eight of the largest ships ever seen in the Mediterranean, though they minimized their confrontations with Christians due to the loss of so many experienced sailors at Lepanto.

In 1574, the Ottomans retook the important city of Tunis from Spanish control.

Just as a century and a half earlier the Muslims took advantage of the political rivalry between the Italian city-states of Venice and Genoa to advance on Constantinople, the Muslims in 1579 took advantage of the political distrust between Spain and France to advance again into the western Mediterranean, recapturing Fez, Morocco from the Portuguese.

The Muslim Ottomans controlled the entire coast of the Mediterranean from the Straits of Gibraltar to Croatia and Slovenia, with the exception of a few strategic Spanish settlements.

∽

SPANISH ARMADA

After the battles against the Muslims in the Mediterranean, Spain turned its attention to stopping the spread of the Protestant Reformation by sending its Armada to capture England and Holland in 1588. With 130 ships, 18,000 soldiers, 7,000 sailors, 1,500 brass guns and 1,000 iron guns, it was planning to transport an additional 30,000 Spanish soldiers from the Netherlands to invade Queen Elizabeth's England.

Spain's battle plan was to board the English ships in combat as they had the Muslim ships at Lepanto, but Sir Francis Drake's smaller, more maneuverable vessels proved difficult to catch. Drake dispersed the Spanish fleet by waiting till night and floating burning ships downwind toward the anchored Spanish ships. In the confusion, the Armada was scattered. A hurricane destroyed two dozen more Spanish ships.

With Spain's Armada destroyed, its dominance of the seas declined, as did its monopoly on colonizing the New World. Soon England, Holland, Sweden, and France began colonies in America.

∽

CAPTAIN JOHN SMITH

Americans are aware of the story of the founding of Jamestown, Virginia, in 1607, where Captain John

Smith was about to be killed by Chief Powhatan but was saved by the pleading of 11-year-old Pocahontas. Smith wrote in his *New England's Trials* (1622):

> God made Pocahontas, the King's daughter the means to deliver me.

The True Travels, Adventures and Observations of Captain John Smith in Europe, Asia, Africa and America, (1630), record that six years before he came to America, John Smith joined the Austrian forces and fought in the "Long War" against the Muslim Ottoman Turks in Hungary.

Mehmed III (1566-1603) became the Ottoman Sultan in 1595 and immediately had his 16 brothers strangled to death to eliminate rivalry to his throne. He raised an army of 60,000 and in 1596 conquered the Hungarian city of Erlau. Mehmed III defeated the Austrian Habsburg and Transylvanian forces at the *Battle of Mezõkeresztes.*

The Complete Works of Captain John Smith, 1580-1631, edited by Philip L. Barbour (Institute of Early American History & Culture, UNC Press, 1986) reported that at age 21, John Smith joined the ranks of Austrian Hapsburg Earl of Meldritch, being assigned to the General of Artillery, Baron Kisell.

The book, *Captain John Smith* by Charles Dudley Warner of *Harper's Magazine* (1881, chap. 2-3), tells of Smith marching with German, French, Austrian and Hungarian troops to fight the Muslims, who had captured Budapest and were invading Lower Hungary, Wallachia, Moldovia, Romania and Transylvania near the Black Sea.

In 1600-1601, during the campaign of Romanian Prince, Michael the Brave, John Smith introduced ingenious battle tactics. When Muslims were besieging the garrison at Oberlymback, Smith devise a method of signaling messages with torches and using gunpowder to create diversions. The resulting victory earned him the rank of captain with a command of 250 horsemen.

Fighting with the Duc de Mercoeur at the siege of Alba Regalis, Smith devised makeshift bombs. Earthen pots filled with gunpowder, musket shot and covered with pitch were catapulted into the city, contributing to the Muslim evacuation.

Muslims had captured the city of Regall, located in a pass between Hungary and Transylvania, "the Turks having ornamented the walls with Christian heads when they captured the fortress."

Smith fought under General Moyses, serving the Prince of Transylvania, Sigismund Bathory, to lead a campaign to regain the city. During a lull in the fighting, the bashaw (officer) of the Turks put out a challenge.

In a "David and Goliath" style contest, the 23-year-old John Smith was chosen to fight. He defeated the bashaw, cutting off his head. To avenge the bashaw's death, another Muslim challenged Smith and lost his head. This happened a third time, resulting in Smith being awarded a "coat-of-arms."

General Moyses, with Captain John Smith, soon recaptured Regall, then Veratis, Solmos and Kapronka. At Weisenberg, Prince Sigismund Bathory conferred on John Smith a shield-of-arms with "three Turks' heads."

John Smith continued in the regiment of Earl Meldritch, fighting in 1602 for Radu Serban to defend Wallachia against invading Turkish Muslims. In the battle, the Earl of Meldritch was killed along with 30,000 soldiers. John Smith was wounded and left for dead:

> Smith among the slaughtered dead bodies, and many a gasping soul with toils and wounds lay groaning among the rest, till being found by the pillagers he was able to live, and perceiving by his armor and habit, his ransom might be better than his death, they led him prisoner with many others.

At Axopolis, Smith was sold with other prisoners at the slave market to Bashaw Bogall, "so chained by the necks in gangs of twenty they marched to Constantinople."

There, Smith was pitied by Bashaw Bogall's mistress, who sent him to her brother, Tymor Bashaw.

Unfortunately, Tymor "diverted all this to the worst cruelty," stripped Smith naked, shaved him bald, riveted an iron ring around his neck, clothed him in goat skins and, as slave of slaves, was given only goat entrails to eat.

Following a beating while he was thrashing in a field, Smith seized the opportunity and killed his master. He hid the body in the straw, put on his master's clothes, took a bag of grain and rode off toward Russia. After 16 days he reached a Muscovite garrison on the River Don, where the iron ring was removed from his neck.

With their help he found his way through Poland back to his troops in Transylvania. After being released from service with a large reward, John Smith traveled through Europe to Morocco in Northern Africa to fight Muslim Barbary pirates in the Mediterranean Sea. In 1605, at the age of 26, he returned to England.

In 1606, Captain John Smith set sail to help found Jamestown, Virginia, the first permanent English colony in North America. In 1614, six years before the Pilgrims arrived, Smith explored Maine and Massachusetts Bay.

In his *Advertisements for Unexperienced Planters*, published in London, 1631, John Smith wrote:

> When I first went to Virginia, I well remember, we did hang an awning (which is an old saile) to three or foure trees to shadow us from the Sunne, our walls were rales of wood, our seats unhewed trees, till we cut plankes, our Pulpit a bar of wood nailed to two neighboring trees, in foule weather we shifted into an old rotten tent, for we had few better…this was our Church, till we built a homely thing like a barne…
>
> We had daily Common Prayer morning and evening, every day two Sermons, and every three moneths the holy Communion, till our Minister died, [Robert Hunt] but our Prayers daily, with an Homily on Sundaies.

PILGRIM SHIP TAKEN BY MUSLIM TURKS

Between 1606-1609, Algerian corsairs captured 466 British and Scotish ships. The Pilgrims, who landed in Massachusetts in 1620, had borrowed money from English adventurers (investors) to finance their voyage and buy supplies. It took forty years worth of beaver skins and dried fish to repay the debt, due to exorbitant interest rates and losses at sea. One such loss happened in the year 1625. Governor William Bradford wrote of the incident in his *History of the Plymouth Settlement 1608-1650* (rendered in Modern English by Harold Paget, 1909, chapter 6, pages 165-167):

The adventurers...sent over two fishing ships...The pinnace was ordered to load with corfish...to bring home to England...and besides she had some 800 lbs. of beaver, as well as other furs, to a good value from the plantation.

The captain seeing so much lading wished to put aboard the bigger ship for greater safety, but Mr. Edward Winslow, their agent in the business, was bound in a bond to send it to London in the small ship...The captain of the big ship...towed the small ship at his stern all the way over. So they went joyfully home together and had such fine weather that he never cast her off till they were well within the England channel, almost in sight of Plymouth.

But even there she was unhapply taken by a Turkish man-of-war and carried off to Saller [Morocco], where the captain and crew were made slaves and many of the beaver skins were sold for 4d. a piece. Thus all their hopes were dashed and the joyful news they meant to carry home was turned to heavy tidings... In the big ship Captain Myles Standish... arrived at a very bad time...a plague very deadly in London...The friendly adventurers were so reduced by their losses last year, and **now by the ship taken by the Turks...that all trade was dead.**

Giles Milton wrote in *White Gold: The Extraordinary Story of Thomas Pellow and North Africa's One Million European Slaves* (UK: Hodder & Stoughton Ltd, 2004), that Muslim corsair pirates raided England in 1625, even sailing up the Thames River.

Attacking the coast of Cornwall, they captured 60 villagers at Mount's Bay and 80 at Looe. Muslims took Lundy Island in Bristol Channel and raised the standard of Islam. By the end of 1625, over 1,000 English subjects were sent to the slave markets of Sale, Morocco.

Between July 4-19, 1627, Algerian and Ottoman Muslim pirates, led by Murat Reis the Younger, raided Iceland, carrying into slavery an estimated 400 from the cities of Reykjavik, Austurland and Vestmannaeyjar. One captured girl, who had been made a slave concubine in Algeria, was rescued back by King Christian IV of Denmark.

On June 20, 1631, the entire village of Baltimore, Ireland was captured by Muslim pirates, led by Murat Reis the Younger. Only two ever returned. (see: Des Ekin's *The Stolen Village: Baltimore and the Barbary Pirates*, O'Brien Press, 2006). Thomas Osborne Davis wrote in his poem, "The Sack of Baltimore" (1895):

> The yell of 'Allah!' breaks above the shriek
> and roar; O'blessed God! the Algerine is lord
> of Baltimore.

Robert C. Davis' book, *Christian Slaves, Muslim Masters: White Slavery in the Mediterranean, the Barbary Coast and Italy 1500-1800* (Palgrave Macmillian, 2003), gives the record Francis Knight, an Englishman who had been kidnapped and enslaved in Algiers, then made a slave on Algerian galleys for seven years:

> January the 16th day, in the year before
> nominated [1631]; I arrived in [Algiers,] that Citie
> fatall to all Christians, and the butchery of
> mankind...my condolation is for the loss of many

Christians, taken from their parents and countries, of all sorts and sexes. Some in Infancy, both by Land and by Sea, being forced to abuses (most incorrigible flagitions) not onely so, but bereaft of Christian Religion, and means of grace and repentence. How many thousands of the Nazarian nations have beene and are continually lost by that monster, what rational creature can be ignorant of?

In the 16th and 17th centuries, more Europeans were carried away south across the Mediterranean into the Muslim slavery of North Africa, than Africans who were purchased at Muslim slave markets and carried west across the Atlantic.

Upon arrival in North Africa, infidel Christian slaves were jeered and pelted with stones by children as they were marched to the auction block. Men were made galley slaves and women were made servants or paraded naked and sold as sex slaves. The whiter the skin, the higher the bid.

Robert Davis described the end of the 17th century:

> The Italian peninsula had by then been prey to the Barbary corsairs for two centuries or more, and its coastal populations had largely withdrawn into walled hilltop villages or larger towns like Rimini, abandoning miles of once populous shoreline.

The Calabrian coast suffered 700 captured in 1636, 1,000 in 1639, and 4,000 in 1644. Some coastal areas lost their entire child-bearing population. Muslims corsair raiders desecrated churches and stole church bells to silence the distintive sound of Christianity.

By 1640, hundreds of English ships and over 3,000 British subjects were enslaved in Algiers and 1,500 in Tunis. In three centuries, over a million Europeans were enslaved by Muslim Barbary Pirates.

Giles Milton wrote of Thomas Pellow, born in an English fishing village in 1704.

At the age of 11, Pellow was captured by Muslim Barbary Pirates when his uncle's ship was taken. He became property of Sultan Moulay Ismail, and, along with 25,000 other white slaves, was put to work building the Sultan's grand palace in Meknes, called the "Versailles of Morocco."

Sultan Ismail ordered soldiers to push Christian slaves off a high wall they were building because they did not synchronize their hammer strokes. He beat his slaves "in the cruelest manner imaginable, to try if they were hard" and murdered some for "hiding pieces of bread." He had 500 wives, mostly captured European women, who bore him a record 1,042 children.

An account of Sultan Moulay Ismail, titled A Journey to Mequinez (Meknes), written by John Windus (published in London, 1825), stated:

> His trembling court assemble, which consists of...blacks, whites, tawnies and his favourite Jews, all barefooted...
>
> He is...known by his very looks...and sometimes the colour of the habit that he wears, yellow being observed to be his killing colour; from all of which they calculate whether they may hope to live twenty-four hours longer..."
>
> When he goes out of town...he will be attended by fifteen or twenty thousand blacks on horseback, with whom he now and then diverts himself at (by throwing) the lance...
>
> His travelling utensils are two or three guns, a sword or two, and two lances, because one broke once while he was murdering;
>
> His boys carry short Brazil sticks, knotted cords for whipping, a change of clothes to shift when bloody, and a hatchet, two of which he took in a Portuguese ship, and the first time they were bought to him, killed a man without any provocation, to try if they were good.

Witnessing tortures, beheadings and forced conversions to Islam, Pellew escaped after 23 years. A distant relative, Sir Edward Pellew, led the British fleet to bombard Algiers in 1816, freeing thousands of slaves.

∽

TAJ MAHAL

In 1648, the Muslim Mughal Emperor, Shah Jahan, completed the Taj Mahal in India, a mausoleum for his favorite of three wives. Intricately engraved with verses from the *Qur'an*, Shah Jahan was so impressed with the architectural masterpiece that the tradition is he cut off the hands of the workers so no building rivaling its beauty could be built.

∽

OTTOMAN TURK EXPANSION

The Muslim Ottoman Empire expanded to its furthest limits in the 17th century. In 1663, under Sultan Mehmed IV, the vizer (commander) of the Ottoman Grand Fleet of the Aegean Sea was Mustafa.

Mustafa captured the Greek Island of Crete in what was possibly the longest siege in history, from 1648 to 1669. Mustafa commanded troops against Poland in 1672 and captured the Cossak region of southern Ukraine.

∽

SECOND SIEGE OF VIENNA

In 1683, Mustafa led 138,000 Muslim Ottoman Turks to surround Vienna, Austria, defended by only 11,000 Hapsburg soldiers. Sultan Mehmed IV sent a message to Austrian King Leopold I:

> Await us in your residence...so we can decapitate you.

For two months, attackers starved Vienna's defenders. Pope Innocent XI appealed to Polish King Jan Sobieski, who then left his country undefended and led a coalition of 81,000 Polish-Austrian-German forces to Vienna's rescue on September 11, 1683. In a surprise move, at five o'clock in the afternoon, September 12, Jan Sobieski charged directly into the Muslim army, leading four husaria cavalry groups.

The Turkish battle line suddenly broke and Turks scattered in confusion. Just thirty minutes after the battle began, Sobieski entered into Mustafa's deserted tent.

The Pope hailed Jan Sobieski as the "Savior of Western European civilization" and his statue was erected in Gdansk, Poland. The *Battle of Vienna* ended the 300-year continuous effort of Muslims to conquer Europe. It also cost Mustafa his life. The commander of the Janissaries ordered Mustafa strangled with a silk rope and his head brought to Sultan Mehmed IV in a velvet bag - the standard punishment for high-ranking Ottoman officials who fell from favor. Mustafa's last words were "Make sure you tie the knot right."

Hilaire Belloc (1870-1953) wrote in *The Great Heresies* (1938):

> Less than 100 years before the American War of Independence a Mohammedan army was threatening to overrun and destroy Christian civilization...Vienna was almost taken and only saved by the Christian army under the command of the King of Poland on a date that ought to be among the most famous in history - September 11, 1683.

After 16 years of fighting, Austrian Hapsburgs with German, Polish, and Serbian troops, freed Neuhausel, Gran, Budapest, Mohacs, Belgrade, Hungary, Ukraine, parts of Greece and Transylvania, forcing the Sultan to sign the Treaty of Karlowitz, 1699.

COFFEE

Muslims fled the *Battle of Vienna* in panic, leaving behind bags of black beans. A Turkish prisoner showed them how to cook the beans into a drink called "coffee" or "kahve," derived from the Arabic word "kafir," which means "infidel," as the beans came from the infidel African countries, such as Ethiopia.

In 1683, Polish officer Jerzy Franciszek Kulczycki opened Vienna's first coffee house and soon coffee became popular across Central Europe, fueling the industrial revolution. The legend is that Pope Clement VIII was petitioned to declare coffee "the drink of the devil" due to its association with Muslims, but the Pontiff tasted it and stated: "This devil's drink is so good, we should cheat the devil by baptizing it."

Another story is that in 1683, Capuchin Franciscan friar, Blessed Marco d'Aviano, was sent to encourage the troops of Vienna. When the confiscated coffee beans tasted bitter, Friar Marco d'Aviano sweetened the drink with honey and milk, thus creating "Cappucino."

◈

CROISSANT

In *Larousse Gastronomique,* edited Alfred Gottschalk, 1938, and Jenifer Harvey Lang, 1988 (NY: Crown, p. 338), the croissant pastry dates to the Turkish siege of Vienna, 1683, or siege of Budapest, 1686:

> The Turks were besieging the city. To reach the center of town, they dug underground passages. Bakers, working during the night, heard the noise made by the Turks and gave the alarm.

> The assailants were repulsed and the bakers who had saved the city were granted the privilege of making a special pastry which had to take the form of a crescent in memory of the emblem on the Ottoman flag.

Alan Davidson wrote in *Oxford Companion to Food* (1999, p. 232):

> According to one of a group of legends...a baker of the 17th century, working through the

night at a time when his city (either Vienna in 1683 or Budapest in 1686) was under siege by the Turks, heard faint underground rumbling sounds which, on investigation, proved to be caused by a Turkish attempt to invade the city by tunneling under the walls.

The tunnel was blown up. The baker asked no reward other than the exclusive right to bake crescent-shaped pastries commemorating the incident, the crescent being the symbol of Islam. He was duly rewarded in this way and the croissant was born.

In the French language, the word for croissant is "Viennoiserie." The Romanian word for croissant is "cornulet" which means "little crescent."

≤≈

BELGRADE & SERBIAN MIGRATION

Belgrade is the capital of Serbia, located at the confluence of the Sava and Danube Rivers. Significant trade was carried on these rivers, resulting in Belgrade being one of the most important cities in Europe.

The largest Serbian Christian Church is the Temple of Saint Sava, named in honor of the first Serbian Archbishop, son of Serbia's founder. Saint Sava died in Bulgaria in 1235, and his remains were moved to Serbia.

In 1521, Belgrade was captured by Muslim Ottoman Turks, led by Suleiman the Magnificent, who largely razed the city to the ground. In 1594, the Serbian Orthodox Christian population tried to get free, but their rebellion was crushed. Muslims burned churches and unearthed remains of their beloved Saint Sava and burnt them at the stake on Vracar hill.

In 1691, Austria freed Belgrade, but the Muslim Ottomans recaptured it and razed the city's buildings. Thousands of Serbian Christians fled, led by the Orthodox Patriarch to the Austrian Hapsburg Empire in the first "Great Serbian Migration."

৽
ATHENS' ACROPOLIS

The Parthenon, built atop the Acropolis hill, is the most well recognized location in Athens, Greece. Complete in 432 BC, it was visited by the Apostle Paul in 54 AD. The Parthenon was turned into a Byzantine Christian Church in 450 AD and a Roman Catholic Church in 1204. In 1458, Muslims Turks turned it into a Mosque in which they stored gunpowder and weapons. In 1687, when Venetian General Francesco Morosini helped free Athens from Muslim occupation, a canon ball hit the Parthenon, causing the gunpowder to explode.

৽
PETER THE GREAT

In 1696, Czar Peter the Great of Russia (1672-1725) captured the fortress of Azov on the Black Sea from Muslim Ottomans. Peter then tried unsuccessfully to rally European powers to fight the Ottoman Turks.

৽
JAMES OGLETHORPE

French King Louis XIV made a treaty with the Turks against the League of Augsburg-King William III, King Leopold I, King Charles II and other princes. The Turks took advantage and recaptured Belgrade. In 1716-17, Prince Eugene of Savoy freed Belgrade. His aid-de-camp was a young British soldier named James Oglethorpe. Afterwards, James Oglethorpe returned to England, entered Parliament, campaigned for prison reform, and in 1732, founded the colony of Georgia in America for poor debtors and Protestant refugees.

৽
JOHN WESLEY

When James Oglethorpe settled the colony of Georgia, Charles Wesley accompanied him as secretary. His brother, John Wesley served as the colony's

Anglican minister, and later founded the Methodist movement. As recorded in *The Doctrine of Original Sin* (*Works*, 1841, ix. 205), John Wesley wrote:

> Ever since the religion of Islam appeared in the world, the espousers of it…have been as wolves and tigers to all other nations, rending and tearing all that fell into their merciless paws, and grinding them with their iron teeth; that numberless cities are raised from the foundation, and only their name remaining; that many countries, which were once as the garden of God, are now a desolate wilderness; and that so many once numerous and powerful nations are vanished from the earth!
>
> Such was, and is at this day, the rage, the fury, the revenge, of these destroyers of human kind.

᷍

SECOND SERBIAN MIGRATION

In 1739, Muslims recaptured Belgrade. The Orthodox Patriach led thousands to the Austrian Hapsburg Empire in the "Second Great Serbian Migration." In 1791, Belgrade was freed from Muslims for a third and final time. In 1999, President Clinton led a NATO attack against the Christian Serbian capital of Belgrade and many ancient churches were destroyed.

᷍

JONATHAN EDWARDS

Jonathan Edwards, first President of Princeton, wrote in *A History of the Work of Redemption*, 1739:

> Those mighty kingdoms of Antichrist and Mohammed...have trampled the world under foot...The two great works of the devil which... are...his Anti-Christian and Mahometan kingdoms...swallowed up the Ancient Roman Empire...Satan's Mohometan kingdom [swallowing up] the Eastern Empire.

∾

PERSIAN SHI'A SACK DELHI

In 1739, Persian Shi'a Muslims sacked Delhi, ending the Mughal Muslim power in India. Persians created the modern state of Iran in 1921 under Reza Khan.

∾

VOLTAIRE

Voltaire wrote the play *Mahomet*, 1746, explaining to Pope Benedict XIV, August 17, 1745, it was:

>...written in opposition to the founder of a false and barbarous sect to whom could I with more propriety inscribe a satire on the cruelty and errors of a false prophet.

∾

MONTESQUIEU

Montesquieu wrote (*Spirit of the Laws*, 1748, Bk 24):

>Moderate government is most agreeable to the Christian Religion, and a despotic government to the Mahometan...
>The Mahometan Religion, which speaks only by the sword, acts still upon men with that destructive spirit with which it was founded.

∾

THE BLACK HOLE OF CALCUTTA

In 1756, the Muslim ruler of Bengal captured the British East India trading post-Fort William. The 69 British soldiers were forced into a tiny, 14x18 foot windowless cell and left overnight. The next morning, 43 of them were dead. The incident was called "the Black Hole of Calcutta."

∾

FIRST RUSSO-TURKISH WAR 1768-1774

Catherine the Great of Russia (1729-1796), and her General, Grigori Potemkin (1739-1791), annexed from

Muslim Turkish control the Crimea, an area on the northern shore of the Black Sea. The *Battle of Chesma*, July 5-7, 1770, was the most disastrous defeat for the Ottoman navy since the *Battle of Lepanto* in 1571. At the same time, 38,000 Russians defeated 80,000 Muslim Tatar cavalry and infantry in the *Battle of Larga*. Sultan Mustfa III (1717-1774), who had given himself the title of Cihangir "World Conquerer," is said to have died upon receiving the news.

∽

MUSLIM BARBARY PIRATES

President Obama stated in Cairo, June 4, 2009: "The first nation to recognize my country was Morocco." For centuries, Muslim pirates of Morocco, Tripoli, Tunis and Algiers - countries along North Africa's Barbary Coast, captured thousands of Europeans at sea. Catholic Orders, such as the Trinitarians (Mathurins), had as their sole mission the collecting of alms from across Europe to ransom captives from Muslim dungeons.

European countries, such as England and France, arranged to pay the Muslim Barbary Pirates an annual tribute, equivalent to millions of dollars, to bribe Muslims to leave their countries' ships alone. American vessels were protected by British tribute until the conclusion of the Revolutionary War in 1783. For a few years, American ships were protected under France's tribute.

Finally, Muslim Barbary Pirates insisted the U.S. pay its own tribute. In 1784, Barbary pirates captured the U.S. schooner *Maria*. The crew and passengers were paraded through the streets of Algiers, jeered as "infidels" and thrown in prison. In 1785, Muslims of Algiers captured two American ships and held their crews as prisoners, demanding $60,000 in ransom.

Muslim ransoms varied from $300 for a seaman to $1,000 for a captain. Tripoli offered a short-term peace for a $66,000 plus commissions and a long-term peace for $160,000 plus commissions. Similar tributes were demanded by other Muslim nations, totaling $1.3 million. Paying a tribute, though, did not guarantee peace. (Gary DeMar, *America's 200 Year War with Islamic Terrorism-The Strange Case of the Treaty of Tripoli*, www.AmericanVision.org)

To arrange a ransom, the U.S. Ministers in France, Jefferson and Adams, consulted with the Catholic Order of Mathurins, an order later disbanded during the anti-clerical French Revolution. Congress directed Jefferson and Adams to negotiate a tribute of $80,000, borrowed from Dutch bankers.

∽

JEFFERSON'S RESPONSE TO ISLAM

Jefferson asked Tripoli ambassador Abdrahaman what the U.S. had done to provoke the Muslims. In *American Sphinx-The Character of Thomas Jefferson* (Vintage, 1998), Joseph J. Ellis recorded Jefferson's dialog:

> Several muslim countries along the North African coast had established the tradition of plundering the ships of European and American merchants in the western Mediterranean and eastern Atlantic, capturing the crews and then demanding ransom from the respective governments for their release.
>
> In a joint message to their superiors in Congress, **Adams and Jefferson described the audacity of these terrorist attacks, pirates leaping onto defenseless ships with daggers clenched in their teeth.**
>
> They had asked the ambassador from Tripoli, Adams and Jefferson explained, **on what grounds these outrageous acts of unbridled savagery could be justified:**
>
> **"The Ambassador answered us that it was founded on the laws of the prophet, that it was written in their *Qur'an*, that all nations who should not have acknowledged their islam's authority were sinners, that it was their right and duty to make war upon them**

wherever they could be found, and to make
slaves of all they could take as prisoners,
and every Musselman who should be
slain in battle was sure to go to Paradise."

∿

JOHN PAUL JONES

In 1788, during the 2nd Russo-Turkish War (1787-1792), Jefferson arranged for John Paul Jones (1747-1792), the "Father of the American Navy," to fight for Russia's Catherine the Great against the Muslim Ottoman navy.

In his *Narrative of the Campaign of the Liman*, John Paul Jones wrote of victoriously sailing his flagship *Vladimir* against the Turks by the Black Sea's Dnieper River. Shortly before he died, Jones was appointed as a U.S. Consul in Paris to negotiate the release of captured U.S. Navy officers held in the dungeons of Algiers.

∿

NAPOLEON INVADES EGYPT

Juan Cole wrote in *Napoleon's Egypt-Invading the Middle East* (NY: Palgrave MacMillian, 2007), of how France had been in a treaty with the Ottoman Empire and planned to send artillery personnel to upgrade their military, including a young artillery officer, Napoleon.

Napoleon resigned in protest, as he wanted to fight, not train others. The French Army relented and Napoleon soon won fame through his brilliant use of artillery in his Italian campaign. One can only speculate how history would have been different if Napoleon's artillery expertise had been used by the Muslim Ottoman Empire.

After the French Revolution began in 1789, the idea of equality and liberty found its way to the slaves in the prosperous French Colony of Haiti. This led to a slave rebellion in 1791. Later, fearing a similar rebellion, Napoleon sold the Louisana Territory to the United States. After the loss of Haiti, France wanted to replace its tropical colony, so Napoleon sailed to colonize Egypt, thus challenging England's trade with India.

Napoleon first stopped at the Christian held Island of Malta asking for safe harbor. Once inside, he captured the Island and evicted the Knights of Saint John who had been keeping the Muslim Barbary Pirates in check. Napoleon then invaded Ottoman Egypt on July 1, 1798, which broke France's treaty with the Ottoman Empire and renewed Muslim pirate attacks on French vessels. Within weeks of being in Egypt, Napoleon's skilled use of artillery defeated the Muslim Mamluk cavalry.

Napoleon was unable to bring "democracy" to Egypt as there were no Arabic words for such concepts - the land being ruled for centuries by the sword. When British Admiral Horatio Nelson destroyed Napoleon's fleet in the *Battle of the Nile*, August 2, 1798, Napoleon was forced to accommodate the Muslims, but this was perceived as weakness and led to repeated uprisings. He abandoned Egypt a year later.

∽

FIRST BARBARY WAR

In 1793, Muslim Barbary pirates captured the U.S. cargo ship *Polly*. The ship was plundered and the crew was imprisoned. The Muslim captain justified their brutal treatment: "for your history and superstition in believing in a man who was crucified by the Jews and disregarding the true doctrine of God's last and greatest prophet, Mohammed."

In 1795, Muslim Barbary Pirates of Algiers captured 115 American sailors. The United States was forced to pay nearly a million dollars in ransom. A Treaty of Tripoli in 1798 failed. (Lines of this treaty are often quoted out of context by secularists.) In 1801, the year Jefferson became President, Muslim Barbary Pirates demanded $225,000, plus an annual tribute of $25,000. When Jefferson refused, the Pasha (Lord) of Tripoli declared war. This was the first war the U.S. was in after becoming a nation.

Jefferson sent U.S. frigates to the Mediterranean to protect American shipping.

In his First Annual Message, December 8, 1801, Thomas Jefferson stated:

> Tripoli, the least considerable of the Barbary States, had come forward with demands unfounded either in right or in compact, and had permitted itself to (announce) war on our failure to comply before a given day.
>
> The style of the demand admitted but one answer. I sent a small squadron of frigates into the Mediterranean, with assurances to that power of our sincere desire to remain in peace, but with orders to protect our commerce against the threatened attack.
>
> The measure was seasonable and salutary.
>
> The Bey (lord) had already declared war. His cruisers were out. Two had arrived at Gibraltar. Our commerce in the Mediterranean was blockaded and that of the Atlantic in peril.
>
> The arrival of our squadron dispelled the danger. One of the Tripolitan cruisers having fallen in with and engaged the small schooner *Enterprise*, commanded by Lieutenant Sterret, which had gone as a tender to our larger vessels, was captured, after a heavy slaughter of her men, without the loss of a single one on our part.
>
> The bravery exhibited by our citizens on that element will, I trust, be a testimony to the world.

On December 29, 1803, the new 36-gun *USS Philadelphia* ran aground. Muslims imprisoned Captain William Bainbridge and his 307 man crew for 18 months. To keep this powerful ship from being used by Muslim pirates, Lieut. Stephen Decatur, in what was described as the "most bold and daring act of the age," sailed his ship, *Intrepid*, February 16, 1804, into the Muslim harbor and set the *USS Philadelphia* ablaze.

After negotiations, the surviving 296 crewmen of the *USS Philadelphia* were released in exchanged for $60,000 and 89 Muslim prisoners taken in skirmishes.

The 11 missing U.S. sailors of the original 307 crewmen included 6 who had died in captivity and 5 who converted to Islam, much to the annoyance of the rest of the crew. When the Bashaw of Tripoli offered the 5 converts the choice of staying in Tripoli as Muslims or returning to America, 4 decided to renounce Islam and return home. The insulted Bashaw ordered them taken away. Horror covered their faces as guards removed them and they were never seen again.

In Hadith al-Bukhari "Mohammed said, 'Whoever changes his Islamic religion, kill him.'" Jefferson owned a *Qur'an* to understand the enemy. He sent Marines to capture Tripoli, led by Commodores Edward Preble, John Rogers and Captain William Eaton.

The Muslim's terrorist attacks were stopped, giving rise to **the Marine Anthem: "From the Halls of Montezuma to the shores of Tripoli..."** The curved Marine sword is from the confiscated Muslim scimitars, called **"mamluke" swords.** Marines were called **"leathernecks"** for the wide leather straps worn around their necks to prevent being beheaded, as Sura 47:4, states: "When you meet the infidel in the battlefield, strike off their heads."

◈

2ND BARBARY WAR 1812-1816

Muslims broke their treaty and in 1815 the Second Barbary War began. Congress authorized naval action and, together with six European countries, fought against Morocco, Algiers, Tunis and Tripoli.

Commodore Stephen Decatur, hero of the War of 1812, and Commodore William Bainbridge, led ten warships to the Mediterranean.

Under Decatur's guns, the Dey (ruler) of Algiers was forced to stop demanding tribute from other countries, to pay reparations for damages and forced to release American prisoners. Similar promises were forced from Tunis and Tripoli.

Of the negotiations, Frederick C. Leiner wrote in *The End of the Barbary Terror-America's 1815 War Against the Pirates of North Africa* (Oxford University Press):

> Commodore Stephen Decatur and diplomat William Shaler withdrew to consult in private...**The Algerians were believed to be masters of duplicity, willing to make agreements and break them as they found convenient...**
> Commodore Stephen Decatur and Captain William Bainbridge both recognized that the peace could only be kept by force or the threat of force.

Muslims again broke their treaty, resulting in the Dutch and British, under Sir Edward Pellew, bombarding Algiers in 1816, forcing them to release 3,000 European prisoners.

Algiers again renewed its piracy and slave-taking, causing the British to bombard them again in 1824. It was not until 1830, when the French conquered Algiers, did Muslim Barbary Piracy come to cease.

Theodore Roosevelt wrote in his book *Fear God and Take Your Own Part* (NY: George Doran Co., 1916, p. 351):

> Centuries have passed since any war vessel of a civilized power has shown such **ruthless brutality toward noncombatants,** and especially toward women and children.
> **The Muslim pirates of the Barbary Coast behaved at times in similar fashion until the civilized nations joined in suppressing them.**

❧

JOHN QUINCY ADAMS - MUSLIM TREATIES

John Quincy Adams wrote "Essays dealing with the Russo-Turkish War and on Greece."

These were published in *The American Annual Register for 1827-28-29* (New York: 1830). Andrew G.

Bosto referenced Chapters X-XIV of Adams' work in his article "John Quincy Adams Knew Jihad" (FrontPageMagazine.com, Sept. 29, 2004), as did Samuel Flagg Bemis in *John Quincy Adams and the Foundations of American Foreign Policy* (NY: 1949, pp. 571-572), and Lynn H. Parsons in *John Quincy Adams-A Bibliography* (Westport, CT: 1993, p. 41, entry #194) John Quincy Adams wrote of Muslim treaties:

The **victorious may be appeased by a false and delusive promise of peace** and the faithful follower of the prophet may submit to the imperious necessities of defeat, **but the command to propagate the Moslem creed by the sword is always obligatory when it can be made effective...**

The **commands of the prophet may be performed alike, by fraud or by force.**

Of Mahometan good faith, we have had memorable examples ourselves.

When our gallant Commodore Stephen Decatur had chastised the pirate of Algiers, till he was ready to renounce his claim of tribute from the United States, he signed a treaty to that effect: **but the treaty was drawn up in the Arabic language, as well as in our own; and our negotiators, unacquainted with the language of the Koran, signed the copies of the treaty, in both languages, not imagining that there was any difference between them.**

Within a year the Dey (Omar Bashaw) demands, under penalty of the renewal of the war, an indemnity in money for the frigate taken by Decatur; our Consul demands the foundation of this pretension; and **the Arabic copy of the treaty, signed by himself is produced, with an article stipulating the indemnity, foisted into it, in direct opposition to the treaty as it had been concluded.**

The **arrival of Commodore Isaac Chauncey, with a squadron before Algiers, silenced the fraudulent claim of the Dey**, and he signed a new treaty in which it was abandoned;

but he disdained to conceal his intentions; My power, **said he, has been wrested from my hands; draw ye the treaty at your pleasure, and I will sign it; but beware of the moment, when I shall recover my power, for with that moment, your treaty shall be waste paper.**

He avowed what they always practised, and would without scruple have practised himself.

Such is the spirit, which governs the hearts of men, to whom **treachery and violence are taught as principles of religion.** (JQA, Essays on Turks, p. 274-275)

JQA examined the Muslim treaty with Russia:

Had it been possible for a sincere and honest peace to be maintained between the Osmanli and his Christian neighbors, then would have been the time to establish it in good faith. **But the treaty was no sooner made than broken. It never was carried into effect by the Turkish government...**

From the time when the disaster of Navarino had been made known to him, the **Reis Effendi [Ottoman diplomat to Russia] had assumed the tone of the aggrieved party,** and made formal demands of indemnity and the punishment of the offending admirals...

Upon the departure of the ambassadors, the Sultan, who must have been...preparing...for that event, immediately determined upon...a war with Russia...**and a dallying attempt to protract the negotiation and gain time of preparation for the conflict.** (JQA, Essays on Turks, p. 276, 298)

JQA compared Muslim correspondence:

[Reis Effendi, Ottoman diplomat to Russia, wrote] "The Sublime Porte (Ottoman court) has...**no other desire or wish than to preserve peace**...and that the event in question has been brought about entirely by the act of the said minister, we hope that you will endeavor, to do every occasion, to fulfill the duties of friendship."
But precisely at the time when this...gently expostulary epistle was dispatched for St. Petersburg, another state paper was issued, addressed by the Sultan...sent to the Pashas of all the provinces, **calling on all the faithful Mussulmen of the empire to come forth and "fight for their religion, and their country, against the infidel despisers of the Prophet."**

The comparison of these two documents with each other, will afford the most perfect illustration of the Ottoman faith, as well as of their temper towards Russia. (JQA, Essays on Turks, p. 299-300)

John Quincy Adams studied Muslim diplomacy:

The Hatti Sheriff commenced..."It is well known **(said the Sultan) to almost every person, that if the Mussulmen naturally hate the infidels,** the infidels, on their part, are the enemies of the Mussulmen: that Russia, more especially, bears a particular hatred to Islamism, and that she is the principal enemy of the Sublime Porte."
This appeal to the natural hatred of the Mussulmen towards the infidels is in just accordance with the precepts of the Koran. The document does not attempt to disguise it, nor even pretend that the enmity of those whom it styles the infidels, is any other than the necessary consequence of the hatred borne by the Mussulmen to them- the paragraph itself, is **a forcible example of the contrasted character of the two religions.**

The fundamental doctrine of the Christian religion, is the extirpation of hatred from the human heart. It forbids the exercise of it, even towards enemies. There is no denomination of Christians, which denies or misunderstands this doctrine...

It has mitigated the horrors of war - it has softened the features of slavery - it has humanized the intercourse of social life. The unqualified acknowledgment of a duty does not, indeed, suffice to insure its performance.

Hatred is yet a passion, but too powerful upon the hearts of Christians. **Yet they cannot indulge it, except by the sacrifice of their principles, and the conscious violation of their duties.** No state paper from a Christian hand, could, without trampling the precepts of its Lord and Master, have commenced by an open proclamation of hatred to any portion of the human race.

The Ottoman lays it down as the foundation of his discourse. (JQA, Essays on Turks, p. 299)

JQA wrote on the Sultan's appeal to fanaticism:

The last **appeal of the Sultan to the fanaticism** of his people, and to the protection of his prophet, has been vain. He told them, that since the happy time of their great prophet, the faithful Mussulmen had never taken into consideration the numbers of the infidels.

He reminded them, too truly reminded them, how often they had put millions of Christians to the sword; how many states and provinces they had thus **conquered, sword in hand.** (JQA, Essays on Turks, p. 302)

The Ottoman Sultan stated, as quoted by Adams:

All infidels are but one nation...This war must be considered purely a religious and

national war. Let all the faithful, rich or poor, great or little, know, that to fight is a duty with us...Let us execute zealously the duties which the honor of Islamism imposes on us - let us unite our efforts, and labor, body and soul, for the support of religion, until the Day of Judgment. **Mussulmen have no other means of working out salvation in this world and the next.** (JQA, Essays on Turks, p. 303)

JQA wrote on Christians' fate in Muslim lands:

Those provinces are the abode of ten millions of human beings, two thirds of whom are Christians, groaning under the intolerable oppression of less than three millions of Turks. Those provinces are in some of the fairest regions of the earth.

They were Christian countries, subdued during the conquering period of the Mahometan imposture, by the ruthless scymetar of the Ottoman race; and under their iron yoke, have been gradually **dwindling in population, and sinking into barbarism.**

The time of their redemption is at hand. (JQA, Essays on Turks, p. 303)

JQA showed Muslim duplicity with Russia:

With regard to the Hatti Sheriff of the 20th of December, **summoning the whole Ottoman nation to arms against Russia,** the Sultan now thinks proper to say, that it was only a proclamation which the Sublime Porte, for certain reasons, circulated in its states; an internal transaction, of which the Sublime Porte alone knows the motives, and that **the language held by a government to its own subjects cannot be a ground for another government to pick a quarrel with it** - especially, as the Grand Vizier had, immediately after the departure of the Russian envoy, written a letter to the prime minister of Russia, declaring the desire of the Sublime Porte to maintain peace.

That if Russia had conceived suspicions, from the Sultan's address to his subjects, she might have applied amicably to the Porte to ascertain the truth and clear up her doubts. (JQA, Essays on Turks, p. 311)

JQA criticized Britain's King George IV:

In the king's speech...opening of the session of Parliament, on the 29th of January, he said that, "for several years a contest had been carried on between the Ottoman Porte, and the inhabitants of the Greek provinces and islands, which **had been marked on each side, by excesses revolting to humanity.**" (JQA, Essays on Turks, p. 304)

Still more extraordinary was it to the ears of Christendom **to hear a British king**, in a speech to his parliament, **style the execrable and sanguinary head of the Ottoman race, his ancient ally...**But the last member of the paragraph from his majesty's speech, which we have quoted, to those accustomed to **the mystifications of royal speeches** and diplomatic defiances, explained these apparent disparities.

He declares the great objects to which all his efforts have been directed...are the termination of the contest between the hostile parties; the permanent settlement of their future relations to each other, and maintenance of the repose of Europe, upon the basis on which it has rested since the last general peace. (JQA, Essays on Turks, p. 305)

JQA decried the King's fear to confront the enemy:

And where is the protection to the commerce of his majesty's subjects! And **where is the determination to launch all the thunders of Britain at half a dozen skulking piratical cockboats, driven by the desperation of famine** to seek the subsistence of plunder, assigned in the protocols, the treaty and the communications to the Ottoman Porte, as the great objects of his majesty's interference between a legitimate sovereign and his revolted rayahs?...

In all these documents, issuing from the profound and magnanimous policy of the British warrior statesman, nothing is more remarkable, than the more than stoical apathy with which they regard the cause for which the Greeks are contending; the more than epicurean indifference with which they **witness the martyrdom of a whole people, perishing in the recovery of their religion and liberty...**

The royal speech of January, 1828 indicates that...the government of **George IV, had outwitted themselves, and were the dupes of their own policy.** It presents the **singular spectacle of a sovereign,** wincing at the success of his own measures, and repining at the triumph of his own arms.

From that time the partialities of England in favor of the ancient ally, have been little disguised; and the disposition to take sides with the Porte has only been controlled, by the unwelcome necessity of adhering to the faith of treaties...**The Hatti Sheriff (made) an appeal to the Ottoman people, a bold and candid avowal of the precepts of the Koran.** (JQA, Essays on Turks, pp. 306-309)

John Quincy Adams wrote on Greek Revolution:

If ever insurrection was holy in the eyes of God, such was that of the Greeks against their Mahometan oppressors. Yet for six long years, they were suffered to be overwhelmed by the whole mass of the Ottoman power; cheered only by the sympathies of all the civilized world, but **without a finger raised to sustain or relieve them by the Christian governments of Europe; while the sword of extermination, instinct with the spirit of the Koran, was passing in merciless horror over the classical regions of Greece,** the birth-place of philosophy, of poetry, of eloquence, of all the arts that embellish, and all the sciences that dignify the human character. The monarchs of Austria, of France, and England, inflexibly persisted in seeing in the Greeks, only revolted subjects against a lawful sovereign.

The ferocious Turk eagerly seized upon this absurd concession, and while sweeping with his besom (broom) of destruction over the Grecian provinces, answered every insinuation of interest in behalf of that suffering people, by assertions of the unqualified rights of sovereignty, and by triumphantly retorting upon the legitimates of Europe, the consequences naturally flowing from their own perverted maxims. (JQA, Essays on Turks, p. 278)

John Quincy Adams referenced the butchery:

This pretended discovery of a plot between Russia and the Greeks is introduced to preface an exulting reference to **the unhallowed butchery of the Greek Patriarch and Priests, on Easter day of 1822, at Constantinople, and to the merciless desolation of Greece, which it calls "doing justice by the sword"** to a great number of rebels of the Morea, of Negropont, of Acarnania, Missolonghi, Athens, and other parts of the continent...**During several years, considerable forces, both naval and military, had been sent against the Greeks**. (JQA, Essays on Turks, p. 301)

∽

HOPE OF ARMENIAN INDEPENDENCE

An incident lingering in world memory is that of Armenia. When the Ottoman Empire declined in the late 1800's, Greece, Romania, Serbia, and other Eastern European countries fought for independence. Armenia being locatied in the heart of Turkey made independence too difficult. Sultan Abdul Hamid killed over 100,000 Armenians between 1894 and 1896.

∽

PRESIDENT CHESTER A. ARTHUR

President Chester A. Arthur wrote in his First Annual Message to Congress, December 6, 1881:

The insecurity of life and property in many parts of Turkey has given rise to correspondence with the Porte looking particularly to the better protection of American missionaries in the Empire. **The condemned murderer of the eminent missionary Dr. Justin W. Parsons has not yet been executed,** although this Government has repeatedly demanded that exemplary justice be done.

∽

PRESIDENT GROVER CLEVELAND

President Cleveland wrote December 11, 1894:

Senate requests the President communicate information of alleged **cruelties committed upon Armenians in Turkey,** and especially whether any such **cruelties have been**

committed upon citizens who have declared their intention to become naturalized in this country or **upon persons because of their being Christians.** And inform the Senate whether **[protests] have been addressed to the Government of Turkey** in regard to such matters...to act in concert with other Christian powers regarding the same.

President Grover Cleveland wrote in his Seventh Annual Message to Congress, December 2, 1895:

Occurrences in Turkey have continued to excite concern. The **reported massacres of Christians in Armenia and the development there and in other districts of a spirit of fanatic hostility to Christian influences** naturally excited apprehension for the safety of the devoted men and women who, as dependents of the foreign missionary societies in the United States, reside in Turkey under the guarantee of law and usage and in the legitimate performance of their educational and religious mission.

No efforts have been spared in their behalf, and their protection in person and property has been earnestly and vigorously enforced...

Intelligence gives assurance of the present personal safety of our citizens and missionaries.

Though thus far no lives of American citizens have been sacrificed, **there can be no doubt that serious loss and destruction of mission property have resulted from riotous conflicts and outrageous attacks.**

By treaty several of the most powerful European powers have secured a right and have assumed a duty not only in behalf of their own citizens and in furtherance of their own interests, but as agents of the Christian world.

Their right to **enforce such conduct of Turkish government as will refrain fanatical**

brutality, and if this fails their duty is to so interfere as to insure against such **dreadful occurrences in Turkey as have lately shocked civilization.**

President Grover Cleveland wrote in his Eighth Annual Message, December 7, 1896:

It would afford me satisfaction if I could assure the Congress that the disturbed condition in **Asiatic Turkey** had during the past year assumed a less **hideous and bloody aspect** and that, either as a consequence of the **awakening of the Turkish Government to the demands of humane civilization** or as the result of decisive action on the part of the great nations having the right by treaty to interfere for the protection of those **exposed to the rage of mad bigotry and cruel fanaticism,** the shocking features of the situation had been mitigated.

Instead, however, of welcoming a softened disposition or protective intervention, **we have been afflicted by continued and not infrequent reports of the wanton destruction of homes and the bloody butchery of men, women, and children, made martyrs to their profession of Christian faith...**

Our citizens in Turkey...often in the midst of **dreadful scenes of danger**, their safety in the future is by no means assured.

Our Government at home and **our minister at Constantinople have left nothing undone to protect our missionaries in Ottoman territory,** who constitute nearly all the individuals residing there who have a right to claim our protection on the score of American citizenship. Our efforts in this direction will not be relaxed; but the deep feelings and sympathy that have been aroused among our people ought not to so far blind their reason and judgment as to lead them to demand impossible things.

The outbreaks of blind fury which lead to murder and pillage in Turkey occur suddenly and without notice...We have made claims against the Turkish Government for the pillage and destruction of missionary property at Harpoot and Marash during the uprisings at those places...A number of Armenian refugees having arrived at our ports, an order has lately been obtained from the Turkish Government permitting the wives and children of such refugees to join them. It is hoped that hereafter no obstacle will be interposed to prevent the escape of all those who seek to avoid the perils which threaten them in Turkish dominions...

I do not believe that the present somber prospect in Turkey will be long permitted to offend the sight of Christendom.

It so mars the humane and enlightened civilization that belongs to the close of the nineteenth century that it seems hardly possible that the earnest demand of good people throughout the Christian world for its corrective treatment will remain unanswered.

PRESIDENT WILLIAM MCKINLEY

President William McKinley wrote in his Second Annual Message to Congress, December 5, 1898:

The...envoy of the United States to the Ottoman Porte carries instructions looking to the disposal of matters in controversy with Turkey...especially to press for a just settlement of our claims for indemnity by reason of the destruction of the property of American missionaries resident in that country during the Armenian troubles of 1895.

PRESIDENT THEODORE ROOSEVELT

President Theodore Roosevelt wrote in his Fourth Annual Message to Congress, December 6, 1904:

It is inevitable that such a nation should desire eagerly to give expression to its horror on an occasion of...**such systematic and long-extended cruelty and oppression of which the Armenians have been the victims, and which have won for them the indignant pity of the civilized world.**

Theodore Roosevelt, in his book *Fear God and Take Your Own Part* (NY: George H. Doran Co., 1916), wrote:

As a nation we...proved our worth...when we championed orderly freedom in Cuba...**We ought now to champion Russia...and Serbia against Turkey and Bulgaria.** (T. Roosevelt, *Fear God*, p. 44-45)

Armenians, who for some centuries have sedulously avoided militarism and war, and have practically applied advanced pacifist principles...are so suffering precisely and exactly because they have been pacifists whereas their neighbors, the Turks, have not been pacifists but militarists... It is probably hopeless ever to convince the majority of these men except by actual disaster that the course they follow is not merely wicked...but from their own standpoint utterly shortsighted-**as the fate of the Armenians...of the present day shows.**(T. Roosevelt, *Fear God*, p. 61, 64)

During the last year...unoffending, industrious and law-abiding peoples like the **Armenians, have been subjected to wrongs far greater than** any that have been committed since the close of the **Napoleonic Wars**...the **wars of Genghis Khan** and **Tamerlane** in Asia.

Yet this government has not raised its hand to do anything to help the people who were wronged or to antagonize the oppressors.

It is not an accident, it betokens a certain sequence of cause and effect, that this course of national infamy on our part began when the last Administration surrendered to the peace-at-any-price people, and started the negotiation of its foolish and wicked all-inclusive arbitration treaties.

Individuals and nations who preach the doctrine of milk-and-water invariably have in them a softness of fiber which means that they fear to antagonize those who preach and practice the doctrine of blood-and-iron. (T. Roosevelt, *Fear God*, p. 111)

Our country has shirked its clear duty. **Our outspoken and straightforward declaration by this government against the dreadful iniquities perpetrated...Armenia and Serbia would have been worth to humanity a thousand times as much as all that the professional pacifists have done in the past fifty years.** (T. Roosevelt, *Fear God*, p. 114)

Let any man who doubts read the statement of **an American eye-witness of the fearful atrocities,** Mr. Arthur H. Gleason, in the New York Tribune of Nov. 25, 1915. **Serbia is at this moment passing under the harrow of torture and mortal anguish. Now, the Armenians have been butchered under circumstances of murder and torture and rape that would have appealed to an old-time Apache Indian...**In the case of the Armenians some of the professional pacifists and praisers of neutrality have ventured to form committees and speak about-not act about-the **"Armenian atrocities."** (T. Roosevelt, *Fear God*, p. 133, 134)

My dear Mr. Samuel T. Dutton, Esq., (Chairman of the Committee on the Armenian Outrages, 70 Fifth Ave. New York, Nov. 24, 1915) Even to nerves dulled and jaded by the heaped-up horrors of the past year and a half, **the news of the terrible fate that has befallen the Armenians must give a fresh shock of sympathy and indignation.** Let me emphatically point out that the sympathy is useless unless it is accompanied with indignation, and that the indignation is useless if it exhausts itself in words instead of taking shape in deeds...**If this people through its government had not shirked its duty...we would now be able to take effective action on behalf of Armenia.** Mass meetings on behalf of the Armenians amount to nothing whatever if they are mere methods of giving a sentimental but ineffective and safe outlet to the emotion of those engaged in them...

The principles of the peace-at-any-price men, of the professional pacifists...will be as absolutely ineffective for international righteousness...This crowning iniquity of the wholesale slaughter of the Armenians...must be shared by the neutral powers headed by the United States for their failure to protest when this initial wrong was committed...

The devastation of Poland and Serbia has been awful beyond description and has been associated with infamies surpassing those of the dreadful religious and racial wars of the seventeenth-century Europe...

Weak and timid milk-and-water policy of the professional pacifists is just as responsible as **the blood-and-iron policy of the ruthless and unscrupulous militarist for the terrible recrudescence of evil on a gigantic scale in the civilized world.**

The crowning outrage has been committed by the Turks on the Armenians. They have suffered atrocities so hideous that it is difficult to name them, atrocities such as those inflicted upon conquered nations by the followers of Attila and of Genghis Khan.

It is dreadful to think that these things can be done and that this nation nevertheless remarks "neutral not only in deed but in thought," between right and the most hideous wrong, neutral between despairing and hunted people, people **whose little children are murdered and their women raped, and the victorious and evil wrong-doers...**

I trust that all Americans worthy of the name feel their deepest indignation and keenest **sympathy aroused by the dreadful Armenian atrocities.** I trust that they feel...that a peace obtained without...righting the wrongs of the Armenians would be worse than any war...

Wrongdoing will only be stopped by men who are brave as well as just, who put honor above safety, who are true to a lofty ideal of duty, who prepare in advance to make their strength effective, and who shrink from no hazard, not even the final hazard of war, if necessary in order to serve the great cause of righteousness.

When our people take this stand, we shall also be able effectively to take a stand in international matters which shall prevent such **cataclysms of wrong as have been witnesses...on an even greater scale in Armenia.** (T. Roosevelt, *Fear God*, pp. 377-383)

✥

THE YOUNG TURKS

In 1908, Bulgaria was liberated from Turkish rule by Russia. That year, the Young Turk revolution began, led by three military officers, "The Three Pashas":

Mehmed Talat Pasha, Ismail Enver, and Ahmed Djemal. They forced out the Sultan and wrote a constitution.

The initial joy felt by Armenians, thinking the terror of Sultan Abdul Hamid was over, was turned to horror. The Three Pashas exercised dictatorial powers and promoted the idea of a homogeneous Turkey of one race and one belief. They decided to expel or exterminate non-Muslim, non-Turkish ethnic groups, specifically Greek and Armenian Christians - an example followed 30 years later by Adolph Hitler's Nazi military who decided to expel or exterminate non-Aryan ethnic groups, such as the Jews.

The Young Turks wanted to reestablish the greatness of the old Ottoman Empire and prevent any more non-Turkish ethnic groups from gaining independence, specifically: Greeks in Eastern Thrace, Western Asia Minor and Pontos; Armenians in Eastern Asia Minor; and Kurds in Southeastern Asia Minor. The Young Turks' new "constitutional" government was more abusive and brutal than the Sultan's.

During World War I, the western world focused on Germany, France and England. This provided Turkey with the perfect cover to carry out their premeditated massacre of the ethnic minorities. One of "The Three Pashas," Talat Pasha, minister of the interior, was the mastermind of the pogroms. He organized systematic genocidal massacres of hundreds of thousands of Greek and Armenian Christians.

His first step was to recruit into the military the Armenian young men, who were soon relegated to "noncombat" duties of digging roads and acting as pack animals. Starved to exhaustion, they were eventually marched into the woods and shot in cold blood.

U.S. Ambassador to Turkey, Henry Mongenthau, wrote of some 2,000 Armenian workmen being dispatched from the city of Harpoot for a "road construction project":

> Every one of the 2,000 were massacred...A few days later another 2,000 were sent to Diarbekir. The only purpose of sending these

men out in the open country was that they might be massacred...

Government agents went ahead on the road, notifying the Kurds...

Not only did the Kurdish tribesmen pour down the mountain upon this starved and weakened regiment, but Kurdish women came with butcher's knives in order that they might gain that merit in Allah's eyes that comes from killing a Christian.

Vahakn Dadrian wrote in *The History of the Armenian Genocide* (Berghahn Books, 1885):

By removing all able-bodied Armenian males from their cities, villages, hamlets...the Armenian communities were reduced to a condition of near helplessness, thus an easy prey for destruction. It was a masterful stroke.

Turks disarmed the Armenian population. Talat Pasha punished so severely those who did not turn in weapons, that Armenians bought guns from Muslims at exorbitant prices so they could have one to turn in. The entire government administration participated in the jihad extermination process. The Armenians were the first targeted for genocide because they had no international state which would rush to their aid, as the Greeks inside Turkey had the nearby country of Greece.

Looting, expulsions and murder began under the pretext of the Balkan Wars (1912-1913), but afterwards grew more intense, causing the Orthodox Patriarch, May 25, 1914, to declare that Christian Church was under attack. All activities which drew public attention, such as Greek Church services and Greek schools, were stopped.

Armenian men, women and children were marched into the desert without water until they dropped and died. Armenians were thrown off cliffs, drowned or burned alive. Russians came to their aid till the Bolshevik revolution began. Only a small area of Armenia that came under Russian control still exists.

Over 1.5 million Armenian men, women and children were killed, 750,000 Syrians, and 1 million Greeks, Albanians and other ethnic minorities, in addition to the previous 7 centuries of Turks systematically massacring millions of Greeks, Armenians, Kurds, Syrians, Serbs, and Bulgarians.

Henry Morgenthau, American Ambassador at Constantinople from 1913 to 1916, wrote:

> I am confident that the whole history of the human race contains no such horrible episode as this. The great massacres and persecutions of the past seem almost insignificant when compared with the sufferings of the Armenian race in 1915.

Referring to the massacre and destruction of Greeks and Armenians, French Prime Minister George Clemanceau commented, June 25, 1919:

> We do not find even one example in Europe, Asia, or Africa, where the imposition of Turkish sovereignty had not been followed by a decline in material prosperity, and by the impoverishment of its culture.
>
> Also there does not exist one example where liberation from Turkish control was not followed by the advancement of material prosperity and an improvement of the cultural level.
>
> Whether dealing with Christians or Muslims, the Turk has managed to bring destruction wherever he conquered.
>
> The Turk has never been able to develop in peace that which he won through conquest.

The London Times, October 3, 1911, reported on the Young Turks' Union and Progress Council:

> The Ottomanization of all Turkish citizens, which never succeeded through persuasion, had to be done by the force of arms.

∽

PRESIDENT WOODROW WILSON

After World War I, Armenia sent representatives to the Paris Peace Conference pleading for help, but Western Europe was recovering from the devastations of war and were divided in their interests.

The situation was similar to when Mehmet II was conquering Constantinople and the western European nations did not come to the rescue because they were preoccupied with the Hundred Years' War, the Papal Schism, the Reconquista and the Bubonic Plague.

Through the League of Nations, France assumed the Mandate for Syria and Lebanon. Britain assumed the Mandate for Palestine and Iraq.

The League of Nations wanted the U.S. to assume the Mandate for Armenia. President Woodrow Wilson wanted to make Armenia an American Protectorate, similar to Puerto Rico, Guam or the Virgin Islands.

In his special message to Congress requesting permission to assume the mandate for Armenia under the League of Nations (Document 791), dated May 24, 1920, President Woodrow Wilson stated:

> Whereas the testimony adduced at the hearings conducted by the subcommittee of **the Senate Committee on Foreign Relations have clearly established the truth of the reported massacres and other atrocities from which the Armenian people have suffered;** and
>
> Whereas the people of the United States are deeply impressed by the **deplorable conditions of insecurity, starvation, and misery now prevalent in Armenia**; and
>
> Whereas the independence of the Republic of **Armenia** has been duly recognized by the Supreme Council of the Peace Conference and by the Government of the United States of America: Therefore be it...Resolved,
>
> That in order to afford **necessary protection for the lives and property** of citizens of the

United States at the port of Batum [on the Black Sea] and along the line of the railroad leading to Baku [Azerbaijan], the President is hereby requested, if not incompatible with the public interest, **to cause a United States warship and a force of marines to be dispatched to such port with instructions to such marines to disembark and to protect American lives and property.**

I received and read this document with great interest and with genuine gratification, not only because it embodied my own convictions and feelings **with regard to Armenia** and its people, but also, and more particularly, because it seemed to me **the voice of the American people expressing their genuine convictions and deep Christian sympathies**, and intimating the line of duty which seemed to them to lie clearly before us.

I cannot but regard it as providential...that almost at the same time I received information that the conference of statesmen now sitting at San Remo...had formally resolved to address **a definite appeal to this Government to accept the mandate for Armenia...**

It was recognized that certain communities formerly belonging to the Turkish Empire have reached a stage of development where their existence as independent nations can be provisionally recognized, subject to the rendering of administrative advice and assistance by a Mandatory Power until such time as they are able to stand alone.

It is in pursuance of this principle and with a desire of affording Armenia such advice and assistance that the statesmen conferring at San Remo have formally requested this Government to assume the duties of mandatory in Armenia...

In response to the in**vitation of the Council
at San Remo, I urgently advise and request that
the Congress grant the Executive power to accept
for the United States a mandate over Armenia.**

I make this suggestion in the earnest belief
that it will be the wish of the people of the
United States that this should be done.

**The sympathy with Armenia has
proceeded from no single portion of our
people, but has come with extraordinary
spontaneity and sincerity from the whole of
the great body of Christian men and women
in this country by whose freewill offerings
Armenia has practically been saved at the
most critical juncture of its existence.**

At their hearts this great and generous people
have made the cause of Armenia their own.

It is to this people and to their Government
that the hopes and earnest expectations of t**he
struggling people of Armenia turn as they
now emerge from a period of indescribable
suffering and peril, and I hope that the
Congress will think it wise to meet this hope
and expectation with the utmost liberality.**

I know from unmistakable evidences given
by responsible representatives of many
peoples struggling towards independence and
peaceful life again that the Government of the
United States is looked to with extraordinary
trust and confidence, and I believe that it
would do nothing less than arrest the hopeful
processes of civilization if we were to refuse
the request to become the helpful friends and
advisers of such of these people as we may be
authoritatively and formally reque**sted to
guide and assist.**

I am conscious that **I am urging upon the
Congress a very critical choice,** but I make the
suggestion in the confidence that **I am speaking**

in the spirit and in accordance with the wishes of the greatest of the Christian peoples.

The sympathy for Armenia among our people has sprung from untainted consciences, pure Christian faith, and an earnest desire to see Christian people everywhere succored in their time of suffering, and lifted from their abject subjection and distress and enabled to stand upon their feet and take their place among the free nations of the world.

Our recognition of the independence of Armenia will mean genuine liberty and assured happiness for her people, if we fearlessly undertake the duties of guidance and assistance involved in the functions of a Mandatory Power.

It is, therefore, with the most earnest hopefulness and with the feeling that I am giving advice from which the Congress will not willingly turn away that I urge the acceptance of the invitation now formally and solemnly extended to us by the Council at San Remo, into whose hands has passed the difficult task of composing the many complexities and difficulties of government in the onetime Ottoman Empire and the maintenance of order and tolerable conditions of life in those portions of that Empire which it is no longer possible **in the interest of civilization** to leave under the government of the Turkish authorities themselves.

The Republican controlled Congress was in an isolationist mood after World War I and so the 2nd Session of the 66th Congress voted down the plan to help Armenia. This was partly due to the League of Nations plan infringing on U.S. sovereignty.

◈

TREATY OF SEVRES

After Congress rejected the League of Nations "Mandate for Armenia," President Wilson continued trying to help the Armenians by negotiating the Treaty of Sevres in which the international community of nations was to pressure Turkey to stop the killings, disarm and recognize the right of Armenia to exist.

This was the model for later United Nations' Sanctions, such as the ones against terrorist states in the Middle East. The last major endeavor before he died, President Woodrow Wilson's Treaty of Sevres, August 10, 1920, was intended to provide protection for Armenians without United States involvement.

The Treaty of Sevres was to be the crowning effort of Woodrow Wilson's plan for world peace, but the defiant Muslim leader Ataturk simply ignored it, as he realized western powers lost the political will to intervene in what appeared to the west as a civil war.

During the 40 months of war, Ataturk not only failed to stop the killing, he actually secured foreign assistance to defeat the Greek military front in Anatolia.

In 1920, Alexander Millerand, president of the Supreme Allied Council stated:

> The Turkish government not only failed in its duty to protect its non-Turkish citizens from the looting, violence and murders, but there are many indications that the Turkish government itself was responsible for directing and organizing the most cruel attacks against the populations, which it was supposed to protect.
>
> For these reasons, the Allied powers have decided to liberate from the Turkish yoke all the lands where the majority of the people were non-Turks.

SMYRNA

Like the unarmed freedom demonstrators in Tiananmen Square, who were crushed by the Communist Government immediately after the United States made it clear it would not intervene, the unarmed peaceful Armenians in Smyrna were crushed by the Muslim Ottoman Turks once the United States made it clear it would not intervene.

The Turks stormed into the Armenian and Greek areas of Asia Minor and, on September 8, 1922, overran the city of Smyrna, the largest city in Asia Minor called "Pearl of the Aegean Sea." The city was overburdened with refugees from the other war-torn parts of Asia Minor.

United States, British, and French ships were anchored offshore watching in dismay as the massacre unfolded before their eyes. The screams for help went unanswered, as the ships had no orders to intervene.

The Turks set the city on fire and in a wild jihad began their mass genocide. In unbelievable horror, so many Greeks and Armenians men, women and children were killed that the water at the pier turned red.

The Orthodox bishop of Smyrna, Chrysostomos, was seized from his church service in the cathedral, dragged into the street, publicly humiliated, murdered and dismembered.

Defying description, the horrible atrocities were photographed and recounted by the American Consul in Smyrna, George Horton, in his book "The Blight of Asia" (Indianapolis: Bobb and Merryl, 1925).

George Horton's photographs were of:

Greeks of Asia Minor massacred by Turks in 1915-1922
Photo of the massacres of the Greeks of Asia Minor
Photo of a grandfather and grandson slain together
Photo of the order of Nourredin for the slaughter of the
 Greek population
Smyrna in flames

Boats the only hope for salvation; Inhabitants in panic
preferring drowning to slaughter
Complete destruction of the French hospital by the fire
Some of the 1,500,000 refugees
Destruction of the Temple of Artemis (one of the seven
marvels of the ancient world)
Church of Taxiarchis turned to a liquor storehouse

৵

ARMENIANS EXPELLED BY TREATY

Instead of abiding by the Treaty of Sevres, 1920, the Turks insisted on the Treaty of Lausanne, 1923, which required all non-Muslims to be expelled from Smyrna and the Armenian areas.

Christians were expelled from ancient areas familiar to Christianity, where stood the seven churches mentioned in the Book of Revelation – Smyrna, Ephesus, Pergamum, Thyatira, Sardis, Laodicea and Philadelphia.

This was the area where the Apostles Paul and John ministered, which spoke Armenian, a language derived from Aramaic-the language Jesus spoke, where early Christians lived in labyrinth caves to hide from Roman persecutions, the first nation to declare itself Christian, where the Council of Nicea took place and the Nicene Creed was written, where stood ancient churches and monasteries, where lived Saint Nicholas, Saint Basil, Saint George, Saint John Chrysostom and others, where Christian men, women and children suffered through invasion after invasion from Mongols, Muslim Seljuks, Muslim Ottomans, and were sold as slaves in bazaars, and where young Christian boys were confiscated to be made into Muslim soldiers.

Now, after all they had endured for centuries, every Christian was ordered expelled.

After three years of fighting, Greece declared itself an independent republic in 1924.

After the war, there were around 1,400,000 Greeks still in Turkey. They wanted to stay but the 1923 Treaty of Lausanne imposed their mandatory deportation, even though some could not even speak Greek and thousands were orphans. The Treaty also required 300,000 Turks to be deported from Greece.

Armenian buildings, libraries and architecture which stood for thousands of years were demolished. The Armenian cities of Harper, Van and Ani were completely leveled. The Greek people of Asia Minor had not even been consulted about this Treaty, yet they were forced to abandon their ancestral homes where their families had lived as Christians for almost 2,000 years and as Greeks for almost 4,000 years.

A modern example of this policy was when thousands of Jews were forcibly removed from the Gaza strip in 2005 so Muslims could take control.

᪐

FEW CHRISTIANS ALLOWED TO STAY

According to the Treaty of Lausanne, only the Greeks in Constantinople, Imvros and Tenedos were given permission to stay. The total number of Greeks which remained in Turkey in 1924 were 300,000.

In direct violation to the Treaty of Lausanne, the Turks closed the Halki Seminary on the Princes' Islands in the Sea of Marmara. It was the main school of theology for the Eastern Orthodox Church's Patriarch of Constantinople.

A *New York Times* Editorial, Sunday, December 3, 1922, Page 6, Col. 2, Section 2, reported:

> A BLACK FRIDAY. There have been many Black Fridays in recent history. Most of them have been days of financial panic.
>
> There has been none of blacker foreboding than last Friday. And the blackness is not loss or fear of loss in stocks and bonds.
>
> It is the blackness of loss of home, the blackness of exile and suffering and the peril of death.

But that which deepens the darkness that has come upon the earth in the broad daylight of the twentieth century is civilization's prompt acceptance of the Turks' decree of banishment not only of a million Greeks, but incidentally of all Christian minorities within the Turkish realm beyond the Hellespont, which the Aryan crossed over three thousand years ago.

On December 4, 1922, the *New York Times* printed on page 16, col. 3:

STATESMANSHIP OF EXTERMINATION
What The Times thinks about the morality of the Turkish plan to drive every Greek and Armenian out of Turkey — which means that a great many of them will die or be murdered on the way, and that others will fall victims to famine or pestilence in their places of refuge — has already been said.

It has been pointed out, too, that the serious thing is not so much the morality of the Turk, which has been fairly well-known to the world for several centuries but that of the so-called Christian Powers which stood by and were consenting.

The British Government protested in the name of humanity when the Greek revolutionaries shot a group of ex-Ministers and Generals.

But when the Turks announce that a million Greeks are to be expelled from the country where they have lived since two thousand years before the Turks were heard of, and driven out to die, Lord Curzon's moral scruples are satisfied with a request for two weeks delay.

Politicians it seems can be knocked by killings only when the victims are other politicians.

PRESIDENT WARREN G. HARDING

President Warren G. Harding wrote in a speech released for publication in San Francisco, July 31, 1923:

> We were never technically at war with Turkey...which threatened to set the Near East aflame.
> **But...we did not fail to voice American sentiment of behalf of Christian minorities, and we did assist in reaching a settlement calculated to assure their future protection.**

In less than two short decades, the Armenian population in Turkey was reduced from ten percent to less than one percent.

∽

THEODORE ROOSEVELT ON ISLAM

Theodore Roosevelt wrote a book titled *Fear God and Take Your Own Part* (NY: George H. Doran Company, 1916), with a dedication to Julia Ward Howe. On pages 196-197, Theodore Roosevelt wrote:

> Christianity is not the creed of Asia and Africa at this moment solely because the seventh century **Christians of Asia and Africa had trained themselves not to fight, whereas the Moslems were trained to fight.**
> Christianity was saved in Europe solely because the peoples of Europe fought.
> If the peoples of Europe in the seventh and eighth centuries, and on up to and including the seventeenth century, had not possessed a military equality with, and gradually a growing superiority over **the Mohammedans who invaded Europe,** Europe would at this moment be Mohammedan and the Christian religion would be exterminated.

Wherever the Mohammedans have had complete sway, wherever the Christians have been unable to resist them by the sword, Christianity has ultimately disappeared.

From the hammer of Charles Martel to the sword of Sobieski, **Christianity owed its safety in Europe to the fact that it was able to show that it could and would fight as well as the Mohammedan aggressor.**

On pages 70-71 of his book *Fear God and Take Your Own Part*, Theodore Roosevelt wrote of his address to the American Sociological Congress:

The civilization of Europe, America and Australia exists today at all only because of the victories of civilized man over the enemies of civilization, because of victories stretching through the centuries from Charles Martel in the eighth century and those of John Sobieski in the seventeenth century.

During the thousand years that included the careers of the Frankish soldier and the Polish king, **the Christians of Asia and Africa proved unable to wage successful war with the Moslem conquerors; and in consequence Christianity practically vanished from the two continents;** and today nobody can find in them any "social values" whatever, in the sense in which we use the words, so far as the sphere of Mohammedan influences are concerned.

There are such "social values" today in Europe, America and Australia only because during those thousand years the Christians of Europe possessed the warlike power to do what the Christians of Asia and Africa had failed to do - that is, to beat back the Moslem invader.

If European militarism had not been able to defend itself against and to overcome the militarism of Asia and Africa, there would have been no "social values" of any kind in our world today, and no sociologists to discuss them.

✍

BISHOP FULTON J. SHEEN

Bishop Fulton J. Sheen wrote in *The World's First Love* (McGraw-Hill, 1952):

The Christian European West barely escaped destruction at the hands of the Muslims. At one point they were stopped near Tours and at another point, later on in time, outside the gates of Vienna. The Church throughout northern Africa was practically destroyed by Muslim power, and at the present hour, the Muslims are beginning to rise again...

Muslimism is a heresy, as Hilaire Belloc believes it to be...There was never a time in which it declined, either in numbers, or in the devotion of its followers. The missionary effort of the Church toward this group has been, at least on the surface, a failure...The hatred of the Muslim countries against the West is becoming a hatred against Christianity itself.

Although the statesmen have not yet taken it into account, there is still a grave danger that the temporal power of Islam may return, and with it, the menace that it may shake off a West which has ceased to be Christian, and affirm itself as a great anti-Christian power.

Muslim writers say, "When the locust swarms darken countries, they bear on their wings these Arabic words: 'We are Allah's host, each of us has ninety-nine eggs, and if we had a hundred, we should lay waste to the world, with all that is in it.'"

The problem is how shall we prevent the hatching of the hundredth egg?

✍

SIR LAWRENCE OF ARABIA

Thomas Edward Lawrence, an Oxford graduate, had studied archeology and ancient architecture in Syria, Palestine, Mesopotamia (now called Iraq), and Turkey beginning in 1909.

In 1916, the Muslim Arabs rebelled against the Muslim Ottoman Turks. Lawrence was instrumental in organizing the disunified Arab tribes to fight the Ottoman Turks.

Lawrence dressed as an Arab and worked with Arab sheik Feisal al Husayn to launch a full-scale revolt. In 1916, Lawrence was captured by the Ottoman Turks. He was tortured with beatings and homosexual rape by the Turkish Governor of Deraa, who Lawrence described as "an ardent pederast."

Lawrence escaped, but was emotionally scarred by the ordeal, later writing "I gave away the only possession we are born into the world with-our bodily integrity."

Lawrence served as a liaison between the Arabs and the British Military. He formed an alliance with Auda abu Tayi, leader of the Howeitat tribe, and fought in the desert of Wadi Rum.

The Ottoman Empire, which was allied with Germany during World War I, was undermined by Lawrence's guerrilla warfare of blowing up sections of the Hejaz Railway and raiding Turkish positions.

Though wounded from dozens of bullet and shrapnel wounds, Lawrence captured the port of Aqaba, July 1917. Lawrence lured Turkish forces into the desert, which opened the way for the British army, led by General Edmund Allenby, to occupy Syria, Palestine and Jerusalem.

After World War I, Lawrence accompanied the Arab delegation to the Paris Peace Conference in 1919. He caused repercussions by advocating that Iraq, Transjordan, Syria and Lebanon be recognized as independent states.

Though Iraq and Transjordian were made British protectorates, and Syria and Lebanon were made

French protectorates, these countries were eventually given independence.

Lawrence became a research fellow at Oxford and served as advisor on the Middle East to Winston Churchill in 1922. Lawrence resigned, but later joined the Royal Tank Corp and the Royal Air Force in 1925. He was stationed in India and Afghanistan. In 1935, he retired and died in a motorcycle accident.

There is a monument to him at the Anglo-Saxon church of St. Martin at Wareham, Dorset. Lawrence's book, *The Seven Pillars of Wisdom*, was the basis of the 1963 movie *Lawrence of Arabia*, starring Peter O'Toole.

∽

ATATURK: REINVENTING TURKEY

When Islam conquers its enemies, there is peace.

After the genocide of the Armenians in Turkey, Ataturk began to reinvent the country by modernizing it and making it more secular.

In 1922, Ataturk declared the Republic of Turkey and ended the religious Caliphate, thus preventing Muslim religious leaders from controlling Government affairs. Ataturk replaced Arabic Islamic names with Turkish names and abolished the use of Arabic script, replacing it with the Latin script.

Ataturk abolished women wearing of scarves and chadors or burkas, (the full-length body dress worn by Muslim women), requiring women to wear skirts. He abolished the fez (the red felt cap with a black tassel worn by men) and required men to wear western pants and suits.

Ataturk banned beards on men, even requiring Muslim prayer leaders, priests and preachers to be beardless. He outlawed the Muezzins call for prayer, making prayer a private affair.

He encouraged the next generation of Turks to not take Islamic names, but ethnic Turkish names, like Bullet Deceit, Target Ozzal, Mast Wilma, Emetine Arabian or Tans Caller.

He made the Turkish military the custodian of secular traditions. During the last ninety years the Turkish military has intervened to stop attempted Islamist takeovers of Turkey.

Unfortunately, Ataturk's effort to transform Turkey outwardly has not removed an underlying anti-Christian sentiment.

᷍

ISTANBUL POGROM

In 1930, Constantinople was renamed Istanbul, which in Turkish means "in the city." This was an effort to remove Greek influences.

As was seen in the sudden outbreak of violence after a Dutch newspaper published a cartoon of Mohammed, there have been similar incidents throughout Muslim history.

In 1932, Turkey passed laws barring Greeks from 30 different trades and professions. In 1942, a capital gains tax was passed to reduce the number of Greek businesses.

Politicians began speaking openly against the 100,000 Greek Christians still living in Constantinople.

The Turkish Prime Minister Adnan Menders orchestrated a plan where a Turkish University Student was to place an explosive charge in the Turkish Consulate and birthplace of Ataturk in Greece and have it blow up on September 3, 1955. The press would blame this on the Greeks and the Muslims would be incited to retaliate. Though the bomb never went off, the newspapers ran with the story and the Greeks in Constantinople were pillaged.

Turkish Prime Minister Menders had government trucks block off the streets to the Greek neighborhood and provided shovels, pickaxes, crowbars, ramming rods and gas, to the 300,000 rioters.

Like the "Kristall Nacht" in Germany on November 9, 1938, when Nazis smashed storefront windows and vandalized Jewish businesses, Turkish mobs on September 6, 1955, destroyed Greek homes, businesses and churches in a mad frenzy for nine hours. They raped dozens of Greek women, beat and forcibly circumcised Greek men (mostly priests), and killed 16 Greek and Orthodox clerics. Turkish rioters destroyed over 1,000 Greek homes, 4,348 Greek-owned businesses, 110 hotels, 27 pharmacies, 23 schools, 21 factories, 3 monasteries, and 73 of the 81 Greek Orthodox Churches in the city. The World Council of Churches estimated the damage at over 150 million dollars. The mob chanted "Massacre the Greek traitors" "Down with Europe" In one church arson attack, Father Chrysanthos Mandas, was burned alive. Greek cemeteries were desecrated with relics of saints burned or thrown to dogs.

Journalist of the *London Daily Mail*, Noel Barber, wrote September 14, 1955:

> The church of Yedikule was utterly smashed, and one priest was dragged from bed, the hair torn from his head and the beard literally torn from his chin.
>
> Another old Greek priest [Fr. Mantas] in a house belonging to the church and who was too ill to be moved was left in bed, the house was set on fire and he was burned alive.
>
> At the church of Yenikoy, a lovely spot on the edge of the Bosporus, a priest of 75 was taken out into the street, stripped of every stitch of clothing, tied behind a car and dragged through the streets.
>
> They tried to tear the hair of another priest, but failing that, they scalped him, as they did many others.

Another eyewitness was Ian Fleming, author of the *James Bond* detective stories, who was in Istanbul for the *London Sunday Times* reporting on an International Police Conference. His column "The Great Riot of Istanbul," appeared in the paper September 11, 1955.

Ian Fleming wrote that "hatred ran through the streets like lava." (Phillip Mansel, *Constantinople: City of the World's Desire,* 1453-1944, Harmondworth, U.K., Penquin, 1995, p. 425).

The riots were reported in the I*llustrated London News, Time Magazine* and *Reader's Digest,* which described Istanbul as "a city gone mad."

After the 1955 Istanbul Pogrom, over 100,000 more Greeks departed. The discrimination continued and in 1958, Turkish nationalist students campaigned for a boycott on all Greek businesses. In 1964, the Turkish government deported 50,000 more Greeks.

In August of 1995, the U.S. Senate passed a special resolution calling on President Bill Clinton to proclaim 6 September a Day of Memory for the victims of the 1955 Istanbul Pogrom. As of 2006, only 5,000 mostly elderly Greek Christians remained in Istanbul.

∽

DISCRIMINATION OF CHRISTIANS

The *New York Times* printed, November 26, 1979:

> According to the most recent statistics, the Christian population in Turkey was diminished from 4,500,000 at the beginning of this century to just about 150,000. Of those, the Greeks are no more than 7,000. Yet, in 1923 they were as many as 1 to 2 million.

The 1998, Religious Freedom in the Majority Islamic Countries Report stated:

> Turkey...Christianity 0.2%
> Evangelizing is hindered because the Christians are equated with the Armenian terrorists and with the Jehovah's Witnesses...
> Religious minorities not recognized by the Treaty of Lausanne of 1923 are not authorized to acquire property for their religious activities. But even those communities that are recognized

are subjected to restrictions, such as the ban on using premises belonging to them...

Properties of the religious communities have been confiscated by the State without any compensation. It is difficult if not impossible to obtain permits to build new places of prayer or even to restore existing churches...

Christians in Turkey have been imprisoned on the pretext that the public expression of their religion might provoke a disturbance of the peace. Eight American citizens were arrested in March 1998 for having distributed copies of the *New Testament* in the streets of Eskisehir...

The majority of the population is Muslim, and there has been a return to the strictest form of Islamism, which manifests itself in outbreaks of intolerance towards Christians.

An elderly Syrian Christian couple, the last remaining couple in Mzizah (close to Midyat) who were in the process of moving - like all the other members of their faith - to the southwest of Turkey, were brutally murdered in their own home.

In Tur Abdin there are 2,300 Syrian Orthodox Christians living today. Less than 40 years ago there were 150,000.

KNA of September 30, 1997 and Menschenrechte of November/December 1997 reported on an appeal...to find a place where these people - the only ones who still speak Aramaic, the language of Jesus Christ - could be allowed to live out their ordinary existence without injustice and violence.

The 1998, Religious Freedom in the Majority Islamic Countries Report continued:

On January 12, 1998, the *Ecumenical News International* reported that a Greek Orthodox sacristan had been found murdered inside the church of Agios Therapontas, one of the most ancient churches in Istanbul, and that icons and precious objects had also been stolen.

The Turkish government, accused of not taking any steps to prevent this, refused all responsibility.

On December 3, 1997, a bomb exploded in the headquarters of the Ecumenical Patriarch, injuring a deacon and damaging the church.

The Islamic fundamentalists, who do not want any Christian sacred places in the city, have been blamed for this, even though there is no concrete proof that they were responsible for the attack on this Greek citizen.

On January 22, 1998, Droits de l'homme sans frontières reported that Chaldean Christians fleeing from the north of Iraq had been the object of a wave of arrests involving around 5,000 people.

These refugees, whose exact numbers are not known and among whom there are also some Kurds, have resettled for the most part in Istanbul but also in other regions of the country.

All the police units are said to have received orders to arrest the refugees and send them back to the frontier - even though this could well mean sending them back to be massacred in a country from which they had fled at the time of the Gulf war.

The 1998, Religious Freedom in the Majority Islamic Countries Report further stated:

According to the *International Catholic Press Agency (Agence de Presse Internationale Catholique* - APIC) of Fribourg in Switzerland, during the night of 30th to 31st of March 1998 more than 72 tombs were profaned in the Christian cemetery of St. Eleutherios. Some 15 tombs had been opened and the bones scattered around.

The Christians in Istanbul are a tiny minority among 10 million Muslims.

Prior to the murder of the sacristan and the bomb attack in December there had been other attacks, one in 1996 and two time bombs in 1994, found before they exploded in the courtyard of the patriarchate.

At the third meeting of the Islamic Council of Eurasia, according to the Fides agency, the delegate responsible for the direction of religious affairs in Turkey referred to Christianity as "a threat" and spoke of the need for "missionary activity" to prevent an increase in this religion.

Faced with the request to include Turkey among the pilgrimage destinations for the Holy Year, the government of this country will also have to face up to the situation of the Christians in its own borders... Christians who live anonymously...

The 1998, Religious Freedom in the Majority Islamic Countries Report concluded:

> *Human Rights Without Frontiers* of September 3, 1998 reported that the Turkish Interior Minister had attempted to strip the current Patriarch Mutafyan of the Armenian Apostolic Orthodox Church of his powers and to replace him with a leader of his own choosing.
>
> The State has forbidden the 65,000 Armenians from electing a new patriarch after the death of the preceding one (which occurred on March 10), while at the same time exerting pressure to secure their own candidate, Sivacyan.
>
> Meanwhile the violence against Christians continues. On November 26, 1998, close to the village of Besbin in southeast Turkey, the 60-

year-old shepherd Hannah Atekti was murdered while he was pasturing his sheep.

With his death, the last Christian head of family in that place was removed, since his brother-in-law, Isa Karakut, who supplied the news to Droits de l'homme sans frontières, had already fled to Belgium in 1995 because of the death threats made against him by Muslims, and only his wife Kitane Ateki, aged 27, and their two children Ziver and Verine, aged seven and five respectively, had remained in the village.

It is the men, in fact, who are the principal targets of the religious hostility of their neighbors, and his wife wanted to remain close to her family to look after her own parents and to care for the children, who were still too young to face the discomforts of emigration.

Isa Karakut, who was refused asylum by the Belgian authorities, could shortly be forced to return to his country.

From the beginning of the 1990's, thousands of Chaldean Christians have fled this region of the country as a result of the persecutions both by the local authorities and by the Kurds, but Belgium still refuses to recognize their status as refugees.

❦

WAHHABISM, SAUD FAMILY & OIL

In 1744, Muhammad Ibn Abd al-Wahhab began attracting followers, calling for adherence to the *Qur'an's* command for the whole world to submit to Allah.

He forged a pact with Mohammed bin Saud ensuring that the areas conquered by the Saud tribe would be ruled according to Wahhabi's teachings.

For the next 140 years, the Saud family gradually controlled all of Arabia, resulting in the country's name: Saudi Arabia.

In 1924, the Wahhabi sect finally conquered the Muslim holy sites of Mecca and Medina, giving them control of Muslim pilgrimage known as the "hajj."

Wahhabism was a minor current in Islam until the discovery of oil in Saudi Arabia in 1938. Billions of dollars began pouring in from western nations purchasing Saudi oil. This financed the exportation of the Wahhabi version of Islam around the world.

An area impacted by Wahhabi Islam is southern Sudan where, since 1980, millions of mostly African Christians have been killed by Arab Muslims of northern Sudan, and, like Armenia, the world has done nothing.

∽

LEBANESE CHRISTIANS MASSACRED

Maronites took their name from an early Christian hermit, Maron, who died in 410 AD. Though retaining their own liturgy, Maronites have been in communion with the Catholic Church since 1182.

In 1975, the coastal Christian towns of Damour and Jiyya were totally destroyed and their inhabitants massacred or violently evicted from their homes by Muslims. Over the next 17 years, 90,000 mostly Maronite Christian and Greek Catholic inhabitants were killed, thousands mutilated and hundreds of thousands evicted or fled.

Islamization in Lebanon is advancing with the help of the Saudi-backed billionaire Prime Minister Hariri, who buys large amounts of properties from poor Christians. The Iran backed Hezbollah has stated their goal is to have Lebanon be a completely Islamic state.

∽

THE WASHINGTON POST

Nina Shea, director of the Center for Religious Freedom at Freedom House, wrote in her *Washington Post* article, **"This is a Saudi Textbook (after the intolerance was removed),"** May 21, 2006:

Religion is the foundation of the Saudi state's political ideology; it is also a key area of Saudi education in which students are taught the interpretation of Islam known as Wahhabism (a movement founded 250 years ago by Muhammad Ibn Abd al-Wahhab) that is reflected in these textbooks.

Scholars estimate that within the Saudi public school curriculum, Islamic studies make up a quarter to a third of students' weekly classroom hours in lower and middle school, plus several hours each week in high school.

Educators who question or dissent from the official interpretation of Islam can face severe reprisals.

In November 2005, a Saudi teacher who made positive statements about Jews and the *New Testament* was fired and sentenced to 750 lashes and a prison term.

(He was eventually pardoned after public and international protests.)

The Saudi public school system totals 25,000 schools, educating about 5 million students. In addition, Saudi Arabia runs academies in 19 world capitals, including one outside Washington in Fairfax County, that use some of these same religious texts.

Saudi Arabia also distributes its religion texts worldwide to numerous Islamic schools and madrassas that it does not directly operate.

Undeterred by Wahhabism's historically fringe status, Saudi Arabia is trying to assert itself as the world's authoritative voice on Islam — a sort of "Vatican" for Islam, as several Saudi officials have stated — and these textbooks are integral to this effort.

As the report of the commission investigating the Sept. 11 attacks observed, "Even in affluent countries, Saudi-funded Wahhabi schools are often the only Islamic schools" available. Education is at the core of the debate over freedom in the Muslim world. Al-Qaeda leader Osama bin Laden understands this well; in a recent audiotape he railed against those who would "interfere with school curricula."

∽

THE WALL STREET JOURNAL

In *The Wall Street Journal's Opinion Journal,* May 20, 2005, Ali Al-Ahmed, director of the Saudi Institute, Washington, D.C., wrote an article: "Hypocrisy Most Holy-Muslims should show some respect to others' religions":

With the revelation that a copy of the *Qur'an* may have been desecrated by U.S. military personnel at Guantanamo Bay, Muslims and their governments-including that of Saudi Arabia-reacted angrily.

This anger would have been understandable if the U.S. Government's adopted policy was to desecrate our *Qur'an.* But even before the Newsweek report was discredited, that was never part of the allegations.

As a Muslim, I am able to purchase copies of the *Qur'an* in any bookstore in any American city, and study its contents in countless American universities. American museums spend millions to exhibit and celebrate Muslim arts and heritage.

On the other hand, my Christian and other non-Muslim brothers and sisters in Saudi Arabia, where I come from, are not even allowed to own a copy of their holy books.

Indeed, the Saudi government desecrates and burns *Bibles* that its security forces confiscate at immigration points into the kingdom or during raids on Christian expatriates worshipping privately.

Soon after *Newsweek* published an account, later retracted, of an American soldier flushing a copy of the *Qur'an* down the toilet, the Saudi government voiced its strenuous disapproval. More specifically, the Saudi Embassy in Washington expressed "great concern" and urged the U.S. to "conduct a quick investigation."

Although considered as holy in Islam and mentioned in the *Qur'an* dozens of times, the *Bible* is banned in Saudi Arabia.

This would seem curious to most people because of the fact that to most Muslims, the *Bible* is a holy book. But when it comes to Saudi Arabia we are not talking about most Muslims, but a tiny minority of hard-liners who constitute the Wahhabi Sect.

The *Bible* in Saudi Arabia may get a person killed, arrested, or deported.

In September 1993, Sadeq Mallallah, 23, was beheaded in Qateef on a charge of apostasy for owning a *Bible*. The State Department's annual human rights reports detail the arrest and deportation of many Christian worshipers every year.

Just days before Crown Prince Abdullah met President Bush last month, two Christian gatherings were stormed in Riyadh.

Bibles and crosses were confiscated, and will be incinerated. (The Saudi government does not even spare the *Qur'an* from desecration.

On Oct. 14, 2004, dozens of Saudi men and women carried copies of the *Qur'an* as they protested in support of reformers in the capital, Riyadh. Although they carried the *Qur'ans* in part to protect themselves from assault by police, they were charged by hundreds of riot police, who stepped on the books with their shoes, according to one of the protesters.)

As Muslims, we have not been as generous as our Christian and Jewish counterparts in respecting others' holy books and religious symbols. Saudi Arabia bans the importation or the display of crosses, Stars of David or any other religious symbols not approved by the Wahhabi establishment. TV programs that show Christian clergymen, crosses or Stars of David are censored.

The desecration of religious texts and symbols and intolerance of varying religious viewpoints and beliefs have been issues of some controversy inside Saudi Arabia.

Ruled by a Wahhabi theocracy, the ruling elite of Saudi Arabia have made it difficult for Christians, Jews, Hindus and others, as well as dissenting sects of Islam, to visibly coexist inside the kingdom.

Another way in which religious and cultural issues are becoming more divisive is the Saudi treatment of Americans who are living in that country: Around 30,000 live and work in various parts of Saudi Arabia..

These people are not allowed to celebrate their religious or even secular holidays. These include Christmas and Easter, but also Thanksgiving. All other Gulf states allow non-Islamic holidays to be celebrated.

The Saudi Embassy and other Saudi organizations in Washington have distributed hundreds of thousands of *Qur'ans* and many more Muslim books, some that have libeled Christians, Jews and others as pigs and monkeys.

In Saudi school curricula, Jews and Christians are considered deviants and eternal enemies.

By contrast, Muslim communities in the West are the first to admit that Western countries-especially the U.S.-provide Muslims the strongest freedoms and protections that allow Islam to thrive in the West.

Meanwhile Christianity and Judaism, both indigenous to the Middle East, are maligned through systematic hostility by Middle Eastern governments and their religious apparatuses.

The lesson here is simple: If Muslims wish other religions to respect their beliefs and their Holy book, they should lead by example.

TOLERANCE VIEWED AS SUBMISSION

In an effort to extend tolerance to Muslims, President **George W. Bush** was the first President to **mention the** *Qur'an* **in an Inaugural Address**, January 20, 2005; first to **celebrate Muslim Ramadan in the White House**, November 19, 2001; first to **speak at an Islamic Center**, December 5, 2002; first to **issue an Islamic postage stamp, "Eid mubarak,"** during his Administration, August 1, 2001; first to **appoint a Muslim U.S. ambassador to the United Nations**, Zalmay Khalilzad, April 17, 2007, and first to **put a Qur'an in the Presidential Library.**

Nancy Pelosi is the **first U.S. House Speaker to submit to Islamic Law and cover her head with a Hijab (veil)** while visiting Syria, April 5, 2007. **Keith Ellison (MN-5th) became the first Muslim Congressman,** swearing upon a *Qur'an.* **Andre Carson (IN-7th) became the second Muslim Congressman. On September 25, 2009, a thousand Muslims gathered on the Capital lawn to bow toward Mecca.**

Barack Obama, whose **grandfather, father and stepfather were Muslim,** is the first President with a Muslim name, **Hussein. In 2009, he bowed to Saudi King Abdullah; said America is not a Christian nation; said America was one of the largest Muslim countries; did not celebrate the National Day of Prayer; celebrated Ramadan with a White House dinner and a broadcast**

to Muslims of the world; appointed devout Muslims Arif Alikhan and Kareem Shora to the Department of Homeland Security; appointed devout Muslims Dalia Mogahed and Rashad Hussain to the White House staff. The hope is that America's tolerance of Islam will result in Muslims being more tolerant of non-Muslims. **Unfortunately,** a consequence is emerging, that **tolerance actually emboldens some moderate Muslims to become fundamental by convincing them that their long awaited desire of the West submitting to Allah is imminent.**

On the 5th anniversary of the terror attacks, President Bush addressed the nation, September 11, 2006:

> Since the horror of 9/11, **we've learned a great deal about the enemy. We have learned that they are evil and kill without mercy — but not without purpose.** We have learned that they form a global network of **extremists who are driven by a perverted vision of Islam** — a totalitarian ideology that hates freedom, **rejects tolerance, and despises all dissent.**
>
> And we have learned that **their goal is to build a radical Islamic empire** where women are prisoners in their homes, men are beaten for missing prayer meetings, and terrorists have a safe haven to plan and launch attacks on America and other civilized nations.
>
> **The war against this enemy is more than a military conflict. It is the decisive ideological struggle of the 21st century, and the calling of our generation.** Our nation is being tested in a way that we have not been since the start of the Cold War. We saw what a handful of our enemies can do with box cutters and plane tickets. We hear their threats to launch even more terrible attacks on our people.
>
> And we know that if they were able to get their hands on weapons of mass destruction, they would use them against us.

We face an enemy determined to bring death and suffering into our homes.

America did not ask for this war, and every American wishes it were over. So do I.

But the war is not over — and it will not be over until either we or the extremists emerge victorious.

If we do not defeat these enemies now, we will leave our children to face a Middle East overrun by terrorist states and radical dictators armed with nuclear weapons.

We are in a war that will set the course for this new century — and determine the destiny of millions across the world...

If we yield Iraq to men like bin Laden, our enemies will be emboldened... The terrorists fear freedom as much as they do our firepower.

They are thrown into panic at the sight of an old man pulling the election lever, girls enrolling in schools, or families worshipping God in their own traditions.

They know that given a choice, **people will choose freedom over their extremist ideology.**

So their answer is to deny people this choice by raging against the forces of freedom and moderation. This struggle has been called a clash of civilizations. **In truth, it is a struggle for civilization.**

≪ঌ

MULTICULTURALSIM RADICALIZES

The British Newspaper, *Daily Mail,* (*Associated Newspapers Ltd,* www.dailymail.co.uk) published an article titled "Multiculturalism drives young Muslims to shun British values," January 29, 2007:

Multiculturalism has alienated an entire **generation of young Muslims and made them increasingly radical...**

In contrast with their parents, growing numbers sympathise with extreme teachings of Islam, with **almost four in ten wanting to live under Sharia law in Britain.**

The study identifies significant support for wearing the veil in public, Islamic schools and **even punishment by death for Muslims who convert to another religion.** Most alarmingly, **13 per cent of young Muslims said they "admired" organisations such as Al Qaeda** which are prepared to "fight the West."

The poll exposes a fracture between the attitudes of Muslims aged 16 to 24, most of whom were born in Britain, and those of their parents' generation, who are more likely to have been immigrants. A report published alongside the poll, commissioned by the think tank Policy Exchange and carried out by Populus, said **the doctrine of multi-culturalism was at least partly responsible.**

A series of Labour ministers have broken recently with the idea that different communities should not be forced to integrate but should be allowed to maintain their own culture and identities.

Trevor Phillips, head of the Commission for Racial Equality, and Dr. John Sentamu, the Archbishop of York, have also expressed **serious doubts about multiculturalism.**

Academic Munira Mirza, lead author of the report, said: **"The emergence of a strong Muslim identity in Britain is, in part, a result of multi-cultural policies implemented since the 1980s** which have emphasised difference at the expense of shared national identity and divided people along ethnic, religious and cultural lines."

The poll of 1,000 Muslims, weighted to represent the population across the UK, found that a growing minority of youngsters felt they had less in common with non-Muslims than their parents did.

While only 17 per cent of over-55s said they would prefer to live under Sharia law, that increased to 37 per cent of those aged 16 to 24.

Sharia law, which is practised in large parts of the Middle East, specifies **stonings and amputations as routine punishments for crimes.**

It also acts as a religious code for living, covering dietary laws and dress codes. **Religious police are responsible for bringing suspects before special courts.**

The poll found that just 19 per cent of Muslims over 55 would prefer to send their children to Islamic state schools.

That increased to 37 per cent of those aged 16 to 24. **If a Muslim converts to another religion, 36 per cent of 16-to-24-year-olds thought this should be punished by death,** compared with 19 per cent of 55s and over.

According to the poll, **74 per cent of those aged 16 to 24 prefer Muslim women to wear the veil,** compared with only 28 per cent of over 55s.

The report by Miss Mirza, British-born daughter of Pakistani immigrants, concludes that some **Muslim groups have exaggerated the problems of "Islamophobic"** sentiment among non-Muslim Britons, which has fuelled a sense of victimhood.

The vast majority of Muslims–84 per cent–believed they had been treated fairly in British society.

And just over a quarter – 28 per cent – believed that authorities in Britain had gone "over the top" in trying not to offend Muslims...

No one has been convicted under legislation introduced to deal with such figures. **One radical cleric, Abu Hamza, was** allowed to encourage extremism for years before finally being prosecuted – but under separate laws and only under threat of him being extradited to the U.S.

Muslim Labour MP Shahid Malik said the poll findings were disturbing.

"There are evil voices out there and this poll shows some of them are definitely having an impact. People are still turning a blind eye and hoping it will all go away. It cannot and it will not of its own accord.

Of course the Government has a role, but with the Muslim community itself more has to be done to acknowledge that this challenge exists...

"It's my view that the mainstream, umbrella Muslim organisations have not risen to the challenge and don't accept the depth of the problem that's facing them."

Mr. Malik said one legal change which could help address radicalisation was to make committees of faith leaders who run **mosques legally responsible for inflammatory statements made on their premises.**

Baroness Uddin, the only female Muslim peer...said many young **Muslims who had been born in the UK did have completely different attitudes to their parents and grandparents, who migrated into this country from overseas.**

"Whereas we said, 'This isn't our home, we have to fit in, we have to contribute', young people do have a sense that this is now their home and they are prepared to say what they don't like about it.

"They have asserted their identity and gone deeper into their religion. It would have been unheard of for someone like me, as a 16-year-old, to have complained about England.

"But now, when young people go through difficulties in terms of job opportunities and education, they do make their opinions known."

Baroness Uddin said she agreed with the "majority view" that British foreign policy had also aggravated Muslim grievances.

The Labour MP for Birmingham Perry Barr, Khalid Mahmood, said: **"Our young people have been allowed to fall into the hands of fringe organisations who are getting at them at universities, schools, colleges and mosques. They are being manipulated.**

"It's difficult for the Government to prescribe a way forward for the Muslim community. I don't think it can do that.

"It's up to the mainstream, national Muslim organisations, who frankly have failed."

(See Telegraph.co.uk article "Extremism flourished as UK lost Christianity" by Michael Nazir-Ali, Jan. 1, 2008)

ৎ৯

EUROPEAN PARLIAMENT

Gerard Batten, Member of the European Parliament from the UK Independence Party, addressed the European Parliament, February 14, 2007:

Mr. President...The free democratic world is not engaged in a war on terrorism.

This is a misconception repeated in this report. **We are engaged in a war on ideology** – a war we did not start.

The ideology is that of fundamentalist and extreme Islam, an ideology without any humanitarian or civilised constraint.

Thankfully, the United States of America is leading the resistance against it.

FIRST MUSLIM IN CONGRESS

Raised Catholic and a graduate of University of Detroit Jesuit High School, Keith Ellison converted to Islam at age 19 while attending Detroit's Wayne State University. Associate Press writer Frederic J. Frommer, Jan. 4, 2007, wrote that Ellison's mother, Clida Ellison, described herself as a practicing Catholic, saying: "I go to Mass every day."

In 2006, with votes split between Independence, Green and Republican Party candidates, Democrat Keith Ellison, who downplayed his religion during his campaign, made history by being the first Muslim elected to the U.S. Congress (Minnesota 5th District).

Keith Ellison referenced the *Qur'an:*

> Before you begin to think that some hardship has befallen you, you need to stop and thank Allah. Because this controversy [over the *Qur'an* oath] has...made people dust off their Constitution and actually read it.

✧

IF TERRORISTS HAD A CANDIDATE?

Franklin D. Roosevelt, in a Fireside Chat addressing the subject of Nazi terrorist agents, Washington, D.C., December 29, 1940, stated:

> There are also American citizens, many of them in high places, who, unwittingly in most cases, are aiding and abetting the work of these agents.
>
> I do not charge these American citizens with being foreign agents, but I do charge them with doing exactly the kind of work that the dictators want done in the United States.

In an interview with Pat Kessler on CBS affiliate WCCO-TV, Jan. 4, 2007, the first Muslim Congressman, Keith Ellison, discussed his views on the war on terror:

Kessler: Should we remove our troops immediately as you advocated during the campaign?

Ellison: Yes.

Kessler: What do you mean?

Ellison: ...I think that our troops in Iraq are not adding to the peace and we are in a civil war in Iraq...

Kessler: As you know, the president is considering a surge in troops — 15,000 to 30,000 more troops — to quell the violence immediately around Baghdad.

Ellison: Well it's a bad idea...

Kessler: Do you support the impeachment of the president because of this?

Ellison: Well, Pat...I think that it's certainly justifiable. I certainly think that there is ample reason to do so. But the leadership, the speaker has said, that it is not what she wants to do...and I'm going to follow her leadership on this.

But I do think...this question of what to do about impeachment should at least come up...

FOX News' Joseph Abrams reported Jan. 9, 2009:

Minnesota Rep. Keith Ellison's groundbreaking pilgrimage to Mecca last month was paid for by an American Muslim organization that has ties to Islamic radicals and is "the Muslim equivalent of the neo-Nazi party...It is the de facto arm of the Muslim Brotherhood in the U.S.," said Steve Emerson, director of the Investigative Project on Terrorism.

WASHINGTON'S FOREIGN POLICY

Should America be concerned with a growing population having "a passionate attachment" to what could be considered a foreign influence? Since Islam is not just a religion, but also a political and military system, could a Muslim's bowing five times a day be the equivalent of pledging allegiance to Mecca? Does it affect a Muslim's loyalty to America to have one of Islam's five pillars be the Hajj, a pilgrimage once in their life to a city in Saudi Arabia?

George Washington warned in his Farewell Address, September 19, 1796:

> **A passionate attachment of one Nation for another produces a variety of evils**...infusing into one the enmities of the other...
>
> It gives to ambitious, corrupted, or deluded citizens...**facility to betray, or sacrifice the interests of their own country**, without odium, sometimes even with popularity: gilding with the appearances of a virtuous sense of obligation, a commendable deference for public opinion, or a laudable zeal for public good, the base or foolish compliances of ambition, corruption or infatuation.
>
> As avenues to **foreign influence** in innumerable ways, such attachments **are particularly alarming to the truly enlightened and independent Patriot.**
>
> How many opportunities do they afford to tamper with domestic factions, to practice the arts of seduction, **to mislead public opinion,** to influence or awe the public Councils!...
>
> Against **the insidious wiles of foreign influence,** (I conjure you to believe me fellow citizens) the jealously of a free people to be constantly awake; since history and experience prove that foreign influence is one of the most baneful foes of Republican Government.
>
> **Real Patriots, who may resist the intrigues of the favorite, are liable to become suspected and odious;** while its tools and dupes usurp the applause and confidence of the people, to surrender their interests...
>
> Taking care always to keep ourselves, by suitable establishments, on a respectably

defensive posture....

'Tis folly in one Nation to look for disinterested favors from another...it must **pay with a portion of its Independence** for whatever it may accept...

In offering to you, my Countrymen these counsels of an old and affectionate friend, I dare not hope they will make the strong and lasting impression, I could wish....**to warn against the mischiefs of foreign Intrigue.**

◌ঌ

PATRICK HENRY'S FOREIGN POLICY

Patrick Henry stated in a courtroom speech, as recorded by his grandson, William Wirt Henry in *Patrick Henry: Life, Correspondence and Speeches* (NY: Charles Scribner's Sons, 1891, Vol. 3, p. 606):

I know, sir, how well it becomes a liberal man and a **Christian to forget and forgive.**

As individuals professing a holy religion, **it is our bounden duty to forgive injuries done us as individuals.**

But **when the character of Christian you add the character of patriot, you are in a different situation.**

Our mild and holy system of religion inculcates an admirable maxim of forbearance. **If your enemy smite one cheek, turn the other to him.**

But you must stop there. You cannot apply this to your country. As members of a social community, this maxim does not apply to you.

When you consider injuries done to your country your political duty tells you of vengeance. **Forgive as a private man, but never forgive public injuries.**

Observations of this nature are exceedingly unpleasant, but it is my duty to use them.

◌

POLITICAL / MILITARY SYSTEMS

Setting aside the religious aspect of Islam for a moment and examining it as a political/military system, it has a global conquest aspect to it and wherever it takes over, non-Muslims are not treated as equal to Muslims.

What other political/military systems has America had to face in the last 100 years that had a global conquest aspect to them and wherever they took over, non-adherents were not treated as equal to adherents?

Americans love Germans, but during WWII, America had to resist the political/military system of Nazism. Why? Because Nazism had a global conquest aspect to it and wherever it took over, non-Nazis, such as Jews, were not treated as equal to Nazis.

Americans love Japanese, but had to resist the political/military system of Japanese Imperialism.

Americans love Italians, but had to resist the political/military system of Mussolini's Fascism.

Americans love Russians, but had to resist the political/military system of Communism.

Americans love Chinese, but had to resist the political/military system of Chinese Collectivism.

Americans love Arabs, Turks, Persians, Egyptians and Indonesians, but America has to resist the political/military system of Islam.

Why? Because it has a global conquest aspect to it and wherever Islam takes over, non-Muslims are not equal.

◌

COLIN POWELL ON FOREIGN POLICY

Secretary of State Colin Powell stated:

Obama's Muslim heritage feeds the broader suspicion that he is too casual about the threat from America's Islamist enemies.

◌

PRESIDENT TAFT'S FOREIGN POLICY

President William Howard Taft stated in his Annual Message to Congress, December 6, 1912:

> We would go as far as any nation in the world to avoid war, but **we are a world power**, our responsibilities in the Pacific and the Atlantic, our defense of the Panama Canal, together with our enormous world trade and **our missionary outposts on the frontiers of civilization**, require us to recognize our position as one of the foremost in the family of nations,
>
> And **to clothe ourselves with sufficient naval power to give force to our reasonable demands, and to give weight to our influence in those directions of progress that a powerful Christian nation should advocate.**

∽

ENFORCING DHIMMI STATUS IN USA

Islam has a 1,400 year track record of reducing non-Muslims to second-class status called "dhimmi." Dhimmi-status citizens must not say anything critical of Islam.

On December 4, 2006, the Council on American-Islamic Relations (CAIR), which has ties with terrorist organizations, wanted to enforce "dhimmi" status on columnist Dennis Prager by forcing him to be removed from serving on the U.S. Holocaust Memorial Council simply because he was critical of Rep. Keith Ellison's unprecedented act of swearing in on a *Qur'an*.

∽

QUR'AN: ARE ALL PEOPLE EQUAL?

Rep. Keith Ellison swore upon Jefferson's *Qur'an* - the same Jefferson who penned the words "All men are created equal," yet Islamic law says all men are NOT equal. The *Qur'an* reveals Allah's will that infidels are not equal before the law with faithful Muslims.

Muslim courts will not accept the testimony of a Christian or Jew against a Muslim. Blood money retribution for killing a Christian is half of the blood money for killing a Muslim. Christians and Jews are degraded to second-class citizenship called "dhimmi" and required to submit to their Muslim masters and pay a tax called "jizyah" in order to not be killed:

> Fight those who believe not in Allah nor the Last Day, nor hold that forbidden which hath been forbidden by Allah and His Messenger, nor acknowledge the religion of Truth, (even if they are) of the People of the Book, until they pay the Jizya with willing submission, and feel themselves subdued. (Sura 9:29)

Swearing upon a book implies believing what is in that book. Can a politician swear to uphold equality upon a book that does not teach equality?

✧

THIS IS A SAUDI TEXTBOOK

Jeremy Paxman of BBC's *Newsnight*, Feb. 6, 2007, asked Dr. Sumaya Alyusuf of the Islamic King Fahd Academy in Acton, England, if she recognized the Saudi textbooks which called Jews apes and Christians pigs.
Dr. Sumaya Alyusuf replied:

> Yes, I do recognize these books, of course.
> We have these books in our school.

The Washington Post, May 21, 2006, published excerpts from these Saudi textbooks in an article by Nina Shea titled **"This is a Saudi textbook (after the intolerance was removed)":**

> FIRST GRADE
> "Every religion other than Islam is false."
> "Fill in the blanks with the appropriate words (Islam, hellfire): Every religion other

than _____ is false. Whoever dies outside of Islam enters _____."

FOURTH GRADE

"True belief means...that you hate the polytheists and infidels."

FIFTH GRADE

"Whoever obeys the Prophet and accepts the oneness of Allah cannot maintain a loyal friendship with those who oppose Allah and His Prophet, even if they are his closest relatives."

"It is forbidden for a Muslim to be a loyal friend to someone who does not believe in Allah and His Prophet."

"A Muslim, even if he lives far away, is your brother in religion. Someone who opposes Allah, even if he is your brother by family tie, is your enemy in religion."

SIXTH GRADE

"Just as Muslims were successful in the past when they came together in a sincere endeavor to evict the Christian crusaders from Palestine, so will the Arabs and Muslims emerge victorious, Allah willing, against the Jews and their allies."

EIGHTH GRADE

"As cited in Ibn Abbas: **The apes are Jews, the people of the Sabbath; while the swine are the Christians, the infidels of the communion of Jesus."** [swine (pigs) are abhorrent to faithful Muslims]

"Some of the people of the Sabbath were punished by being turned into apes and swine.

"Some of them were made to worship the devil, and not Allah, through consecration, sacrifice, prayer, appeals for help, and other types of worship.

"Some of the Jews worship the devil. Likewise, some members of this nation worship the devil, and not Allah."

"The Jews, whom Allah has cursed and with whom He is so angry that He will never again be satisfied with them."

"Activity: The student writes a composition on the danger of imitating the infidels."

NINTH GRADE

"The clash between this [Muslim] community (umma) and the Jews and Christians has endured, and it will continue as long as Allah wills."

"It is part of Allah's wisdom that the struggle between the Muslim and the Jews should continue until the hour [of judgment]."

"Muslims will triumph because they are right."

TENTH GRADE

"Blood money is retribution paid to the victim or the victim's heirs for murder or injury.

Blood money for a free infidel is half of the blood money for a male Muslim... Blood money for a woman is half of the blood money for a man."

ELEVENTH GRADE

"The greeting 'Peace be upon you' is specifically for believers. It cannot be said to others."

"Do not yield to Christians and Jews on a narrow road out of honor and respect."

TWELFTH GRADE

"Jihad in the path of Allah — which consists of battling against unbelief, oppression, injustice, and those who perpetrate it — is the summit of Islam. **This religion arose through jihad and through jihad was its banner raised high."**

✧

QUR'AN & WOMEN

The *Qur'an* necessitates two women to testify in court against one man, Sura 2:282:

And let two men from among you bear witness to all such documents.

But if two men are not available, there should be one man and two women to bear witness so that if one of the women forgets (anything), the other may remind her.

The *Hadith*, narrated Abu Said Al-Khudri, states:

The Prophet said, "Isn't the witness of a woman equal to half of that of a man?" The women said, "Yes." He said, "This is because of the deficiency of a woman's mind." (Volume 3, Book 48, Number 826)

The *Qur'an* says in Sura 4:11:

The share of the male shall be twice that of a female.

TIME Magazine (2001) reported in Iran: "The legal age for marriage is 9 for girls." A Muslim man can take 4 wives, not counting slave-mistresses and concubines:

Marry women of your choice, two, or three, or four. (Sura 4:3)

Islam permits sex outside of marriage if it is with slaves and captives of war.

Married women (are forbidden unto you) save those (captives) whom your right hands possess. It is a decree of Allah for you. Lawful unto you are all beyond those mentioned. (Sura 4:24, Pickthal Translation)

If a woman is raped, she is guilty of tempting the man and receives 100 lashes.

The woman...guilty of adultery or fornication,- flog...with a hundred stripes: Let not compassion move you in their case, in a matter prescribed by Allah, if ye believe in Allah and the Last Day: and let a party of the Believers witness their punishment. (Sura 24:2)

A Muslim man can divorce any of his wives, yet a Muslim woman does not have the same right, and if she is put away, she has no custody of her children.

In July 2007, a Muslim in Jordan spent only 6 months in jail for killing his pregnant sister in order to "uphold his family's honor." On February 17, 2009, Muzzammil Hassan, founder of Bridges TV, was arrested for the "honor killing" of beheading his wife. In October 2009, a Muslim in Arizona ran over his daughter with his car for becoming "too Westernized."

In 2009, 17-year-old Rifqa Barry converted to Christianity and fled to Florida for fear of being killed by her father. The Pakistan Institute of Medical Sciences reported 90 percent of Pakistani women have been subjected to physical or sexual abuse, as the *Qur'an* (Sura 4:34) dictates:

If you experience rebellion from the women, you shall first talk to them, then (you may use negative incentives like) deserting them in bed, then you may (as a last alternative) beat them. If they obey you, you are not permitted to transgress against them. Allah is Most High, Supreme. (Rashad Khalifa Translation)

A translation by Hassan Qaribullah & Ahmad Darwish says husbands can "smack them (without harshness)." The *Yusufali Translation* says to "beat them (lightly),"as with a rod no thicker than a thumb - "the Rule of Thumb."

Hadith Sahih al-Bukhari, by 'Imran bin Husain:

The Prophet said, "I looked at Paradise and found poor people forming the majority of its inhabitants; and I looked at Hell and saw that the majority of its inhabitants were women." (*Hadith Sahih al-Bukhari,* Vol. 7, No. 125)

The *Qur'an* dictates a woman's dress and walk:

Believing women...shall not reveal any parts of their bodies, except that which is necessary...They shall not strike their feet when they walk in order to shake and reveal certain details of their bodies. All of you shall repent to Allah, O you believers, that you may succeed. (Sura 24:31)

Prayer is annulled by a dog, a donkey or a woman passing in front of you. (Hadith Sahih al-Bukhari vol. 1, bk. 9, no. 490)

∽

AYAAN HIRSI ALI

Raised as a Muslim in Somalia, Ayaan Hirsi Ali sought political asylum in the Netherlands in 1992 and in 2003 was elected to States-General of the Netherlands.

In 2004, she helped Dutch filmmaker Theo van Gogh produce a 10 minute movie about the subordinate role of women in Islamic society with women who showed signs of physical abuse. Ayaan Hirsi Ali is particularly an opponent of female genital mutilation practiced in many Muslim countries.

Mohammed Bouyeri, a member of the radical Muslim Hofstad Group, shot Van Gogh in Amsterdam on November 2, 2004, and stabbed a note into his dead body with a death threat to Ayaan Hirsi Ali. She later resigned from Dutch government and went into hiding.

In 2005, Ayaan Hirsi Ali was in *TIME Magazine's* list of the 100 Most Influential People of the World.

In 2007, Ayaan Hirsi Ali wrote the book "Infidel: My Life: The Story of My Enlightenment" (*Free Press*, 2007). In an interview with Glen Beck on *Headline Prime*, February 10, 2007, Ayaan Hirsi Ali stated: "Anyone who is not a Muslim is a target."

⊰

QUR'AN & SLAVERY

Hundreds of verses in the *Qur'an, Hadith* and *Sirah Rasul Allah* reference slavery. Muslim apologists cannot condemn slavery as Mohammed owned slaves. Selling captives from war into slavery was a lucrative means of funding Islamic expansion.

Mohammed allowed women taken in battle to be enslaved, instructing his men not to interrupt raping them, as they were in the habit of doing because pregnant women fetched less at the slave market.

O Allah's Apostle! We get female captives as our share of booty and we are interested in their prices, what is your opinion about coitus interruptus (Al-'Azi)? The Prophet said...It is better for you not to do it. No soul that which Allah has destined to exist, but will surely come into existence. (*Hadith Sahih Bukhari* Vol. 3, Bk. 34, No. 432; Vol. 5, Bk. 59, No. 459; Vol. 7, Bk. 62, No. 137; Vol. 9, Book, 93, No. 506)

Warriors were drawn to jihad for religion and because women could be captured for sexual exploitation.

Married women are forbidden unto you except those captives whom your right hand possesses. It is a decree of Allah for you. (Sura 4:24)

Slavery of women and castrated men and boys for use in male homosexual pederasty and as eunuchs in harems has a history in Islam. In *Islam's Black Slaves* (Farrar, Straus & Giroux, 2001), Ronald Segal wrote:

Islam conquered the Persian Sassanid Empire and much of the Byzantine Empire, including Syria and Egypt in the 7th Century... Female slaves were required in considerable numbers...many were in demand as concubines. Harems of rulers could be enormous. The harem of Abdal Rahman III (912-961) in Cordoba contained over 6,000 concubines. And the one in the Fatimid Palace in Cairo had twice as many.

Arabian Nights has stories of harems and eunuchs:

Tale of the First Eunuch Baukhayt;
Tale of the Second Eunuch Kafur;
Masrur the Eunuch and Ibn Al-Karibi;
The Tale of Kafur the Black Eunuch.

Not only were thousands of Christians captured and enslaved by Muslim Barbary Pirates from ships and coastal towns of Italy, France, Spain and Portugal, but most African slaves brought to the New World were purchased from Muslim slave traders

Elikia M'bokolo wrote in the French journal *Le Monde diplomatique*, April 2, 1998:

The African continent was bled of its human resources...At least ten centuries of slavery for the benefit of the Muslim countries...millions exported via the Red Sea...through Swahili ports of the Indian Ocean...along trans-Saharan caravan routes.

An estimated 180 million Africans were enslaved by Islam over 1,400 years. So many, in fact, that the Arabic word "abd" means both African and slave.

Muslim slave markets sold 10-15 million Africans to slave traders bound for the Caribbean Islands, Central and South America. Only 500,000 African slaves were brought to the United States.

As 10 percent of slaves died crossing the Atlantic, 80 percent of slaves perished crossing the Sahara Desert.

∽

FIGHTING SLAVERY

Jesus began his ministry in Nazareth by reading a scripture on freeing slaves from Isaiah 61:1: "The Spirit of the Lord is upon me, because He has anointed me to...proclaim liberty to the captives...to set at liberty those who are oppressed." (Luke 4:18 NKJV)

Patrick Henry wrote to Robert Pleasants in 1773, expressing his disapproval of the slave trade:

> I take this opportunity to acknowledge the receipt of Anthony Benezet's Book against the slave trade. I thank you for it....
>
> Is it not amazing, that at a time when the rights of humanity are defined and understood with precision in a country above all others fond of liberty, that in such an age and in such a country, we find men professing a religion most humane, mild, meek, gentle and generous, adopting a Principle as repugnant to humanity, as it is inconsistent to the *Bible* and destructive to liberty?....I will not, I cannot justify it....
>
> I believe a time will come when an opportunity will be offered to abolish this lamentable evil....It is a debt we owe to the purity of our Religion to show that it is at variance with that law which warrants slavery.
>
> I know not when to stop. I would say many things on this subject, a serious review of which gives gloomy perspective to future times.

Slave trade ended in Britain in 1807 and slaves were emancipated in 1833, due to the Christian influences of John Newton, the slave trader who converted and wrote the song "Amazing Grace," and politician William Wilberforce, who wrote in his diary October 28, 1787:

> God Almighty has set before me two great objects, the suppression of the slave trade and the Reformation of society.

Importing slaves to the United States stopped in 1807 and slaves were emancipated in 1865. In his Gettysburg Address, Lincoln, 1863, wrote:

> Fourscore and seven years ago our fathers brought forth upon this continent a new nation, conceived in liberty, and dedicated to the proposition that all men are created equal. Now we are engaged in a great civil war, testing whether that nation, or any nation so conceived and so dedicated, can long endure.

International pressure caused Saudi Arabia and Yemen to end public trading of slaves as recently as 1962 and Mauritania in 1980, though many Muslim countries still are clandestinely involved.

Slavery, forced marriages, sexual slaves and child sex trafficking continues in countries with large Muslim populations, such as: Sudan, Niger, Nigeria, Benin, Togo, United Arab Emirates, Pakistan, Albania, Bosnia, Turkey and Indonesia.

Organizations tracking modern slavery are: Anti-Slavery International, Human Rights Watch, American Anti-Slavery Group, National Underground Railroad Freedom Center, Free the Slaves, Christian Freedom International, International Labor Rights and Education Fund, Human Rights Commission of Pakistan, and Anti-Slavery Society. (freetheslaves.net, anti-slaverysociety.addr.com, freedomcenter.org, antislavery.org, iabolish.org)

⊰

DRIVE-NEUTRAL-REVERSE

An automobile shifts from DRIVE into NEUTRAL before it can shift into REVERSE.

In the same way, **Western Civilization had to shift from Judeo-Christian to Secular-Atheist before it can shift to Fundamental Islam.** This has been demonstrated in Europe, which for centuries had been Catholic and Protestant, with a remnant of Jews. Believing all are "made in the image of God," Jewish teaching "Be nice to the stranger as you were once a stranger in Egypt" and Christian teaching "Do unto others as you would have them do unto you," though not always lived up to, challenged consciences to treat others equally.

The French Revolution shifted Europe to Neutral. The Secular-Atheistic view was to do whatever you wanted because there is no God, and if he does exist, he is so distant that he does not care. This evolved into pluralism, diversity, political correctness, hate-crime legislation and multiculturalism, which acts as the AIDS virus of Western Civilization.

Teaching all belief systems are equal and should be embraced, Europe has allowed in Fundamental Islam, which believes it is blasphemy to believe one is made in the image of Allah and obedience to Allah requires subduing infidels. Fundamental Islam allows husbands to beat their wives, commit honor-killings of daughters who dishonor their families, force women to wear veils (hijab), enslave non-Muslims and instigate violence.

Europeans are awakening to find 70 percent of immigrants are Muslim, large areas of Paris are hostile to non-Muslims and "Mohammed" is the most popular name given to newborn boys in England, Brussels, Amsterdam and Rotterdam. Muslim population in Europe is 50 million and expected to double by 2025.

Muslim men gang-rape European women because they are "not veiled." A Copenhagan Islamic muffti publicly declared women who refuse to wear headscarves are "asking for rape." In Norway, similar to Denmark and Sweden, rapists are six times more likely to be Muslim.

Despite this, Swedish "hate crime" laws imprisoned Bjorn Bjorkqvist, May 25, 2004, for writing

I don't think I am alone in feeling sick when reading about how Swedish girls are raped by immigrant hordes.

Muslim countries prohibit public Judeo-Christian expression and those promoting the Secular-Atheist-Gay agenda want to prohibit public Judeo-Christian expression. There is an unholy alliance between radical Muslims and radical Secularists/Atheist/Gays, as they all are working to erase Judeo-Christian culture.

Secular-Atheism is actually a temporary state, facilitating Western Civilization's transition from Judeo-Christian values to Islamic values.

Secular-Atheism's theme song, John Lennon's *Imagine,* has a line: "Nothing to kill and die for, and no religion too." In other words, producing a Secular-Atheist utopia eliminates the will of anyone to defend it. Brussels newspaper, *De Standard*, printed an Op-Ed by self-declared gay humanist author, Oscar Van Den Boogaard:

> I am not a warrior...I never learned to fight for my freedom. I was only good at enjoying it.

∽

HOW AGENDAS ARE PROMOTED

Social agendas are promoted through media, public education, courts and buying of political office. The first step is to "deconstruct" traditional values and history. Next, education, movies and television programs portray an unacceptable social behavior in a humorous way, then progressively show that behavior in a positive light, then finally ridicule and intimidate those who oppose that behavior.

When the public considers that behavior normal, contributions are given to politicians who advocate changing laws to accept that behavior. Then laws are passed to discriminate and eventually criminalize those refusing to embrace the new behavior.

Previously unacceptable behaviors, such as gambling, drug use, adultery and homosexuality have successfully used these methods. The Islamic agenda is now employing these methods, as in Canada's television series, "Little Mosque on the Prairie," portraying struggles of a Muslim family in America.

The world's 4th-richest man, Prince Al-Waleed bin Talal, the Saudi Warren Buffett, donated $27 million to families of suicide bombers, $500,000 to CAIR (a Hamas terrorist-related group), funded $20 million each Islamic centers at Harvard and Georgetown, and in 2005 became the second largest shareholder of News Corp, which owns Fox News and the Wall Street Journal. When President Jimmy Carter's "Carter Center" neared bankruptcy, Prince Alwaleed bin Talal and a brother of Osama bin Laden, Bakr Bin Laden, donated $5 million. Jimmy Carter subsequently criticized Israel and defended terrorists.

As media today is influenced to "spin" news stories, Islam has "spun" their mistreatment of non-Muslims over the centuries. The classic example is Muslims harassing infidel communities till they defend themselves. Infidels are then accused of "fighting Allah," which justifies Muslims in declaring holy war.

In addition to media jihad is legal jihad, called "lawfare," where warfare is waged through the courts.

Islam teaches "infidels" are not treated equally with Muslims. To preserve equality, America must discourage value systems that deny equality. Dwight Eisenhower was quoted in *TIME Magazine*, October 13, 1952: "**The Bill of Rights contains no grant of privilege for a group of people to destroy the Bill of Rights. A group...dedicated to the ultimate destruction of all civil liberties,** cannot be allowed to claim civil liberties as its privileged sanctuary from which to carry on subversion of the Government."

∽

CHRISTIAN AGENDA OF TOLERANCE

Patricia U. Bonomi, Professor Emeritus of New York University, in her article *The Middle Colonies as the Birthplace of American Religious Pluralism*, wrote: "The colonists were about 98 percent Protestant."

Americans drew their understanding of tolerance from the different Christian groups which founded the original colonies:

Anglicans founded Virginia & Carolinas
Puritans founded Massachusetts
Congregationalists founded Connecticut & New Hampshire
Dutch Reformed founded New York
Baptists founded Rhode Island
Catholics founded Maryland
Lutherans founded Delaware & New Jersey
Quakers & Presbyterians founded Pennsylvania
Protestants founded Georgia

Initially not getting along, these denominations had to work together to fight the Revolution against King George III. After the Revolutionary War tolerance gradually extended to Catholics. In the early 1800's tolerance extended to "liberal" Christian denominations, such as Unitarians and Universalists.

In the middle 1800's persecuted Jews from Europe immigrated and were tolerated. In the late 1800's anyone who believed in a monotheistic God was tolerated.

In the early 1900's tolerance began to extend to polytheists and many new religions. In the middle 1900's tolerance extended to atheists.

Finally, tolerance extended to anti-religious, radical homosexual and radical Muslim groups, who teach intolerance toward the Judeo-Christian beliefs which began the entire progression of tolerance. (Suggested reading: *The Original 13-A Documentary History of Religion in America's First Thirteen States; and BACKFIRED-A Nation Born For Religious Tolerance No Longer Tolerates Religion.*)

WHY FOUNDERS SPREAD TOLERANCE

On June 1, 2009, a U.S. Army recruiter was murdered by Muslim convert Abdulhakim Mujahid in Little Rock, Arkansas. When interviewed, he said it was "Islamic justified," adding: "We believe in eye for an eye. We don't believe in turning the other cheek."

This is different from the Golden Rule which Jesus spoke of in his Sermon on the Mount:

> **Do unto others what you would have them do unto you.**

There are no Suras commanding Muslims to do to infidels what they want infidels to do to them.

President Madison proclaimed, July 9, 1812:

> With a reverence for the unerring precept of our holy religion, to **do to others as they would require that others should do to them.**

In "An Address on the Bank of North America," 1785, Gouverneur Morris stated:

> How can we hope for public peace and national prosperity, if the faith of governments so solemnly pledged can be so lightly infringed?...It is He who tells you, **"do unto others as ye would that they would do unto you."**

President Andrew Jackson, in his 3rd Annual Message, December 6, 1831, stated:

> Our submission to the divine rule of **doing to others what we desire they should do unto us.**

The word "christian" was synonymous with "tolerance," as Samuel Adams mentioned in *The Rights of the Colonists*, 1772, that "the spirit of toleration" was the "chief characteristical mark of the church":

> In regards to religion, mutual toleration in the different professions...is what all good and candid

minds in all ages have ever practiced...**it is now generally agreed among Christians that this spirit of toleration...is the chief characteristical mark of the church.**

The concept of "Christian Forbearance" is "patience, long-suffering, indulgence toward offenders or enemies, not giving in to violence, rage or anger, mildness." This is mentioned by name in the "The Virginia Bill of Rights, written in 1776 by George Mason with the help of James Madison and Patrick Henry:

> That Religion, or the Duty which we owe our Creator, and the Manner of discharging it, **can be directed only by Reason and Convictions, not by Force or Violence**; and therefore all Men are equally entitled to the free exercise of Religion, according to the Dictates of Conscience; and that **it is the mutual Duty of all to practice Christian Forbearance, Love, and Charity towards each other.**

Patrick Henry, as recorded by his grandson, William Wirt Henry in *Patrick Henry: Life, Correspondence & Speeches* (NY: Charles Scribner's Sons, 1891, Vol. 3, p. 606), stated in a courtroom :

> I know, sir, how well it becomes a liberal man and **a Christian to forget and forgive**.
>
> As individuals professing a **holy religion**, it is our bounden duty to **forgive injuries done us** as individuals...**Our mild and holy system of religion inculcates an admirable maxim of forbearance. If your enemy smite one cheek, turn the other to him**.

Patrick Henry is attributed with this explanation why "peoples of other faiths" are given "freedom of worship here":

> It cannot be emphasized too strongly or too often that this great nation was founded, not

by religionists, but by Christians; not on religions, but on the *Gospel* of Jesus Christ. **For this very reason peoples of other faiths have been afforded asylum, prosperity, and freedom of worship here.**

Franklin D. Roosevelt, October 1, 1938, greeted Archbishop Rummel of New Orleans:

I doubt if there is any problem in the world today - social, political or economic - that would not find happy solution if approached in the spirit of the **Sermon on the Mount.**

May your prayers hasten the day when both men and nations will bring their lives into conformity with the teaching of Him Who is the Way, the Light and the Truth.

INSIDE OUT OR OUTSIDE IN

The U.S. Supreme Court Building, completed in 1935, has marble relief sculptures around the ceiling of the Courtroom depicting lawgivers throughout history.

The South Wall frieze has lawgivers who lived before Jesus and the North Wall has lawgivers after Jesus, including Mohammed, pictured holding his Arabic Qur'an and a scimitar sword. The Congress approved portrayal of Mohammed by sculptor, Adolph A. Weinman (1870-1952), reflects the historical understanding of Islam as a religion of the sword.

Czech Cardinal Vlk explained: **"Islam assumes state power and rules people."** Dutch Member of Parliament, Geert Wilders, stated: **"Islam is a political ideology...Islam wants to dictate every aspect of life...If you want to compare Islam to anything, compare it to communism or national-socialism (Nazism). These are all totalitarian ideologies."**

America's founders believed in a different religion that was not to be forced from the outside in, but emanated from the inside out, as the Baptist founder of Rhode Island Roger Williams wrote:

That religion cannot be true which needs such instruments of violence to uphold it.

Quaker founder of Pennsylvania William Penn wrote in *England's Present Interest Considered*, 1675:

Force makes hypocrites, 'tis persuasion only that makes converts.

Jesus taught that religion should be voluntary from the inside out, whereas Mohammed taught that religion could be forced from the outside in. Rather than force people to follow him, Jesus was willing to let his followers leave, as demonstrated in instance in the *Gospel of John* (6:60-67), where after Jesus' teaching:

Many of his disciples...said, "This is a hard saying; who can hear it?" When Jesus knew in himself that his disciples murmured at it, he said unto them, "Doth this offend you?"...From that time many of his disciples went back, and walked no more with him.

Then said Jesus unto the twelve, "Will ye also go away?" Then Simon Peter answered him, "Lord, to whom shall we go? thou hast the words of eternal life."

Mohammed said:

Whoever changes his Islamic religion, kill him. (*Hadith Sahih al-Bukhari,* Vol. 9, No. 57)

Hadith Sahih al-Bukhari, narrated by Abdullah:

Allah's Apostle said, "The blood of a Muslim...cannot be shed except...in three cases...the one who reverts from Islam (apostate) and leaves the Muslims. (*Hadith Sahih al-Bukhari,* Vol. 9, Book 83, No. 17)

Hadith Sahih al-Bukhari, narrated by Ikrima, stated:

Ali burnt some people [hypocrites]...

No doubt, I would have killed them, for the Prophet said, "If somebody (a Muslim) discards his religion, kill him." (*Hadith Sahih Bukhari*, Vol. 4:260, Vol. 9, Book 84, No. 57)

Hadith Sahih al-Bukhari stated:

The punishment for apostasy (riddah) is well-known in Islamic Sharee'ah.

The one who leaves Islam will be asked to repent by the Sharee'ah judge in an Islamic country; if he does not repent and come back to the true religion, he will be killed as a kafir and apostate, because of the command of the Prophet (peace and blessings of Allah be upon him): "Whoever changes his religion, kill him. (*Hadith Sahih al-Bukhari*, 3017)

In strict Islamic nations rulers do not care if individuals have a warm feeling in their heart for Allah, they insist on outward submission, even using police to beat women who are not dressed right, or those who do not close their stores and bow to Mecca five times a day.

ROGER WILLIAMS

Roger Williams founded the Colony of Rhode Island and the first Baptist Church in America. He explained that belief in Jesus can only come from the inside out, not forced from the outside in. In his *Plea for Religious Liberty*, 1644, Roger Williams argued that for Christianity in America to be truly Christian it must allow anti-Christian beliefs:

In holding an enforced uniformity of religion in a civil state, we must necessarily disclaim our desires and hopes of the Jew's conversion to Christ... It is the will and command of God that (since the coming of his Son the Lord Jesus) a permission of the most paganish, Jewish, Turkish, or antichristian consciences and worships, be granted to all men in all nations and countries; and they are only to be fought against with that sword which is only (in soul matters) able to conquer, to wit, the sword of God's Spirit, the Word of God...

I acknowledge that to molest any person, Jew or Gentile, for either professing doctrine, or practicing worship merely religious or spiritual, it is to persecute him, and such a person (whatever his doctrine or practice be, true or false) suffereth persecution for conscience...

The sufferings of false and antichristian teachers harden their followers, who being blind, by this means are occasioned to tumble into the ditch of hell after their blind leaders, with more inflamed zeal of lying confidence...

To batter down idolatry, false worship, heresy, schism, blindness, hardness, out of the soul and spirit, it is vain, improper, and unsuitable to bring those weapons which are used by persecutors, stocks, whips, prisons, swords...

but against these spiritual strongholds in the souls of men, spiritual artillery and weapons are proper, which are mighty through God to subdue and bring under the very thought to obedience.

Roger Williams continued:

An enforced uniformity of religion throughout a nation or civil state, confounds the civil and religious, denies the principles of Christianity and civility, and that Jesus Christ is come in the flesh.

The doctrine of persecution for cause of conscience is most contrary to the doctrine of Christ Jesus the Prince of Peace.

The blood of so many hundred thousand souls of Protestants and Papists, spilt in the wars of present and former ages, for their respective consciences, is not required nor accepted by Jesus Christ the Prince of Peace....

God requireth not a uniformity of religion to be enacted and enforced in any civil state; which enforced uniformity (sooner or later) is the greatest occasion of civil war, ravishing of conscience, persecution of Christ Jesus in his servants, and of the hypocrisy and destruction of millions of souls.

Permission of other consciences and worships than a state professeth only can (according to God) procure a firm and lasting peace...

True civility and Christianity may both flourish in a state or kingdom, notwithstanding the permission of divers and contrary consciences, either of Jew or Gentile.

It is as necessary, yea more honorable, godly, and Christian, to fight the fight of faith, with religious and spiritual artillery, and to contend earnestly for the faith of Jesus, once delivered to the saints against all opposers...

I add that a civil sword is so far from helping forward an opposite in religion to repentance that magistrates sin grievously against the work of God and blood of souls by such proceedings.

JESUS' EXAMPLE

America's leaders put into law Jesus' example of never forcing anyone to believe in him, realizing that the only worship pleasing to God was a voluntary free-will offering from "the impulse of their hearts and the dictates of their consciences." Justice Joseph Story, appointed to the Supreme Court by the "Father of the Constitution," James Madison, wrote in his *Commentaries on the Constitution*, 1833, Section 1871:

The real object of the amendment was, **not to countenance, much less to advance**

Mahometanism, or Judaism, or infidelity, by prostrating Christianity; but to exclude all rivalry among Christian sects…

It thus cut off the means of religious persecution, (the vice and pest of former ages,) and of the subversion of the rights of conscience in matters of religion, which had been trampled upon almost from the days of the Apostles to the present age.

James Madison alluded to this in his Proclamation of a National Day of Public Humiliation & Prayer, July 23, 1813:

If the **public homage of a people** can ever be worthy of the favorable regard of the Holy and Omniscient Being to whom it is addressed, **it must be...guided only by their free choice, by the impulse of their hearts and the dictates of their consciences;** and such a spectacle must be interesting to all Christian nations as proving that **religion, that gift of Heaven for the good of man is freed from all coercive edicts.**

Jefferson's Statute for Religious Freedom in Virginia, 1786, appealed to "the plan of the Holy Author of religion...not to propagate it by coercion":

Well aware that **Almighty God hath created the mind free**, and manifested His Supreme Will that free it shall remain by making it altogether insusceptible of restraints; **that all attempts to influence it by temporal punishments, or burdens, or by civil incapacitations**, tend only to begat habits of hypocrisy and meanness, and **are a departure from the plan of the Holy Author of religion,** who **being Lord both of body and mind, yet chose not to propagate it by coercions on either, as was in his Almighty power to do, but to extend it by its influence on reason alone.**

Who was Jefferson's "Holy Author of religion"? He could not have been referring to polytheistic Hinduism or Buddhism or Greek Mythology, as he used the singular "Author" not the plural "Authors." Besides, there were no Buddhists or Hindus in America at that time.

He could not have been referring to Islam, as there were virtually no Muslims living in the United States at the time, additionally, they had a reputation of propagating through "coercion," with Mohammed himself leading an army which killed many who would not submit.

Jews were not known for "propagating," though their faith did spread through "reason."

Jefferson's phrase "Holy Author of religion" is similar to George Washington's phrase engraved in St. Paul's Chapel, the oldest continuously used structure in New York City. Directly across from the World Trade Center, St. Paul's Chapel was miraculously undamaged during the September 11, 2001, terrorist attack. Washington's Prayer engraved in St. Paul's Chapel refers to "characteristics" and "example" of the "Divine Author of our blessed Religion":

> Almighty God; We make our earnest prayer that Thou wilt keep the United States in Thy Holy protection...
>
> That Thou wilt most graciously be pleased to dispose us all to do justice, to love mercy, and **to demean ourselves with that Charity, humility, and pacific temper of mind which were the Characteristics of the Divine Author of our blessed Religion**, and without a humble imitation of whose example in these things we can never hope to be a happy nation.
>
> Grant our supplication, we beseech Thee, through Jesus Christ our Lord. Amen.

Cotton Mather used the term "Holy Author of that Religion" in his *Magnalia Christi Americana*, 1702:

I write the wonders of the Christian religion, flying from the depravations of Europe, to the American strand: and, assisted by **the Holy Author of that Religion.**

Pennsylvania Frame of Government, April 25, 1682, which required office holders to believe in the *Old and New Testament,* included the phrase:

The same Divine Power that is both the **Author and Object of Pure Religion.**

JEFFERSON VS. MOHAMMED

Mohammed and his followers spread Islam through enforcement, causing infidels to be restrained, molested and burdened. In contrast, Thomas Jefferson opposed "hate crime" legislation which burdened people for their "religious opinions."

Jefferson continued in his Statute for Religious Freedom in Virginia, 1786:

No man shall be compelled to frequent or support any religious worship, place, or ministry, whatsoever, nor shall be enforced, restrained, molested, or burdened in his body or goods, nor shall otherwise suffer, on account of his religious opinions or belief; but that all men shall be free to profess and by argument to maintain their opinions in matters of religion, and that the same shall in no wise diminish, enlarge, or affect their civil capacities.

This is similar to what Rhode Island founder Roger Williams wrote in his *Plea for Religious Liberty,* 1644:

The civil magistrate either respecteth that religion which...is true, or...that which is false.
If that which the magistrate believeth to be true, be true, I say he owes a threefold duty...
First...according to Isa. 49, Revel. 21, a tender respect of truth and the professors of it.

Secondly, personal submission of his own soul to the power of the Lord Jesus in that spiritual government and kingdom...Matt. 18, 1 Cor. 5.

Thirdly, protection of such true professors of Christ, whether apart, or met together, as also of their estates from violence and injury...Rom. 13.

Now, secondly, if it be a false religion (unto which the civil magistrate dare not adjoin, yet) he owes:

First, permission (for approbation he owes not what is evil) and this according to Matthew 13:30, for public peace and quiet's sake.

Secondly, he owes protection to the persons of his subjects (though of a false worship), that no injury be offered either to the persons or goods of any.

RHODE ISLAND CONSTITUTION 1663-1842

Pursuing...their...religious intentions, of Godly edifying themselves...in the Holy Christian faith and worship as they were persuaded...

And whereas...it is much on their hearts...that a most flourishing civil state may...best be maintained... with **a full liberty in religious concernments; and that true piety rightly grounded upon** *Gospel* **principles**, will give the best security...

Now know ye, that we being willing to...secure them in **the free exercise...of all their civil and religious rights...and to preserve unto them that liberty, in the true Christian faith and worship of God, which they have sought with so much travail...**

And because **some of the... inhabitants** of the same colony **cannot, in their private opinions, conforms to the public exercise of religion, according to the liturgy, forms and ceremonies of the Church of England...**

Have therefore thought fit...that **no person within the said colony...shall be...molested, punished, disquieted, or called in question, for any differences in opinion in matters of religion...**

That...every person...may... enjoy...their own judgments and consciences, in matters of religious concernments...behaving themselves peaceably...not using this liberty to licentiousness and profaneness, nor to the civil injury or outward disturbance of others.

The U.S. Supreme Court, in *Church of the Holy Trinity v. United States*, 1892, used two different references to "Christianity." The first being "an established church" with "particular religious tenets," and the second being "general Christianity" with a "liberty of conscience for all men":

In *Updegraph v. The Commonwealth*, it was decided that, "Christianity, **general Christianity, is, and always had been, a part of the common law**...not Christianity founded on any particular religious tenets; **not Christianity with an established church**, and tithes, and spiritual courts, but Christianity with liberty of conscience to all men."

Historian Alexis de Tocqueville wrote in *The Republic of the United States of America & Its Political Institutions*, 1851:

From the earliest settlement of the emigrants, politics and religion contracted an alliance which has never been dissolved...

The **Americans combine the notions of Christianity and of liberty so intimately in their minds, that it is impossible to make them conceive the one without the other.**

SHARING THE *GOSPEL*

Another reason America's founders allowed people of other faiths into the country was evangelism. The idea of going across the world to another culture to evangelize non-Christians was not common until 1812, when America's first foreign missionaries, Adonirum and Ann Judson, left for Rangoon, Burma.

Prior to 1812, the concept of communicating the *Gospel* to those of other religions was to invite them to live in one's community. James Madison used this reasoning in his *Memorial & Remonstrance* to the Virginia Assembly, 1785.

Though other States, such as Massachusetts, Maryland and New Hampshire, supported Christian teachers of piety and religion, Madison opposed the measure in Virginia because: 1) Those responsible for hiring would be tempted to hire teachers from their own denomination, effectively setting up a State church;

and 2) Establishing a State religion would discourage those "still remaining under the dominions of false religions" from immigrating and being reached with "the light of Christianity...the light of Truth."

In *Memorial & Remonstrance*, 1785, Madison wrote:

The policy of the bill is adverse to the diffusion of the light of Christianity. The first wish of those who ought to enjoy this precious gift, ought to be, that **it may be imparted to the whole race of mankind.**

Compare the number of those who have as yet received it, with the number still remaining under **the dominions of false religions**, and how small is the former!

Does the policy of the bill tend to lessen the disproportion? No; **it at once discourages those who are strangers to the light of Truth, from coming into the regions of it.**

Madison continued:

Whilst we assert for ourselves a **freedom to embrace, to profess, and to observe the Religion which we believe to be of divine origin,** we **cannot deny an equal freedom to those whose minds have not yet yielded to the evidence which has convinced us.**

If this freedom be abused, it is an offense against God, not against man: To God, therefore, not to man, must an account of it be rendered.

◈

JEFFERSON'S *QUR'AN*

Jefferson collected books on many topics. He owned a *Qur'an* to understand how to fight Muslim Pirates during the Barbary Wars. It was one of 6,400 books in his library, which he sold to the U.S. Government in 1815 to pay his debts and replenish the Library of Congress after the British burned it during the War of 1812.

The *Associated Press* reported, January 3, 2007:

Rep.-elect Keith Ellison, the first Muslim elected to Congress, will use a *Qur'an* once owned by Thomas Jefferson during his ceremonial swearing-in Thursday. Some critics have argued that only a *Bible* should be used for the swearing-in.

Last month, Virginia Republican Rep. Virgil Goode warned that unless immigration is tightened, 'many more Muslims' will be elected and follow Ellison's lead.

Ellison spokesman Rick Jauert said the new congressman 'wants this to be a special day, and using Thomas Jefferson's *Qur'an* makes it even more special...Jefferson's *Qur'an* dates religious tolerance to the founders of our country,' he added.

A *Washington Post* article by Amyu Argetsinger and Roxanne Roberts, January 3, 2007, stated:

"He wanted to use a *Qur'an* that was special," said Mark Dimunation, chief of the rare book and special collections division at the Library of Congress, who was contacted by the Minnesota Dem early in December...

Ellison will take the official oath of office along with the other incoming members in the House chamber, then use the *Qur'an* in his individual, ceremonial oath with new Speaker Nancy Pelosi.

"Keith is paying respect not only to the founding fathers' belief in religious freedom but the Constitution itself," said Ellison spokesman Rick Jauert.

One person unlikely to be swayed by the book's illustrious history is Goode, who released a letter two weeks ago objecting to Ellison's use of the *Qur'an*.

"I believe that the overwhelming majority of voters in my district would prefer the use of the *Bible*," the Virginia Republican told Fox News, and then went on to warn about what he regards as the dangers of Muslims immigrating to the United States and Muslims gaining elective office.

Associated Press reported, January 4, 2007:

Keith Ellison made history Thursday, becoming the first Muslim member of Congress and punctuating the occasion by taking a ceremonial oath with a *Qur'an*.

Question: Does swearing upon a book imply believing what is in that book?

In light of fundamentalist Muslim threats on the U.S., it is understandable that non-Muslim Americans are disquieted about Rep. Ellison swearing upon a book which advocates inequality towards them, in the same way Jews in Nazi Germany would be unsettled by party members swearing upon "Mein Kampf."

Concerns exist because in other countries fundamental Muslims have used the democratic process to get elected, then, once in office, restricted democratic involvement of those who disagree with them, (as in Lebanon, Algeria, Palestine Authority and Nigeria.)

In America, politicians and judges are beginning to let Muslims who move into a community practice their own clandestine laws called Sharia. With this line of reasoning, the Bloods, Crips, MS-13 Gang, Mafia, drug cartels, or the KKK who take over a neighborhood, should be permitted to practice vigilante justice.

If someone says, there is a difference - those groups are not "religious," the Supreme Court answered that in *Welsh v United States* (1970) stating if someone holds "beliefs" about "what is right and wrong," with strength of "convictions," then they are "religious."

A way to remedy the situation would be for politicians to take a simple pledge:

PLEDGE TO STOP CRUELTY AND ABUSE OF WOMEN AND THE DEFENSELESS

I pledge to <u>stand against</u>:

·WIFE-BEATING – allowing a man to bully, batter or be physically abusive to his wife if she refuses to have sex with him or otherwise disobeys him;

·POLYGAMY – allowing a man to have multiple wives;

·PUNISHMENT OF RAPE VICTIMS – whipping, stoning or inflicting of corporal punishment on a woman who has been the victim of a rape;

·SEX SLAVERY–women forced into involuntary marriages;

·NO AGE OF CONSENT – allowing a man to marry a girl who is under the age of consent;

·INEQUALITY – teaching chauvinism, that men are more equal than women before the law;

·NO FREEDOM TO BE ALONE IN PUBLIC – not allowing women to leave their homes without being accompanied by a male relative;

·DETERMINING OF DRESS – discriminating, threatening, uttering of abuse, or committing violence on a woman because she is seen in public not wearing a particular dress or covering;

·DEFENSLESS DIVORCE – facilitating men divorcing their wives without due process of American law, such as by simply saying "I divorce you";

·NO ALIMONY – denying alimony to a woman who has been divorced, without due process of American law;

·NO VISITING RIGHTS – denying a woman who has been divorced access to her own children, without due process of American law;

·KIDNAPPING OF CHILDREN – facilitating a father taking a woman's children to another country which has laws denying her rights to her own children;

·NAME-CALLING – calling any race of people "apes or pigs," or women who are not covered "whores";

·NO DOGS – discriminating against those with seeing-eye dogs, service dogs, or canine campanions;

·DEATH THREATS – issuing death threats on someone for leaving a faith community;

·HONOR KILLINGS – supporting a system which effectively provides cover for a man who kills a wife or child that embarrassed him before his faith community;

·CORPORAL PUNISHMENT – beheadings, amputations, or any form of cutting off parts of a person's body as punishment for a crime;

·MUTILATION - practicing female genital mutilation;

·NO HONESTY – lying to gain access into a group, then using membership, financial contributions and intimidation to subvert the group into not opposing clandestine laws which deny women & children rights;

·GENOCIDE - advocating racism, extermination of ethnic groups, such as Jews, or Africans in south Sudan;

·AMERICAN LAW NOT SUPREME – advocating for foreign laws and traditions to be superior to U.S. laws;

·DISDAIN FOR PLEDGE – disparaging or discouraging American citizens from pledging allegiance to the flag of the United States of America.

JEFFERSON ON JESUS

In an interview with Niraj Warikoo of the *Detroit Free Press*, January 5, 2007, Rep. Keith Ellison said:

> The *Qur'an* is definitely an important historical document in our national history and demonstrates that Jefferson was a broad visionary thinker who not only possessed a *Qur'an*, but read it...
>
> It would have been something that contributed to his own thinking...it shows that from the earliest times of this republic, the *Qur'an* was in the consciousness of people who brought about democracy.

Rep. Ellison praised Jefferson for owning a *Qur'an*, which Jefferson had to understand why Muslim Barbary Pirates were enslaving American sailors. Though he read the *Qur'an*, Jefferson only had praise for the precepts of Jesus, as Jefferson wrote to Jared Sparks, Nov. 4, 1820:

> **I hold the precepts of Jesus as delivered by Himself, to be the most pure, benevolent and sublime which have ever been preached to man.**

On April 9, 1803, Thomas Jefferson wrote to Joseph Priestly concerning Jesus:

> **His system of morality was the most benevolent and sublime probably that has been ever taught,** and consequently **more perfect than those of any of the ancient philosophers.**

Jefferson wrote to William Canby, Sept. 18, 1813:

> **Of all the systems of morality, ancient or modern, which have come under my observation, none appear to me so pure as that of Jesus.**

Jefferson wrote to John Adams, July 5, 1814:

The **doctrines** that flowed from the **lips of Jesus** himself are within the comprehension of a child.

Jefferson lived in Virginia, which had the Anglican Church established from 1606 to 1786. **Establishment meant mandatory membership, mandatory attendance, mandatory taxes to support it, and no one could hold public office unless he was a member.** All other Protestant Christian denominations were considered "dissenters" and Catholics were prohibited from coming into the colony.

With the King of England being the head of the Church of England, there was a conflict of interest for Anglican clergy during the Revolution, most siding with the King. The clergy's use of *Scriptures* to justify themselves contributed toward resentment and skepticism of organized churches by some patriot founders.

On June 17, 1804, Jefferson wrote to Henry Fry:

I consider the doctrines of Jesus as delivered by himself to contain the outlines of the sublimest system of morality that has ever been taught but I hold in the most profound detestation and execration the corruptions of it which have been invented.

In 1813, Jefferson wrote to John Adams:

In extracting the **pure principles which Jesus taught,** we should have to strip off the artificial vestments in which they have been muffled...there will be found remaining **the most sublime and benevolent code of morals which has ever been offered to man.**

On April 21, 1803, Jefferson wrote to Dr. Benjamin Rush, also a signer of the Declaration:

My views...are the result of a life of inquiry and reflection, and very different from the anti-christian system imputed to me by those who know nothing of my opinions.

To the corruptions of Christianity I am, indeed, opposed; but not to the genuine precepts of Jesus himself.

I am a Christian in the only sense in which he wished any one to be; **sincerely attached to his doctrines in preference to all others...**

His system of morals...if filled up in the style and spirit of the rich fragments He left us, would be **the most perfect and sublime that has ever been taught by man...**

1. He corrected the Deism of the Jews, confirming them in their belief of one only God, and giving them juster notions of His attributes and government.

2. **His moral doctrines...were more pure and perfect than those of the most correct of the philosophers...**gathering all into one family under the bonds of love, charity, peace, common wants and common aids. A development of this head will evince **the peculiar superiority of the system of Jesus over all others.**

3. The precepts of philosophy, and of the Hebrew code, laid hold of actions only. **He pushed his scrutinies into the heart of man; erected his tribunal in the region of his thoughts, and purified the waters at the fountain head.**

4. He taught, emphatically, the doctrines of a future state...and wielded it with efficacy as an important incentive, supplementary to the other motives to moral conduct.

Jefferson told Benjamin Waterhouse, June 26, 1822:

The doctrines of Jesus are simple, and tend all to the happiness of man.

1. That there is one only God, and he all perfect. 2. That there is a future state of

rewards and punishments. 3. That to love God with all thy heart and thy neighbor as thyself, is the sum of religion.

These are the great points on which he endeavored to reform the religion of the Jews...

Now, which of these is the true and charitable Christian? He who believes and acts on the simple doctrines of Jesus?..

Had the doctrines of Jesus been preached always as pure as they came from his lips, the whole civilized world would now have been Christian...

How much wiser are the Quakers, who, agreeing in the fundamental doctrines of the gospel, schismatize about no mysteries, and, keeping within the pale of common sense, suffer no speculative differences of opinion...to impair the love of their brethren.

∽

THE JEFFERSON BIBLE

Congressman Keith Ellison brought attention to Jefferson's *Qur'an*, but Ellison did not mention *The Jefferson Bible-The Life and Morals of Jesus of Nazareth Extracted Textually from the Gospels in Greek, Latin, French and English*, compiled by Thomas Jefferson in 1816, which stated on the original handwritten cover page:

The Philosophy of Jesus of Nazareth - extracted from the account of his life and doctrines as given by Matthew, Mark, Luke & John - being an abridgement of the New Testament for the use of the Indians unembarrassed with matters of fact or faith beyond the level of their comprehensions.

Jefferson wrote to Charles Thomson, Jan. 9, 1816:

I have made this wee-little book...which I call *The Philosophy of Jesus*. It is a paradigm of his doctrines, made by cutting the texts out of the book and arranging them on the pages of a blank book, in a certain order of time and subject.

A more beautiful or precious morsel of ethics I have never seen; **it is a document in proof that I am a real Christian, that is to say, a disciple of the doctrines of Jesus,** very different from the Platonists, who call me an infidel, and themselves Christians and preachers of the gospel, while they draw all their characteristic dogmas from what its Author never said nor saw.

Franklin Roosevelt said on the 400th Anniversary of the Printing of the *English Bible*, October 6, 1935:

Learned as **Jefferson** was in the best of the ancient philosophers, he turned to the *Bible* as the source of his higher thinking and reasoning...

He held that the *Bible* contained the noblest ethical system the world has known.

His own compilation of the selected portions of this Book, in what is known as *Jefferson's Bible*, bears evidence of the profound reverence in which he held it.

In 1904, the 57th Congress, in order to restrain unethical behavior, voted:

That there be printed and bound, by photolithographic process, with an introduction of not to exceed twenty-five pages, to be prepared by Dr. Cyrus Adler, Librarian of the Smithsonian Institution, for the use of Congress, 9,000 copies of *Thomas Jefferson's Morals of Jesus of Nazareth*, as the same appears in the National Museum; 3,000 copies for the use of the Senate and 6,000 copies for the use of the House.

EXCERPTS FROM THE JEFFERSON BIBLE

JEFFERSON *BIBLE*, CHAPTER 2

24 Ye have heard that it was said by them of old time,
Thou shalt not kill; and whosoever shall kill shall be in
danger of the judgment:

25 But I say unto you, **That whosoever is angry with his
brother without a cause shall be in danger of the judgment...**

43 Ye have heard that it hath been said, **An eye for an
eye, and a tooth for a tooth:**

42 **But I say unto you, That ye resist not evil: but
whosoever shall smite thee on thy right cheek, turn to
him the other also.**

43 And if any man will sue thee at the law, and take
away thy coat, let him have thy cloak also.

44 And whosoever shall compel thee to go a mile,
go with him twain.

45 Give to him that asketh thee, and from him that would
borrow of thee turn not thou away…

46 Ye have heard that it hath been said, Thou shalt love
thy neighbour, **and hate thine enemy.**

47 **But I say unto you, Love your enemies, bless them
that curse you, do good to them that hate you, and pray
for them that despitefully use you, and persecute you;**

48 That ye may be the children of your Father which is
in heaven: for he maketh his sun to rise on the evil and on
the good, and sendeth rain on the just and on the unjust.

49 For if ye love them which love you, what reward
have ye? do not even the publicans the same?

50 And if ye salute your brethren only, what do ye
more than others? do not even the publicans so?

51 And if ye lend to them of whom ye hope to receive,
what thank have ye? for sinners also lend to sinners, to
receive as much again.

52 **But love ye your enemies**, and do good, and lend,
hoping for nothing again; and your reward shall be great,
and ye shall be the children of the Highest: for he is kind
unto the unthankful and to the evil.

53 Be ye therefore merciful, as your Father also is merciful.

JEFFERSON BIBLE, CHAPTER 3

5 And when thou prayest, thou shalt not be as the hypocrites are: for they love to pray standing in the synagogues and in the corners of the streets, that they may be seen of men. Verily I say unto you, They have their reward.

6 ...When thou prayest, enter into thy closet, and when thou hast shut thy door, pray to thy Father which is in secret; and thy Father which seeth in secret shall reward thee openly.

7 But when ye pray, **use not vain repetitions, as the heathen do**: for they think that they shall be heard for their much speaking.

35 Judge not, that ye be not judged.

36 For with what judgment ye judge, ye shall be judged: and with what measure ye mete, it shall be measured to you again.

37 Give, and it shall be given unto you...

38 And why beholdest thou the mote that is in thy brother's eye, but considerest not the beam that is in thine own eye?

39 Or how wilt thou say to thy brother, Let me pull out the mote out of thine eye; and, behold, a beam is in thine own eye?

40 Thou hypocrite, first cast out the beam out of thine own eye; and then shalt thou see clearly to cast out the mote out of thy brother's eye...

50 **Beware of false prophets,** which come to you in sheep's clothing, but **inwardly they are ravening wolves.**

51 **Ye shall know them by their fruits**. Do men gather grapes of thorns, or figs of thistles?

52 Even so every good tree bringeth forth good fruit; **but a corrupt tree bringeth forth evil fruit.**

53 A good tree cannot bring forth evil fruit, neither can a corrupt tree bring forth good fruit.

54 Every tree that bringeth not forth good fruit is hewn down, and cast into the fire.

55 Wherefore by their fruits ye shall know them.

56 A good man out of the good treasure of the heart bringeth forth good things: and **an evil man out of the evil treasure bringeth forth evil things.**

JEFFERSON BIBLE, CHAPTER 8

4 They say unto him, **Master, this woman was taken in adultery,** in the very act.

5 Now **Moses in the law commanded us, that such should be stoned: but what sayest thou?**

6 This they said, tempting him, that they might have cause to accuse him. But Jesus stooped down, and with his finger wrote on the ground, as though he heard them not.

7 So when they continued asking him, he lifted up himself, and said unto them, **He that is without sin among you, let him first cast a stone at her.**

8 And again he stooped down, and wrote on the ground.

9 And they which heard it, being convicted by their own conscience, went out one by one, beginning at the eldest, even unto the last: and Jesus was left alone, and the woman standing in the midst.

10 When Jesus had lifted up himself, and saw none but the woman, he said unto her, Woman, where are those thine accusers? hath no man condemned thee?

11 She said, No man, Lord. And **Jesus said unto her, Neither do I condemn thee: go, and sin no more.**

∽

OTHER PRESIDENTS REFER TO THE *BIBLE*

"Both sides read **the same** *Bible*."-ABRAHAM LINCOLN, Inaugural, March 4, 1865

"One of the factors which I think weighed heaviest on the side of unity - **the** *Bible* **was the one work of literature that was common to all of them. The** *Scriptures* **were read and studied everywhere.**" - CALVIN COOLIDGE, May 3, 1925, speaking on colonial America

"In the formative days of the Republic the directing influence **the** *Bible* exercised upon the fathers of the Nation is conspicuously evident...**We cannot read the history of our rise and development as a Nation, without**

reckoning with the place the *Bible* has occupied in shaping the advances of the Republic. Its teaching is ploughed into the very heart of the race."-FDR, October 6, 1935

"As Commander-in-Chief I take pleasure in commending the reading of the Bible to all who serve in the armed forces of the United States. "-FDR, forword, Military Edition, Gideon's New Testament & Book of Psalms distributed by the millions to U.S. soldiers.

"I hope that you have re-read the Constitution of the United States...**Like the *Bible*, it ought to be read again and again.**"-FDR, Fireside Chat, March 9, 1937

"An ordering of society which relegates religion, democracy and good faith among nations to the background can find no place within it for the **ideals of the Prince of Peace.** The United States rejects such an ordering, and retains its ancient faith."-FDR, January 4, 1939, to Congress

"I surely wish God Almighty would give the Children of Israel an Isaiah, the Christians a St. Paul, and **the Sons of Ishmael a peep at the Golden Rule."**-HARRY S TRUMAN, *Memoirs-Volume Two: Years of Trial and Hope,* 1956, note to his assistant

"We will celebrate this Christmas Day in our traditional American way - because of its deep spiritual meaning to us; because **the teachings of Christ are fundamental in our lives**; and because we want our youngest generation to grow up knowing the significance of this tradition and **the story of the coming of the immortal Prince of Peace."**-FDR, December 24, 1944, Address to the Nation

"The fundamental basis of **this nation's laws was given to Moses on the Mount.** The fundamental basis of our Bill of Rights comes from the teachings we get from **Exodus and St. Matthew, from Isaiah and St. Paul.** I don't think we emphasize that enough these days."- HARRY S TRUMAN, Attorney General's Conference, February 15, 1950

⁓

JESUS & MOHAMMED COMPARED

●Jesus was a **religious leader.**
●Mohammed was **a religious leader, a political leader** and **a military leader.**

●Jesus never killed anyone.
●Mohammed killed an estimated 3,000 people, including beheading 700 Jews in Medina.

●Jesus never owned slaves.
●Mohammed received a fifth of the slaves taken in battle, including African slaves, as he was Arab.

●Jesus never married.
●Mohammed had at least 11 wives, plus slave wives, concubines, and women taken in battle.

Muslim apologists do not deny Mohammed's actions, but respond that King David was a prophet who killed people, led armies, owned slaves and had wives.

The response is still that **Jesus never killed anyone, never owned slaves and never married.** Besides, King David only wanted a small piece of land - there is no command in the *Old Testament* for Jews to subdue the world to Yahweh by force.

●Jesus never forced his followers to believe. When his sayings were not understood, "many of his disciples, when they had heard this said, 'This is a hard saying, who can hear it?'...Many of his disciples went back and walked no more with him. Then Jesus said to the twelve, 'Will ye also go away?' Then Simon Peter answered him, 'Lord, to whom shall we go? Thou hast the words of eternal life.'" (John 6:31-69)

•Mohammed forced his followers to continue believing, saying in the *Hadith al-Bukhari* (Vol. 9, Bk. 84, No. 57): "Whoever changes his Islamic religion, kill him."

•Jesus did not permit followers to lie and rape.
•Mohammed permitted followers to lie to spread Islam and to rape infidel women taken in battle.

•Jesus never avenged insults, but forgave.
•Mohammed avenged insults, ordering Ibn Khatal and his slave girls killed for making fun of him in poems.

•Jesus never tortured anyone.
•Mohammed had the chief of Khaybar tortured to get him to reveal the location of the tribe's treasure.

•None of Jesus' Apostles led armies, but instead spread Christianity throughout the Roman Empire by loving their enemies and dying for their faith.
•All the Caliphs and Sultans led armies.

•In the first 300 years of Christianity, there were ten major persecutions by the Romans, resulting in thousands of Christians being killed in the Coliseum and fed to the lions. Never once did Christians lead an armed resistance against those who attacked them.
•In the first 300 years of Islam, Muslim armies conquered Arabia, Persia, the Holy Land, North Africa, Spain, Southern France, Central Africa, and invaded vast areas of Asia and Asia Minor.

JESUS TEACHES TO TREAT ENEMIES

•Love your enemies, bless them that curse you, do good to them that hate you, pray for them which despitefully use you (Matt. 5:44)
•If someone strikes you on one cheek, turn to them the other (Mat. 5:39)

•Resist not evil (Mat. 5:39)

•If someone takes your coat, give them your shirt (Mat. 5:40)

•If someone make you carry something one mile, carry it two (Mat. 5:41)

•Forgive and you shall be forgiven (Mat. 6:14)

•Judge not, that ye be not judged (Mat. 7:1)

•Blessed are the merciful, for they shall obtain mercy (Mat. 5:7)

•Blessed are the peacemakers (Mat. 5:9)

•Treat others the way you want to be treated (Luke 6:27-36)

•Ye have heard that it was said, Thou shalt not kill, but I say who ever is angry with his brother is in danger of the judgment (Mat. 5:21-22)

•Feed the hungry, clothe the naked, visit the sick, whatever you do to the very least you have done unto me (Mat 25:40)

MOHAMMED TEACHES TO TREAT ENEMIES

•Infidels are your sworn enemies (Sura 4:101)

•Be ruthless to the infidels (Sura 48:29)

•Make war on the infidels who dwell around you (Sura 9:123, 66:9)

•Fight those who believe not in Allah nor the Last Day (Sura 9:29)

•Strike off the heads of infidels in battle (Sura 47:4)

•If someone stops believing in Allah, kill him (al-Bukhari 9:84:57)

•Take neither the Jews nor the Christians for your friends (Sura 5:51, 60:13)

•Never help the disbelievers (Sura 28:86)

•The only reward of those who make war upon Allah and His messenger will be that they will be killed or crucified, or have their hands and feet on alternate sides cut off, or will be expelled out of the land (Sura 5:33)

•Kill the disbelievers wherever we find them (Sura 2:191)

•No Muslim should be killed for killing an infidel (al-Bukhari 1:3:111)

OTHER CONTRASTING TEACHINGS

•Jesus taught that we are children of God and that God was our Father (Mat. 6:10).

•Mohammed considered it blasphemy to call Allah your father, as Allah took no wife and has no children. (Sura 5:18)

•Jesus taught that man was made in God's image. (Matt 22:20, referring to Gen. 1:26-27, 9:6)

•Mohammed taught that Allah has no image. (Sura 42:11, Sura 112:4)

•Jesus taught "Forgive us our trespasses as we forgive those who trespass against us."(Matthew 6:10-15)

•Mohammed taught to avenge trespasses and insults committed against one's honor, family or religion.

•When violence was committed against Jesus, he did not retaliate but allowed himself to be crucified.

•When violence was committed against Mohammed, he retaliated, ordering his enemies killed.

•The concept of a martyr in Christian and Jewish thought is one who would die for their faith.

•The concept of martyr in Islamic thought is one who would die for their faith while killing infidels.

•Jesus taught that religion is from the inside out.

•Mohammed taught that religion could be forced from the outside in.

•Christianity teaches God wants a personal relationship with each individual believer.

•Islam teaches that individual believers cannot have a personal relationship with Allah.

•Jesus' religion is one of forgiveness and love.
•Mohammed's is one of fear and subjugation.

To criticize someone for treating those of other religions harshly is to acknowledge the example of Jesus is superior to the example of Mohammed.

When the Crusades are criticized, a question to be asked is: "Are you condemning or justifying?":

-Are you condemning the Crusades fought in the name of religion?

If so, then you are condemning Mohammed and the Caliphs who fought in the name of religion.

-Or are you justifying Mohammed and Caliphs for fighting in the name of religion by saying other religions did it too?

Either way, the spreading religion by force is contrary to Jesus' example, but not contrary to Mohammed's example.

∽

JQA COMPARED JESUS & MOHAMMED

John Quincy Adams wrote in his "Essays dealing with the Russo-Turkish War and on Greece," (NY: *The American Annual Register for 1827-28-29*; 1830):

[Jesus] declared, that the enjoyment of felicity in the world hereafter, would be reward of the practice of benevolence here.

His whole law was resolvable into the precept of love; peace on earth–good will toward man, was the early object of his mission; and the authoritative demonstration of the immortality of man, was that, which constituted the more than earthly tribute of glory to God in the highest...

The first conquest of the religion of Jesus, was over the unsocial passions of his disciples. It elevated the standard of the human character in the scale of existence...

On the Christian system of morals, man is an immortal spirit, confined for a short space of time, in an earthly tabernacle.

Kindness to his fellow mortals embraces the whole compass of his duties upon earth, and the whole promise of happiness to his spirit hereafter.

THE ESSENCE OF THIS DOCTRINE IS, TO EXALT THE SPIRITUAL OVER THE BRUTAL PART OF HIS NATURE. [Adam's capital letters] (JQA, Essay on Turks, pp. 267-268)

In the seventh century of the Christian era, a wandering Arab of the lineage of Hagar [i.e., Mohammed], the Egyptian, combining the powers of transcendent genius, with the preternatural energy of a fanatic, and the fraudulent spirit of an impostor, proclaimed himself as a messenger from Heaven, and spread desolation and delusion over an extensive portion of the earth.

Adopting from the sublime conception of the Mosaic law, the doctrine of one omnipotent God; he connected indissolubly with it, the audacious falsehood, that he was himself his prophet and apostle.

Adopting from the new Revelation of Jesus, the faith and hope of immortal life, and of future retribution, he humbled it to the dust by adapting all the rewards and sanctions of his religion to the gratification of the sexual passion.

He poisoned the sources of human felicity at the fountain, by degrading the condition of the female sex, and the allowance of polygamy; and he declared undistinguishing and exterminating war, as a part of his religion, against all the rest of mankind.

THE ESSENCE OF HIS DOCTRINE WAS VIOLENCE AND LUST: TO EXALT THE

BRUTAL OVER THE SPIRITUAL PART OF
HUMAN NATURE. [Adam's capital letters]
(JQA, Essay on Turks, p. 269)

John Quincy Adams concluded:

[Mohammed] declared undistinguishing
and exterminating war as a part of his religion
against all the rest of mankind...
The precept of the Koran is perpetual war
against all who deny that Mahomet is the prophet
of God. (JQA, Essay on Turks, p. 267)

Between these two religions, thus contrasted
in their characters, a war of 1200 years has
already raged. The war is yet flagrant...
While the merciless and dissolute dogmas
of the false prophet shall furnish motives to
human action, there can never be peace upon
earth, and good will towards men." (JQA,
Essay on Turks, p. 269)

∽

H.G. WELLS -COMPARING MOHAMMED

In his *Outlines of History*, (NY: MacMillian Co.,
1920, Vol. 2, p. 13), H.G. Wells wrote:

Because Mohammed too founded a great
religion, there are those who write of this
evidently lustful and rather shifty leader as
though he were a man to put beside Jesus of
Nazareth or Gautama or Mani.
But it is surely manifest that he was a being
of commoner clay; he was vain, egotistical,
tyrannous, and a self-deceiver; and it would
throw all our history out of proportion if, out
of an insincere deference to the possible
Moslem reader, we were to present him in
any other light.

∽

ALLAH HAS NO IMAGE

Mohammed taught Allah has no image and that it is blasphemy to believe one is made in God's image:

> And there is none like unto Him. (Sura 112:4, *Yusufali Translation*) The Originator of the heavens and the earth; He made mates for you from among yourselves, and mates of the cattle too, multiplying you thereby; nothing like a likeness of Him; and He is the Hearing, the Seeing. (Sura 42:11, *Shakir Translation*)

Not only were there to be no images of Allah, the *Hadith* stated there should be no images in art:

> Abu'l-Hayyaj al-Asadi told that 'Ali (b. Abu Talib) said to him: Should I not send you on the same mission as Allah's Messenger (may peace be upon him) sent me?
> Do not leave an image without obliterating it, or a high grave without leveling it. This hadith has been reported by Habib with the same chain of transmitters and he said:
> (Do not leave) a picture without obliterating it. (*Hadith Book 4, No. 2115*)

Americans have always believed man was made in God's image, as Thomas Paine demonstrated in his *The American Crisis*, December 23, 1776:

> The Almighty implanted in us these inextinguishable feelings for good and wise purposes. They are the guardians of **His image in our heart.** They distinguish us from the herd of common animals.

On the 150th Anniversary of the Declaration of Independence, July 5, 1926, President Calvin Coolidge said:

> They justified freedom by the text that **we are all created in the divine image.**

George Washington Carver wrote to Rev. Kunzman of Seattle, March 24, 1925:

My lifetime study of nature in its many phases leads me to believe more strongly than ever in the Biblical account of man's creation as found in Gen. 1:27: "**And God created man in his own image, in the image of God created He him; male and female created he them.**"

George Washington Carver wrote to Mr. and Mrs. Woods, who had given him some dahlias, on Sept. 7, 1940:

The great Creator...made man in the likeness of his image to be co-partner with him in creating some of the most beautiful and useful things in the world.

In his State of the Union, January 6, 1942, FDR said:

Our enemies are guided by...unholy contempt for the human race. We are inspired by a faith that goes back through all the years to the first chapter of the Book of Genesis: "**God created man in His own image.**"

President Harry S. Truman stated January 7, 1948:

We believe in the dignity of man. We believe that **he was created in the image of the Father of us all**.

President Harry S. Truman stated in his Inaugural Address, January 20, 1949:

We believe that all men are created equal because **they are created in the image of God.**

Eisenhower addressed via telephone the unification meeting of the AFL and CIO, New York, December 5, 1955:

Man is created in the Divine Image and has spiritual aspirations that transcend the material.

Dwight Eisenhower told the Spiritual Foundation of American Democracy Conference, Nov. 9, 1954:

> Milton asserted that all men are born equal, because **each is born in the image of his God**.
>
> Our whole theory of government finally expressed in our Declaration...said "Man is endowed by his Creator."
>
> When you come back to it, there is just one thing...that a man is worthwhile because he was born in **the image of his God.**

President Eisenhower stated upon his return from the Geneva Conference, July 25, 1955:

> The wide gulf that separates so far East and West...the gulf that lies between the concept of **man made in the image of his God** and the concept of man as a mere instrument of the state.

Douglas MacArthur addressed the cadets at the U.S. Military Academy at West Point, May 12, 1962:

> In the face of danger and death, he discloses those Divine attributes which his Maker gave when **He created man in His own image.**

President Ronald Reagan told the citizens of Hambach, Germany, May 6, 1985:

> Each of us, each of you, is made in the most enduring, powerful image of Western civilization. We're made in the **image of God, the image of God the Creator.**

Ronald Reagan stated the Royal Institute of International Affairs, London, England, June 3, 1988:

> Our faith is in a higher law. Yes, we believe in prayer and its power. And like the Founding Fathers of both our lands, we hold that humanity was meant not to be dishonored by

the all-powerful state, but to live **in the image and likeness of Him who made us.**

Pope John Paul II addressed 50,000 people at Oriole Park in Camden Yards, Baltimore, Maryland, Oct. 8, 1995:

Always be guided by the truth - by the truth about God who created and redeemed us, and by the truth about **the human person, made in the image and likeness of God** and destined for a glorious fulfillment in the Kingdom to come.

President George H.W. Bush proclaimed 1990 the International Year of *Bible* Reading, Feb. 22, 1990:

A biblical view of man-one affirming the dignity and worth of **the human person, made in the image of our Creator**-that inspired the principles upon which the United States is founded.

President George W. Bush stated in his Inaugural Address, January, 20, 2001:

We are guided by a power larger than ourselves, **Who creates us equal in His image.**

George W. Bush, just 48 hours after assuming the presidency, addressed the annual January 22nd March for Life, gathered in Washington, D.C.:

Every person, at every stage and season of life, is created in God's image.

∽

ALLAH HAS NO CHILDREN

The *Qur'an's* many names for Allah include: Abaser, Afflictor, All Compelling Subduer, Avenger, Bringer of Death, Bringer of Judgement, Destroyer, Distressor, Giver of Dishonor, Greatest of All Deceivers, and Harmer.

Nowhere is Allah named "Father."The *Hadith*, narrated Abu Said al-Khudri stated:

Allah has never taken anyone as a wife or a son. (Vol. 6, Book 60, No. 105)

For Muslims, to seek a relationship with Allah as "Father" is condemned by the *Qur'an* (Sura 5:18):

And (both) the Jews and the Christians say: "We are the children of Allah and His loved ones." Say: "Why then does He punish you for your sins?" Nay, you are but human beings, of those He has created...

Americans viewed God as "Father," as Horace Mann wrote in his *12th Annual Report to the Massachusetts Board of Education*, 1848:

It was in consequence of laws that invaded the direct and exclusive jurisdiction which **our Father in Heaven exercises over his children upon earth**, that the Pilgrims fled from their native land to that which is the land of our nativity.

Abraham Lincoln stated in a debate with Stephen A. Douglas in Chicago, July 10, 1858:

The Saviour...did not expect any human being could be perfect...but He said, "As **your Father in Heaven** is perfect, be ye also perfect."

Senator James G. Blaine is quoted in *Columbus and Columbia, a History of the Man and the Nation*:

Brotherhood of man, the Fatherhood of God is becoming the corner-stone of religion, as revealed in Christ, and as clearly traced in human history.

President Calvin Coolidge addressed the Holy Name Society, Washington, D.C., September 21, 1924:

The principle of equality is recognized. It follows inevitably from belief in the **brotherhood of man through the fatherhood of God.**

At the 150th anniversary of the Declaration of Independence, Philadelphia, July 5, 1926, Coolidge stated:

> They preached equality because they believed in the **fatherhood of God and the brotherhood of man.**

President Ronald Reagan stated in observance of the National Day of Prayer, May 6, 1982:

> George Washington on his knees in the snow of Valley Forge...personifies a people who know that it's not enough to depend on our own courage and goodness; we must also seek help from **God, our Father.**

At the National Prayer Breakfast, January 31, 1985, Reagan stated:

> **We are all God's children.**

Ronald Reagan addressed the freed hostages of a hijacked Trans World Airlines jet, July 2, 1985:

> **Our Father**, we just gather before you in humble adoration and praise and thanks.

Lincoln told a Negro deputation, August 14, 1862:

> It is difficult to make a man miserable while he...claims **kindred to the great God who made him.**

∽

RELIGIONS OF THE WORLD

CIA.gov *World Factbook* (2006) listed the world as:

33.03 percent Christian
     17.33 percent Roman Catholic
     5.8 percent Protestant
     3.42 percent Orthodox
     1.23 percent Anglican
     5.25 percent Other Christian

20.12 percent Muslim
    18.11 percent Sunni
    2.01 percent Shi'a (Sufi & other Muslims)
13.34 percent Hindu
12.61 percent other religions
12.03 percent non-religious
 5.89 percent Buddhist
 2.36 percent atheist
 0.39 percent Sikh
 0.23 percent Jewish

JUDEO-CHRISTIAN CIVILIZATION

Have all cultures and civilizations valued human life equally? If not, which have valued human life more and which have valued human life less?

Islam teaches that the life of an infidel is not equal to that of a Muslim, and women do not enjoy the same status as men.

Hinduism's caste system teaches that a person in the lowest caste of "untouchables" (Dalits) does not have the same rights and privileges as a person in the highest caste of Brahmin.

Buddhism's view of women is lower than men. If a woman serves men well, even, as is common in Thailand, as prostitutes, this will produce karma resulting in her being reborn in her next life as a man.

Atheism teaches the utilitarian ethic that one's worth is dependent on their utility. One who contributes to society is valued more than someone who does not contribute. (ie. *Survivor Game Show,* CBS Television)

Jewish Law teaches human life is of equal ("The stranger that dwells with you shall be unto you as one born among you, and thou shalt love him as thyself, for ye were strangers in the land of Egypt."-Lev. 19:34)

Jewish Law teaches that punishment should equal the crime. ("an eye for an eye, a tooth for a tooth"-Ex. 21:24), whereas the *Qur'an* teaches that punishment can be much greater than the crime ("as for the thief, both male or female, cut off their hands"-Sura 4:36).

Jesus gave the highest value to all human life when he taught: "love thy neighbor as thy self" (Mat. 19:19), "do unto others what you would have them do to you" (Mat. 7:12), "whatever you do unto the least of these you have done unto me" (Mat. 25:40) and "the greatest among you shall be the servant of all" (Mk. 9:35).

MARTIN LUTHER KING, JR.

On April 16, 1963, written from Birmingham, Alabama, Martin Luther King, Jr. stated:

Just as the prophets of the 8th century B.C. left their villages and carried their "thus saith the Lord" far afield, and just as the Apostle Paul left his village of Tarsus and carried the gospel of Jesus Christ to the far corners of the Greco-Roman world, so am I compelled to carry the gospel of freedom beyond my own hometown.

Like Paul, I must constantly respond to the Macedonian call for aid....

I must make two honest confessions to you, my Christian and Jewish brothers. First, I must confess that over the past few years I have been gravely disappointed with the white moderate...who is more devoted to "order" than justice...

I began thinking about the fact that I stand in the middle of two opposing forces in the Negro community.

One is a force of complacency made up of Negroes who, as a result of long years of oppression, are...drained of self-respect...

The other force is one of bitterness and hatred, and it comes perilously close to advocating violence. It is expressed in the various black nationalist groups that are springing up across the nation, the largest and

best-known being Elijah Muhammad's Muslim movement.

Nourished by the Negro's frustration over the continued existence of racial discrimination, **this movement is made up of people who have lost faith in America, who have absolutely repudiated Christianity, and who have concluded that the white man is an incorrigible "devil."**

I have tried to stand between these two forces, saying that we need emulate neither the "do-nothingism" of the complacent nor **the hatred of the black nationalist.**

For there is the more excellent way of love and nonviolent protest. **I am grateful to God that, through the influence of the Negro church, the way of nonviolence became an integral part of our struggle....**

I am further convinced that if our white brothers dismiss...those of us who employ nonviolent direct action and if they refuse to support our nonviolent efforts, millions of Negroes will, out of frustration and despair, seek solace and security in **black nationalist ideologies - a development that would inevitably lead to a frightening racial nightmare...**

I say this as a minister of the *Gospel,* who loves the church; who was nurtured in its bosom; who has been sustained by its spiritual blessings and who will remain true to it as long as the cord of life shall lengthen...

One day the South will know that when these disinherited children of God sat down at lunch counters they were in reality standing up for what is best in the American dream and for the most sacred values in our **Judeo-Christian heritage**, thereby bringing our nation back to those **great wells of democracy** which were dug deep by the founding fathers in their formulation of the Constitution and the Declaration of Independence.

FRANKLIN D. ROOSEVELT

Franklin D. Roosevelt stated in his Labor Day Address, September 1, 1941:

Preservation of these rights is vitally important now, not only to us who enjoy them, but to the whole future of **Christian civilization.**

In accepting the Democrat Nomination, July 19, 1940, FDR stated:

We face one of the great choices of history...**the continuance of civilization as we know it** versus the ultimate destruction of all that we have held dear - religion against godlessness.

FDR stated in Brooklyn, NY, Nov. 1, 1940:

Those forces hate democracy and Christianity as two phases of the **same civilization.** They oppose democracy because it is Christian. They oppose Christianity because it preaches democracy.

FDR said at Madison Square Garden, Oct. 28, 1940:

We guard ourselves against all evils - spiritual as well as material - which may beset us. **We guard against the forces of anti-Christian aggression,** which may attack us from without, and the forces of ignorance and fear which may corrupt us from within.

FDR remarked in his State of the Union, January 6, 1942:

The world is too small to provide adequate "living room" for both Hitler and God. In proof of that, the Nazis have now announced their plan for enforcing their new German, pagan religion all over the world - **a plan by which the *Holy Bible* and the Cross of Mercy would be displaced by *Mein Kampf* and the swastika and the naked sword.**

FDR said in a Fireside Chat, April 28, 1942:

This great war effort must be carried through to its victorious conclusion…It shall not be imperiled by the handful of noisy traitors - **betrayers of America, betrayers of Christianity itself** – would-be dictators who in their hearts and souls have yielded to Hitlerism and would have this Republic do likewise.

FDR addressed Congress regarding the Yalta Conference, March 1, 1945:

I had read about Warsaw and Lidice and Rotterdam and Coventry-but I saw Sevastopol and Yalta! And I know that **there is not room enough on earth for both German militarism and Christian decency.**

WINSTON CHURCHILL

Faced with an ideological threat, Winston Churchill addressed Britain's House of Commons, June 18, 1940:

What General Weygand called **the Battle of France is over.** I expect that the Battle of Britain is about to begin. **Upon this battle depends the survival of Christian civilization**. Upon it depends our own British life, and the long continuity of our institutions and our Empire. The whole fury and might of the enemy must very soon be turned on us. Hitler knows that he will have to break us in this island or lose the war.

If we can stand up to him, all Europe may be free and the life of the world may move forward into broad, sunlit uplands.

But if we fail, then the whole world, including the United States, including all that we have known and cared for, will sink into the abyss of a new Dark Age made more sinister, and perhaps more protracted, by the lights of perverted science.
Let us therefore brace ourselves to our duties and so bear ourselves that, if the British Empire and its Commonwealth last for a thousand years, men will still say, "This was their finest hour."

Churchill, in From War to War, (*Second World War*, Vol. 1, ch. 4, p. 50) described **Hitler's** *Mein Kampf* as:

...**the new Koran of faith** and war: turgid, verbose, shapeless, but pregnant with its message.

Winston Churchill, in *The (Nile) River War*, (first edition, Vol. II, 1899, pp. 248-50), wrote:

How dreadful are the curses which **Mohammedanism** lays on its votaries! Besides the fanatical frenzy, which is as dangerous in a man as hydrophobia in a dog, there is this fearful fatalistic apathy.
The effects are apparent in many countries. Improvident habits, slovenly systems of agriculture, sluggish methods of commerce, and insecurity of property exist wherever the followers of the Prophet rule or live...
A degraded sensualism deprives this life of its grace and refinement; the next of its dignity and sanctity. The fact that in **Mohammedan law every woman must belong to some man as his absolute property, either as a child, a wife, or a concubine, must delay the final extinction of slavery until the faith of Islam has ceased to be a great power among men.**

Individual Moslems may show splendid qualities...but the influence of the religion paralyses the social development of those who follow it. No stronger retrograde force exists in the world. Far from being moribund, **Mohammedanism is a militant and proselytizing faith**.

It has already spread throughout Central Africa, raising fearless warriors at every step; and were it not that Christianity is sheltered in the strong arms of science, the science against which it had vainly struggled, the civilisation of modern Europe might fall, as fell the civilisation of ancient Rome.

Hilaire Belloc, one of the four greatest Edwardian Letter writers, along with H.G. Wells, George Bernard Shaw and G.K. Chesterton, wrote in *The Great Heresies* (1938):

"Will not perhaps the temporal power of Islam return and with it the menace of an armed Mohammedan world which will shake off the domination of Europeans – still nominally Christian – and reappear again as the prime enemy of our civilization?"

The future always comes as a surprise but political wisdom consists in attempting at least some partial judgment of what that surprise may be. And for my part I cannot but believe that a main unexpected thing of the future is the return of Islam...

In view of this, anyone with a knowledge of history is bound to ask himself whether we shall not see in the future a revival of Mohammedan political power, and the renewal of the old pressure of Islam upon Christendom; yet over and over again they have suddenly united under a leader and accomplished the greatest things.

Now it is probable enough that on these lines – unity under a leader – the return of Islam may arrive. There is no leader as yet, but enthusiasm might bring one and there are signs enough in the political heavens today of what we may have to expect from the revolt of Islam at some future date perhaps not far distant.

After the Great War the Turkish power was suddenly restored by one such man. Another such man in Arabia, with equal suddenness, affirmed himself and destroyed all the plans laid for the incorporation of that part of the Mohammedan world into the English sphere.

∽

DOES IT MATTER?

Some naively argue that the world's problems are the result of religion, and that government should ban all religions, regardless of what they teach. This is like saying political parties are the problem, that a government policy should ban all political parties regardless of what they stand for.

This atheistic purge has already attempted and resulted in **millions killed in the godless French Revolution's Reign of Terror, Stalin's Soviet Russia, and Mao Zedong's Chinese Cultural Revolution.**

Webster's New World Dictionary **defines "religion" as "a belief-system."** The word "belief" is defined as opinions, convictions or thoughts. **Atheism, then, is a religion.** As long as a person is doing "actions," that person has opinions, convictions or thoughts underlying those actions, and that collection of thoughts is their "belief-system" or "religion."

As long as a government is doing "actions," that government has opinions, convictions or thoughts underlying its actions, and that collection of thoughts is the government's "belief-system" or "religion." Thus it follows that there can never be a separation of belief-system and government.

As long as the government is doing "actions" someone's beliefs underlie those actions. **So the question is not** *whether* **a religion or belief-system should underlie the government's actions, but** *whose* **religion** or belief-system.

What kind of thoughts should underlie a government or country? Forgiveness? Love? Equality? Revenge? Hate? Violence? Should Americans swear into office upon any book? Does it really matter if one swears upon a *Bible*, a *Qur'an*, a *Bhagavad Gita*, a cookbook or a comic book?

Calvin Coolidge stated at the anniversary of the Declaration of Independence, July 5, 1926:

> The principles of human relationship which went into the Declaration of Independence...are found in the texts, the sermons, and the writings of the early colonial clergy who were earnestly undertaking to instruct their congregations in the great mystery of how to live.
>
> **They preached equality because they believed in the fatherhood of God and the brotherhood of man**. They justified freedom by the text that **we are all created in the divine image...**
>
> The Declaration of Independence is a great spiritual document. It is a declaration not of material but of spiritual conceptions.
>
> **Equality, liberty, popular sovereignty, the rights of man** - these are not elements which we can see and touch...**They have their source and their roots in the religious convictions**... Unless the faith of the American in these religious convictions is to endure, the principles of our Declaration will perish. **We can not continue to enjoy the result if we neglect and abandon the cause...Before we can understand their conclusions we must go back and review the course which they followed. We must think the thoughts which they thought...They were**

intent upon religious worship...There was a wide acquaintance with the Scripture...

We live in an age of science and of abounding accumulation of material things. These did not create our Declaration. Our Declaration created them. The things of the spirit come first. Unless we cling to that, all our material prosperity, overwhelming though it may appear, will turn to a barren sceptre in our grasp. **If we are to maintain the great heritage which has been bequeathed to us, we must be like-minded as the fathers who created it.**

We must not sink into pagan materialism. We must cultivate the reverence which they had...We must follow the spiritual and moral leadership which they showed. We must keep replenished, that they may glow with a more compelling flame, the altar fires before which they worshipped.

Laying the cornerstone of the Jewish Community Center, May 3, 1925, President Calvin Coolidge stated:

It is a lesson which our country, and every country based on the principle of popular government, must learn and apply, generation by generation...

The patriots who laid the foundation of this Republic drew their faith from the *Bible*...We cannot escape the conclusion that **if American democracy is to remain the greatest hope of humanity, it must continue abundantly in the faith of the** *Bible*.

In a Fireside Chat, Sept. 11, 1941, FDR stated:

The times call for clear heads and fearless hearts. And with that inner strength that comes to a free people... **conscious of the righteousness of what they do, they will - with Divine help and guidance - stand their ground.**

✍